K-507-S, p. 51

180 RECRE
HOME

IN THIS ISSUE:

HOW TO ORDER BLUEPRINTS

CALL TOLL-FREE TO ORDER!
1-800-547-5570

President	Jeffrey B. Heegaard
Publisher	Roger W. Heegaard
Associate Publishers	Mark Englund, Wendy Schroeder
Editors	Pamela Robertson, Eric Englund, Sharon Teska, Jessica Tolliver, Jason Miller
Specialty Editors	Dianne Talmage, John Lickteig, Carrie Morrison, Leonard Renner
Sales Operations Supervisor	Wayne Ramaker
Marketing Associates	Gene Tubbs, Susan Rowland, Kris Donnelly
Specialty Marketing Associates	Daniel Brown, Michelle Gerling, Tera Girardin, Diana Jasan
Controller	Nancy Ness
Financial Analysts	Barbara Marquardt, Jeanne Marquardt, Tom Klauer, Kirk Anderson
Information Systems Analyst	John Herber
Information Systems Associates	Kevin Gellerman, Jeffrey Tindillier, John Driscoll
Blueprint Consultants	Brad Johnson, Lee Buescher, Cassidy Gammon, Brian Binstock
Blueprint Manager	Chuck Lantis

Staff: Jennifer Banks, Amy Berdahl, Brian Boese, Jeanel Carlson, Joan Jerry, Dorothy Jordan, Sarah Moeller, Monita Mohammadian, Lori Nicolai, Kellie Pierce, Michael Romain, Shelley Safratowich, Jacqueline Scott, Leon Thompson, Steve Verhaest, Laura Voetberg, Rebecca Wadsworth, Karen Zambory

Romantic Retreat   H-858-2, p. 70

Magnificent Windows   HFL-1750-IR, p. 103

Zesty Villa   DD-1779, p. 125

All Decked Out!   CAR-81007, p. 129

Published by HomeStyles Publishing and Marketing, Inc. Company Leaders Jeffrey B. Heegaard and Roger W. Heegaard. For information on advertising, contact Gene Tubbs at 612-338-8155, P.O. Box 50670, Minneapolis, MN 55405.

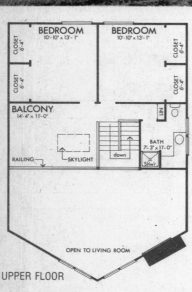

Photo by Bob Hallinen

Soaring Design

- Suitable for level or sloping lots, this versatile design can be expanded or finished as time and budget allow.
- Surrounding deck accessible from all main living areas.
- Great living room enhanced by vaulted ceilings, second-floor balcony, skylights and dramatic window wall.
- Rear entrance has convenient access to full bath and laundry room.
- Two additional bedrooms on upper level share second bath and balcony room.

NOTE: The above photographed home may have been modified by the homeowner. Please refer to floor plan and/or drawn elevation shown for actual blueprint details.

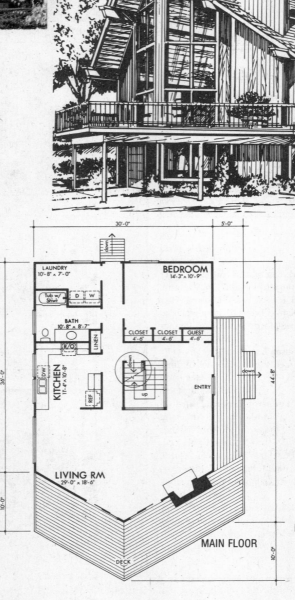

See this plan on our "Best-Sellers" VideoGraphic Tour! Order form on page 9

Upper Floor

- BEDROOM 10'-10" x 13'-1"
- BEDROOM 10'-10" x 13'-1"
- CLOSET 6'-4"
- CLOSET 6'-4"
- CLOSET 6'-4"
- CLOSET 6'-4"
- BALCONY 14'-4" x 11'-0"
- LIN
- BATH 7'-3" x 11'-0"
- Shwr.
- RAILING
- SKYLIGHT
- down
- OPEN TO LIVING ROOM

Main Floor

- 30'-0"
- 5'-0"
- 36'-0"
- 10'-0"
- 44'-8"
- 10'-0"
- down
- LAUNDRY 10'-8" x 7'-0"
- D W
- Tub w/ Shwr
- BATH 10'-8" x 8'-7"
- R/O
- LINEN
- KITCHEN 11'-4" x 10'-8"
- DW
- REF
- CLOSET 4'-6"
- CLOSET 4'-6"
- GUEST 4'-6"
- down
- up
- down
- ENTRY
- BEDROOM 14'-3" x 10'-9"
- LIVING RM 29'-0" x 18'-6"
- DECK

Basement — Plan H-930-1 with basement

- SERVICE ROOM 13'-8" x 12'-8"
- GARAGE / SHOP 14'-2" x 35'-4"
- WH
- heat
- STOR
- up
- RECREATION 14'-6" x 13'-8"

Plan H-930-1A WITHOUT BASEMENT (CRAWLSPACE FOUNDATION)

- STOR

Plans H-930-1 & -1A

Bedrooms: 3	Baths: 2

Space:

Upper floor:	710 sq. ft.
Main floor:	1,210 sq. ft.
Total living area:	**1,920 sq. ft.**
Basement:	605 sq. ft.
Garage/shop:	605 sq. ft.
Exterior Wall Framing:	**2x6**

Foundation options:
Daylight basement (Plan H-930-1).
Crawlspace (Plan H-930-1A).
(Foundation & framing conversion diagram available — see order form.)

Blueprint Price Code:

Without basement:	B
With basement:	D

TO ORDER THIS BLUEPRINT, CALL TOLL-FREE 1-800-547-5570

Plans H-930-1 & -1A

PRICES AND DETAILS ON PAGES 12-15

Unique, Dramatic Floor Plan

- An expansive and impressive Great Room, warmed by a wood stove, features an island kitchen that's completely open in design.
- A passive solar sun room is designed to collect and store heat from the sun, while also providing a good view of the surroundings.
- Upstairs, you'll see a glamorous master suite with a private bath and a huge walk-in closet.
- The daylight basement adds a sunny sitting room, a third bedroom and a large recreation room.

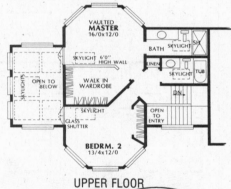

UPPER FLOOR

See this plan on our "Two-Story" VideoGraphic Tour!
Order form on page 9

Plans P-536-2A & -2D	
Bedrooms: 2-3	**Baths:** 2-3
Space:	
Upper floor:	642 sq. ft.
Main floor:	863 sq. ft.
Total living area:	**1,505 sq. ft.**
Basement:	863 sq. ft.
Garage:	445 sq. ft.
Exterior Wall Framing:	2x4

Foundation options:	Plan #
Daylight basement	P-536-2D
Crawlspace	P-536-2A

(Foundation & framing conversion diagram available — see order form.)

Blueprint Price Code:	
Plan P-536-2A	B
Plan P-536-2D	C

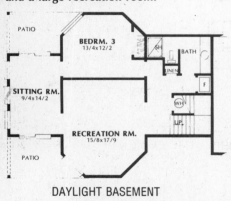

DAYLIGHT BASEMENT

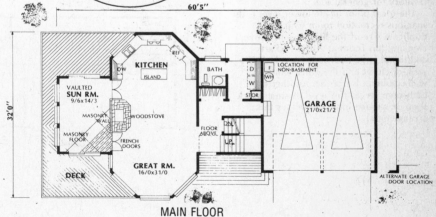

MAIN FLOOR

Attractive Hillside Home

This three-level recreation home is designed to fit comfortably on a slope of approximately 20 degrees, with a fall of 15 to 17 feet for the depth of the building. Naturally the stability of the ground must be taken into consideration, and local professional advice should be sought. Otherwise, this home is designed to meet the requirements of the Uniform Building Code.

The pleasing contemporary nature of the exterior is calculated to blend into the surroundings as unobtrusively as possible, following the natural contours.

The modest roadside facade consisting of garage doors and a wooden entrance deck conceals the spacious luxury that lies beyond. Proceeding from the rustic deck into the skylighted entry hall, one is struck by the immensity of the living-dining room and the huge deck extending beyond. A massive masonry backdrop provides a setting for the pre-fab fireplace of your choice (this same structure incorporates the flue for a similar unit on the lower level).

Before descending from the entry hall, one must take notice of the balcony-type den, library, hobby or office room on this level — a private retreat from the activities below.

The efficient U-shaped kitchen has an adjoining attached breakfast bar for casual dining whenever the roomy dining room facilities are not required. A convenient laundry room is an important part of this housekeeping section.

The master bedroom suite occupies the remainder of the 1,256 sq. ft. contained on this level. The room itself, 12' x 16' in size, is served by a private full bathroom and two huge wardrobe closets. Direct access to the large deck provides opportunity for morning sit-ups or evening conversation under the stars. A final convenience on this level is the small lavatory for general use.

The focal point of the lower level is the spacious recreation room which is a duplicate size of the living room above. Flanking this room at either end are additional large bedrooms, one having a walk-in closet and the other a huge wall-spanning wardrobe. Another full bathroom serves this level. A small work shop or storage room completes this arrangement.

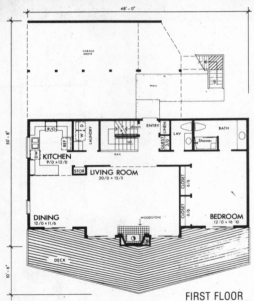

FIRST FLOOR
1256 SQUARE FEET

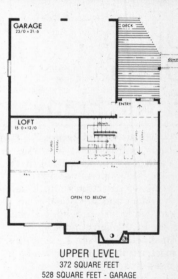

UPPER LEVEL
372 SQUARE FEET
528 SQUARE FEET - GARAGE

PLAN H-966-1B
WITH DAYLIGHT BASEMENT

(Exterior walls framed in 2x6 studs)

Upper level:	372 sq.
Main floor:	1,256 sq.
Basement:	1,256 sq.
Total living area:	2,884 sq.
(Not counting garage)	

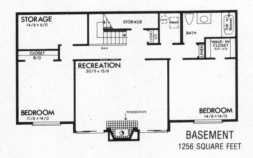

BASEMENT
1256 SQUARE FEET

4   *TO ORDER THIS BLUEPRINT,*
CALL TOLL-FREE 1-800-547-5570

Blueprint Price Code D
Plan H-966-1B

PRICES AND DETAILS
ON PAGES 12-15

All-Season Chalet

A guided tour from the front entry of this home takes you into the central hallway that serves as the hub of traffic to the main floor level. From here, convenience extends in every direction and each room is connected

in a step-saving manner. Besides the master bedroom with twin closets, a full bathroom with stall shower is placed adjacent to a common wall that also serves the laundry equipment.

The living room and dining area are connected to allow for the expandable use of the dining table should the need arise for additional seating. The kitchen is open ended onto the dining area and has all the modern conveniences and built-in details.

A raised deck flanks the gable end of the living zone and extends outward for a distance of 8′.

A full basement is reached via a stairway connecting with the central hallway. The basement provides ample storage plus room for the central heating system. Another interesting feature is the garage placed under the home where the owner may not only store his automobile but such things as a boat and trailer and other sporting equipment.

First floor:	1,008 sq. ft.
Second floor:	462 sq. ft.
Total living area:	1,470 sq. ft.
(Not counting basement or garage)	

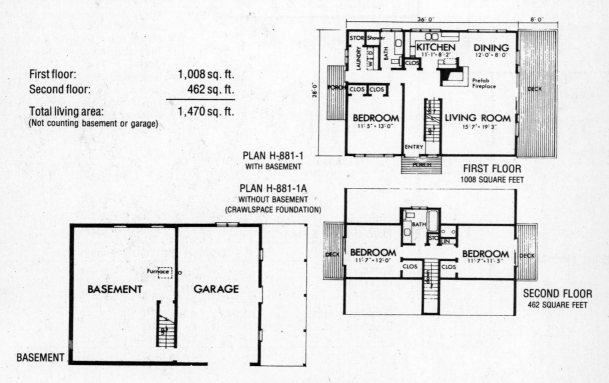

PLAN H-881-1
WITH BASEMENT

PLAN H-881-1A
WITHOUT BASEMENT
(CRAWLSPACE FOUNDATION)

TO ORDER THIS BLUEPRINT,
CALL TOLL-FREE 1-800-547-5570

Blueprint Price Code A
Plans H-881-1 & -1A

PRICES AND DETAILS
ON PAGES 12-15

5

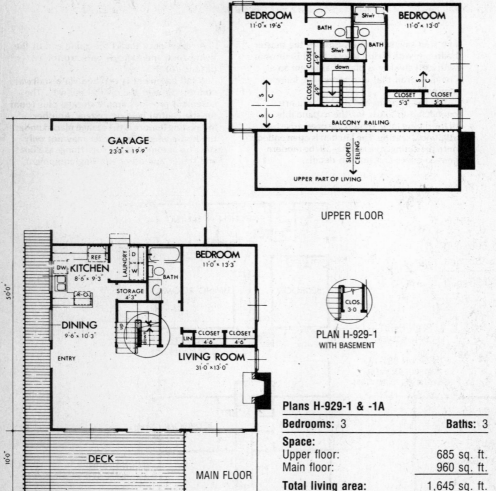

UPPER FLOOR

PLAN H-929-1
WITH BASEMENT

MAIN FLOOR

Contemporary Retreat

- Main floor plan revolves around an open, centrally located stairway.
- Spaciousness prevails throughout entire home with open kitchen and combination dining/living room.
- Living room features a great-sized fireplace and access to two-sided deck.
- Separate baths accommodate each bedroom.
- Upstairs hallway reveals an open balcony railing to oversee activities below.

Plans H-929-1 & -1A

Bedrooms: 3	Baths: 3
Space:	
Upper floor:	685 sq. ft.
Main floor:	960 sq. ft.
Total living area:	**1,645 sq. ft.**
Basement:	approx. 960 sq. ft.
Garage:	459 sq. ft.

Exterior Wall Framing:	2x6
Foundation options:	
Daylight basement (Plan H-929-1).	
Crawlspace (Plan H-929-1A).	
(Foundation & framing conversion	
diagram available — see order form.)	
Blueprint Price Code:	B

Five-Bedroom Chalet

Realizing that there are situations that require the maximum number of bedrooms, we have created this modest-sized home containing five bedrooms. One of these, especially the one over the garage, would serve very well as a private den, card room or library. The plan is available with or without basement.

This is an excellent example of the classic chalet. Close study will reveal how hall space has been kept at an absolute minimum. As a result, a modest first floor area of 952 sq. ft. and a compact second floor plan of 767 sq. ft. make the five bedrooms possible.

Also notice the abundance of storage space and built-ins with many other conveniences. Plumbing is provided in two complete bathrooms, and a washer and dryer has been tucked into one corner of the central hall on the main floor.

A clever technique has been used in the design of the staircase as it progresses halfway up to a landing midway between the two floors. From here it branches in two directions to a bedroom over the garage and to a hallway common to other rooms.

First floor:	952 sq. ft.
Second floor:	767 sq. ft.
Total living area:	1,719 sq. ft.
(Not counting basement or garage)	

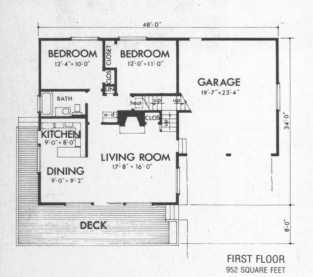

FIRST FLOOR
952 SQUARE FEET

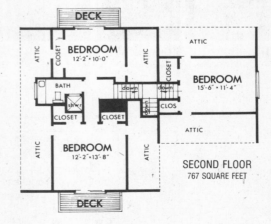

SECOND FLOOR
767 SQUARE FEET

PLAN H-804-2
WITH BASEMENT

PLAN H-804-2A
WITHOUT BASEMENT
(CRAWLSPACE FOUNDATION)

Blueprint Price Code B

Plans H-804-2 & -2A

Make the right choice when it comes to choosing your Dream Home...

SEND FOR YOUR FREE INFORMATION GUIDE!

Written by Jack Bloodgood, one of America's finest home designers.

Send for your FREE "how-to" guide that will help you make the smartest choices when it comes to your biggest investment: your dream home! You'll receive advice from home designer Jack Bloodgood. This illustrated guide is loaded with practical information you've been waiting for on home plan selection!

To receive your *FREE* guide, simply fill out this coupon and send it along with the UPC code from the front cover to:

**HomeStyles Plan Service
P.O. Box 50670
Minneapolis, MN 55405-0670**

Name_____

Address_____

City_____ State_____ ZIP_____

PGW33-A

Photo by Mark Englund/HomeStyles

Take the Plunge!

- From the elegant porte cochere to the striking rooflines, this home's facade is magnificent. But the rear area is equally fine, with its spa, waterfall and pool.
- Double doors lead from the entry into a columned foyer. Beyond the living room is a sunken wet bar that extends into the pool area, allowing guests to swim up to the bar for refreshments.
- The stunning master suite offers views of the pool through a curved window wall, access to the patio and an opulent bath.
- A secluded den, study or guest room is conveniently close to the hall bath.
- The dining room boasts window walls and a tiered pedestal ceiling. The island kitchen easily services both the formal and the informal areas of the home.
- A large breakfast room flows into a warm family room with a fireplace and sliders to the patio and pool.
- A railed staircase leads to the upper floor, where there are two bedrooms, a continental bath and a shared balcony deck overlooking the pool area.
- The observatory features high windows to accommodate an amateur stargazer's telescope. This room could also be used as an activity area for hobbies or games.

NOTE: The above photographed home may have been modified by the homeowner. Please refer to floor plan and/or drawn elevation shown for actual blueprint details.

See this plan on our "Best-Sellers" VideoGraphic Tour! Order form on page 9

UPPER FLOOR

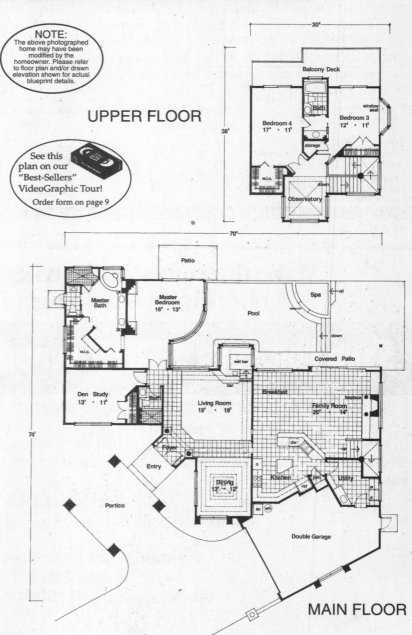

MAIN FLOOR

Plan HDS-99-154	
Bedrooms: 3-4	**Baths:** 3
Living Area:	
Upper floor	675 sq. ft.
Main floor	2,212 sq. ft.
Total Living Area:	**2,887 sq. ft.**
Garage	479 sq. ft.
Exterior Wall Framing:	2x4
Foundation Options:	
Slab	
(Typical foundation & framing conversion diagram available—see order form.)	
BLUEPRINT PRICE CODE:	D

TO ORDER THIS BLUEPRINT, CALL TOLL-FREE 1-800-547-5570

Plan HDS-99-154

PRICES AND DETAILS ON PAGES 12-15

THE "SOURCE 1"

WHAT OUR PLANS INCLUDE

"SOURCE 1" construction blueprints are detailed, clear and concise. All blueprints are designed by licensed architects or members of the A.I.B.D. (American Institute of Building Design), and each plan is designed to meet nationally recognized building codes (either the Uniform Building Code, Standard Building Code or Basic Building Code) at the time and place they were drawn.

The blueprints for most home designs include the following elements, but the presentation of these elements may vary depending on the size and complexity of the home and the style of the individual designer:

1. *Exterior Elevations* show the front, rear and sides of the house, including exterior materials, details and measurements.

2. *Foundation Plans* include drawings for a full, daylight or partial basement, crawlspace, slab, or pole foundation. All necessary notations and dimensions are included. (Foundation options will vary for each plan. If the home you want does not have the type of foundation you desire, a foundation conversion diagram is available from "SOURCE 1".)

3. *Detailed Floor Plans* show the placement of interior walls and the dimensions for rooms, doors, windows, stairways, etc., of each level of the house.

4. *Cross Sections* show details of the house as though it were cut in slices from the roof to the foundation. The cross sections specify the home's construction, insulation, flooring and roofing details.

5. *Interior Elevations* show the specific details of cabinets (kitchen, bathroom, and utility room), fireplaces, built-in units, and other special interior features, depending on the nature and complexity of the item. **Note:** *For cost savings and to accommodate your own style and taste, we suggest contacting local cabinet and fireplace distributors for sizes and style*

6. *Roof Details* show slope, pitch and location of dormers, gables and other roof elements, including clerestory windows and skylights. These details may be shown on the elevation sheet or on a separate diagram. **Note:** *If trusses are used, we suggest using a local truss manufacturer to design your trusses to comply with your local codes and regulations.*

7. *Schematic Electrical Layouts* show the suggested locations for switches, fixtures and outlets. These details may be shown on the floor plan or on a separate diagram.

8. *General Specifications* provide general instructions and information regarding structure, excavating and grading, masonry and concrete work, carpentry and wood, thermal and moisture protection, and specifications about drywall, tile, flooring, glazing, caulking and sealants.

PLANS PACKAGE

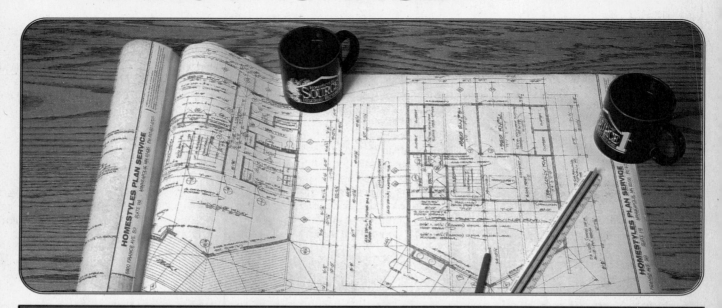

OTHER HELPFUL BUILDING AIDS

Every set of plans that you order will contain the details your builder needs. However, "Source 1" provides additional guides and information that you may order, as follows:

1. *Reproducible Blueprint Set* is useful if you will be making changes to the stock home plan you've chosen. This set consists of original line drawings produced on erasable, reproducible paper for the purpose of modification. When alterations are complete, working copies can be made.

2. *Mirror Reversed Plans* are used when building the home in reverse of the illustrated floor plan. Reversed plans are available for an additional one-time surcharge. Since the lettering and dimensions will read backwards, we recommend that you order only one or two reversed sets in addition to the regular-reading sets.

3. *Itemized List of Materials* details the quantity, type and size of materials needed to build your home. (This list is helpful in acquiring an accurate construction estimate.)

4. *Description of Materials* describes the type and quality of materials suggested for the home. This form may be required for obtaining FHA or VA financing.

5. *Typical "How-To" Diagrams — Plumbing, Wiring, Solar Heating, and Framing and Foundation Conversion Diagrams.* Each of these diagrams details the basic tools and techniques needed to plumb, wire and install a solar heating system, convert plans with 2 x 4 exterior walls to 2 x 6 (or vice versa), or adapt a plan for a basement, crawlspace or slab foundation. ***Note: These diagrams are general and not specific to any one plan.**

NOTE: Due to regional variations, local availability of materials, local codes, methods of installation, and individual preferences, it is impossible to include much detail on heating, plumbing, and electrical work on your plans. The duct work, venting, and other details will vary depending on the type of heating and cooling system (forced air, hot water, electric, solar) and the type of energy (gas, oil, electricity, solar) that you use. These details and specifications are easily obtained from your builder, contractor, and/or local suppliers.

PLEASE READ BEFORE YOU ORDER

WHO WE ARE

"Source 1" is a consortium of 45 of America's leading residential designers. All the plans presented in this book are designed by licensed architects or members of the A.I.B.D. (American Institute of Building Designers), and each plan is designed to meet nationally recognized building codes (either the Uniform Building Code, Standard Building Code or Basic Building Code) in effect at the time and place that they were drawn.

BLUEPRINT PRICES

Our sales volume allows us to offer quality blueprints at a fraction of the cost it takes to develop them. Custom designs cost thousands of dollars, usually 5 to 15% of the cost of construction. Design costs for a $100,000 home, for example, can range from $5,000 to $15,000.

Our pricing schedule is based on "Total heated living space." Garages, porches, decks and unfinished basements are <u>not</u> included.

Number of Sets	Price Code Based on Square Feet						
	A under 1,500	B 1,500-1,999	C 2,000-2,499	D 2,500-2,999	E 3,000-3,499	F 3,500-3,999	G 4,000 & up
1	$280	$315	$350	$385	$420	$455	$490
4	$330	$365	$400	$435	$470	$505	$540
7	$365	$400	$435	$470	$505	$540	$575
Reproducible Set	$440	$475	$510	$545	$580	$615	$650

ARCHITECTURAL AND ENGINEERING SEALS

The increased concern over energy costs and safety has prompted many cities and states to require an architect or engineer to review and "seal" a blueprint prior to construction. There may be a fee for this service. Please contact your local lumber yard, municipal building department, Builders Association, or local chapter of the AIBD or AIA (American Institute of Architecture).

Note: (Plans for homes to be built in Nevada may have to be re-drawn and sealed by a Nevada-licensed design professional.)

EXCHANGE INFORMATION

We want you to be happy with your blueprint purchase. If, for some reason, the blueprints that you ordered cannot be used, we will be pleased to exchange them within 30 days of the purchase date. Please note that a handling fee will be assessed for all exchanges. For more information, call us toll-free. **Note: Reproducible Sets cannot be exchanged for any reason.**

ESTIMATING BUILDING COSTS

Building costs vary widely depending on style, size, type of finishing materials you select, and the local rates for labor and building materials. A local average cost per square foot of construction can give you a rough estimate. To get the average cost per square foot in your area, you can call a local contractor, your state or local Builders Association, the National Association of Home Builders (NAHB), or the AIBD. A more accurate estimate will require a professional review of the working blueprints and the types of materials you will be using.

FOUNDATION OPTIONS AND EXTERIOR CONSTRUCTION

Depending on your location and climate, your home will be built with either a slab, crawlspace or basement foundation; the exterior walls will either be 2x4 or 2x6. Most professional contractors and builders can easily adapt a home to meet the foundation and exterior wall requirements that you desire.

If the home that you select does not offer the foundation or exterior wall requirements that you prefer, HomeStyles offers a typical foundation and framing conversion diagram. (See order form.)

HOW MANY BLUEPRINTS SHOULD I ORDER?

A single set of blueprints is sufficient to study and review a home in greater detail. However, if you are planning to get cost estimates or are planning to build, you will need a minimum of 4 sets. If you will be modifying your home plan, we recommend ordering a Reproducible Blueprint Set.

To help determine the exact number of sets you will need, please refer to the Blueprint Checklist below:

BLUEPRINT CHECKLIST

____**Owner (1 Set)**
____**Lending Institution (usually 1 set for conventional mortgage; 3 sets for FHA or VA loans)**
____**Builder (usually requires at least 3 sets)**
____**Building Permit Department (at least 1 set)**

REVISIONS, MODIFICATIONS AND CUSTOMIZING

The tremendous variety of designs available from "SOURCE 1" allows you to choose the home that best suits your lifestyle, budget and building site. Through your choice of siding, roof, trim, decorating, color, etc., your home can be customized easily.

Minor changes and material substitutions can be made by any professional builder without the need for expensive blueprint revisions. However, if you will be making major changes, we strongly recommend that you order a Reproducible Blueprint Set and seek the services of an architect or professional designer.

**Every state, county and municipality has its own codes, zoning requirements, ordinances, and building regulations. Modifications may be necessary to comply with your specific requirements -- snow loads, energy codes, seismic zones, etc.

COMPLIANCE WITH CODES

Depending on where you live, you may need to modify your plans to comply with local building requirements -- snow loads, energy codes, seismic zones, etc. All "SOURCE 1" plans are designed to meet the specifications of seismic zones I or II. "SOURCE 1" authorizes the use of our blueprints expressly conditioned upon your obligation and agreement to strictly comply with all local building codes, ordinances, regulations, and requirements -- including permits and inspections at the time of construction

LICENSE AGREEMENT, COPY RESTRICTIONS, COPYRIGHT

When you purchase a "SOURCE 1" blueprint, we, as Licensor, grant you, as Licensee, the right to use these documents to construct a single unit. All of the plans in this publication are protected under the Federal Copyright Act, Title XVII of the United States Code and Chapter 37 of the Code of Federal Regulations. Each "Source 1" designer retains title and ownership of the original documents. The blueprints licensed to you cannot be resold or used by any other person, copied or reproduced by any means. **This does not apply to Reproducible Blueprints.** When you purchase a Reproducible Blueprint Set, you reserve the right to modify and reproduce the plan.

BLUEPRINT ORDER FORM

Ordering your dream home plans is as easy as 1-2-3!

Complete this order form in just 3 easy steps. Then mail in your order, or call 1-800-547-5570 for faster service!

Thank you for your order and good luck with your new home!

1. BLUEPRINTS & ACCESSORIES

SAVE $60! **SAVE $135!**

BLUEPRINT CHART

Price Code	1 Set	4 Sets	7 Sets	Reproducible Set*
A	$280	$330	$365	$440
B	$315	$365	$400	$475
C	$350	$400	$435	$510
D	$385	$435	$470	$545
E	$420	$470	$505	$580
F	$455	$505	$540	$615
G	$490	$540	$575	$650

Prices subject to change.

*A Reproducible Set is produced on erasable paper for the purpose of modification. Available for plans with prefix: A, AG, AGH, AH, AHP, APS, AX, B, C, CPS, DCL, DD, DW, E, EOF, FB, GL, GMA, GML, GSA, H, HDG, HDS, HFL, J, K, KLF, LMB, LRD, M, NW, OH, PH, PI, RD, S, SDG, THD, U, UDG, V.

ADDITIONAL SETS: Additional sets of the plan ordered are $40 each. Save $70 to $125 when you order the 4-set or 7-set package shown above!

MIRROR REVERSED SETS: $40 Surcharge. From the total number of sets you ordered above, choose the number of these that you want to be reversed. Pay only $40. *Note: All writing on mirror reversed plans is backwards. We recommend ordering only one or two reversed sets in addition to the regular-reading sets.*

ITEMIZED LIST OF MATERIALS: Available for $40; each additional set is $10. Details the quantity, type and size of materials needed to build your home.

DESCRIPTION OF MATERIALS: Sold only in a set of two for $40. (For use in obtaining FHA or VA financing.)

TYPICAL HOW-TO DIAGRAMS: One set $15.00. Two sets $25. Three sets $35. All four sets only $40. General guides on plumbing, wiring, and solar heating, plus information on how to convert from one foundation or exterior framing to another. *Note: These diagrams are not specific to any one plan.*

2. SHIPPING AND HANDLING

Add shipping and handling costs according to chart below:

	1-3 Sets	4-6 Sets	7 Sets or more	Reproducible Set
U.S. Regular (5-6 working days)	$12.50	$15.00	$17.50	$15.00
U.S. Express (2-3 working days)	$25.00	$27.50	$30.00	$27.50
Canada Regular (2-3 weeks)	$12.50	$15.00	$17.50	$15.00
Canada Express (5-6 working days)	$25.00	$30.00	$35.00	$30.00
Overseas/Airmail (7-10 working days)	$50.00	$60.00	$70.00	$60.00

3. PAYMENT INFORMATION

Choose the method of payment you prefer. Send check, money order or credit card information, along with name and address to:

FOR FASTER SERVICE CALL 1-800-547-5570

---

1. COMPLETE THIS FORM

Plan Number_____ **Price Code**_____

Foundation_____

(Carefully review the foundation option(s) available for your plan -- basement, crawlspace, pole, pier, or slab. If several options are offered, choose only one.)

No. of Sets:
- ☐ One Set
- ☐ Four Sets
- ☐ Seven Sets
- ☐ One Reproducible Set

$_____ (See Blueprint Chart at left)

ADDITIONAL SETS_____ (Quantity) $_____ ($40 each)

MIRROR REVERSED SETS_____ (Quantity) $_____ ($40 Surcharge)

ITEMIZED LIST OF MATERIALS_____ (Quantity) $_____ ($40; $10 for each additional)
(Available on plans with prefix: AH, AHP, APS*, AX*, B*, C, CAR, CDG*, CPS, DD*, DW, E, FB, GSA, H, HDG, HFL, I*, J, K, LMB*, LRD, NW*, P, PH, R, S, THD, U, UDG, VL.)
Not available on all plans. Please call before ordering.

DESCRIPTION OF MATERIALS $_____ ($40 for two sets)
(Available on plans with prefix: AHP, C, DW, H, HFL, J, K, LMB, P, PH, VL.)

TYPICAL HOW-TO DIAGRAMS $_____ (All four only $40)
(One set $15.00. Two sets $25. Three sets $35.)
- ☐ Plumbing
- ☐ Wiring
- ☐ Solar Heating
- ☐ Framing & Foundation Conversion

SUBTOTAL $_____

SALES TAX* $_____ (*MN residents add 6.5% sales tax)

2.

SHIPPING & HANDLING $_____ (See chart at left)

3.

GRAND TOTAL $_____

- ☐ Check/Money Order enclosed (in U.S. funds)
- ☐ VISA ☐ MASTERCARD ☐ DISCOVER ☐ AMEX

Credit Card#_____ **Exp. Date**_____

Name_____

Address_____

City_____**State**_____**Country**_____

Zip_____ **Daytime Phone**(____)_____

Check if you are a builder: ☐ **Home Phone**(____)_____

Mail coupon to: **HomeStyles Plan Service** P.O. Box 50670 Minneapolis, MN 55405

Or Fax to: (612)338-1626

FOR FASTER SERVICE CALL 1-800-547-5570

PGW33-A

Adorable and Affordable

- This charming one-story home has much to offer, despite its modest size and economical bent.
- The lovely full-width porch has old-fashioned detailing, such as the round columns, decorative railings and ornamental molding.
- An open floor plan maximizes the home's square footage. The front door opens to the living room, where a railing creates a hallway effect while using very little space.
- Straight ahead, the dining room adjoins the island kitchen, while offering a compact laundry closet and sliding glass doors to a large rear patio.
- Focusing on quality, the home also offers features such as a 10-ft. tray ceiling in the living room and a 9-ft. stepped ceiling in the dining room.
- The three bedrooms are well proportioned. The master bedroom includes a private bathroom, while the two smaller bedrooms share another full bath. Note that the fixtures are arranged to reduce plumbing runs.

Plan AX-91316

Bedrooms: 3	Baths: 2
Living Area:	
Main floor	1,097 sq. ft.
Total Living Area:	**1,097 sq. ft.**
Basement	1,097 sq. ft.
Garage	461 sq. ft.
Exterior Wall Framing:	2x4

Foundation Options:
Daylight basement
Standard basement
Slab

(All plans can be built with your choice of foundation and framing. A generic conversion diagram is available. See order form.)

BLUEPRINT PRICE CODE: A

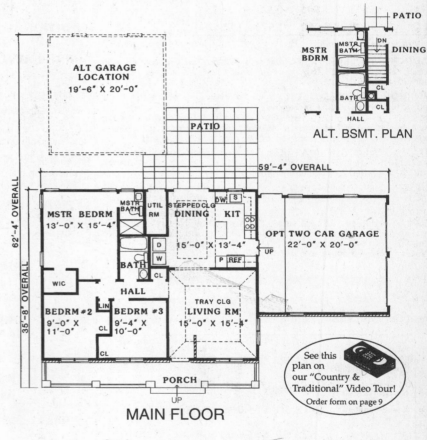

MAIN FLOOR

ALT. BSMT. PLAN

See this plan on our "Country & Traditional" Video Tour! Order form on page 9

VIEW INTO LIVING ROOM AND DINING ROOM

Compact Plan Fits Narrow Building Site

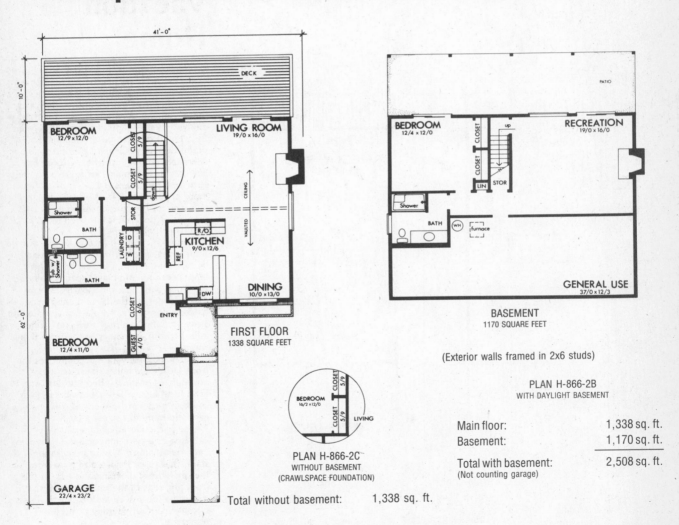

FIRST FLOOR
1338 SQUARE FEET

41'-0"
10'-0"
62'-0"

DECK

BEDROOM
12/9 x 12/0

LIVING ROOM
19/0 x 16/0

CLOSET 5/9
CLOSET 5/9
STOR
down

Shower

BATH

LAUNDRY
W D

KITCHEN
9/0 x 12/6
REF
R/O

VAULTED CEILING

Tub w/ Shower

BATH

CLOSET 6/6

ENTRY

DW

DINING
10/0 x 13/0

GUEST 4/0

BEDROOM
12/4 x 11/0

GARAGE
22/4 x 23/2

PLAN H-866-2C
WITHOUT BASEMENT
(CRAWLSPACE FOUNDATION)

BEDROOM
16/2 x 12/0
CLOSET 5/9
CLOSET 5/9
LIVING

Total without basement: 1,338 sq. ft.

PATIO

BEDROOM
12/4 x 12/0

CLOSET
CLOSET
up

RECREATION
19/0 x 16/0

LIN
STOR

Shower

BATH
WH
furnace

GENERAL USE
37/0 x 12/3

BASEMENT
1170 SQUARE FEET

(Exterior walls framed in 2x6 studs)

PLAN H-866-2B
WITH DAYLIGHT BASEMENT

Main floor:	1,338 sq. ft.
Basement:	1,170 sq. ft.
Total with basement:	2,508 sq. ft.
(Not counting garage)	

Blueprint Price Code D With Basement
Blueprint Price Code A Without Basement

Carefree Vacation Home

Scoffers and non-believers had a field day when the A-Frame first began to appear. Impractical, some said; uncomfortable, declared others; too expensive, ugly and more. And yet people built them and enjoyed them — and like the Volkswagen Bug, found them to be economical and practical, and yes, even beautiful to many beholders. Through the years, there has been a steady demand for these ubiquitous structures, and Plan H-15-1 is one of our more popular models. With this design, you will not be experimenting or pioneering because it has been built sucessfully many times.

Though it covers only 654 sq. ft. of main floor living space, it boasts an oversized living/dining room, a U-shaped kitchen, large bedroom and closet spaces, fully equipped bath plus a standard stairway (not a ladder) to the large second floor balcony dormitory. An old fashioned wood stove or a modern pre-fabricated fireplace adds warmth and cheer to the main living room.

The huge glass wall that dominates the front facade enhances the romantic atmosphere of the vaulted interior. And in ideal locations, where this wall can face south, a surprising amount of solar energy can help minimize heating costs.

One particular advantage of the A-Frame as a part-time or holiday home is easy maintenance. Use of penetrating stains that resist flaking and powdering on the small areas of siding and trim at the front and rear of the building is all that is required. The rest is roofing which resists weather without painting or other treatment.

MAIN FLOOR

26'-0"

DECK

STORAGE

BATH

Shwr

REF

KITCHEN 9'-2" x 8'-8"

DW

R/O

LIN

STOR

up

CLOSET 5'-0"

STORAGE

WOODSTOVE

BEDROOM 11'-8" x 10'-0"

4'-0"

28'-0"

LIVING ROOM 23'-8" x 11'-6"

DECK

10'-0"

PLAN H-15-1
CRAWLSPACE FOUNDATION

UPPER LEVEL

DECK

S. C.

BALCONY ROOM 15'-6" x 12'-4"

RAILINGS

down

OPEN TO LIVING RM.

SLOPED CEILING

Main floor:	654 sq. ft.
Upper floor:	254 sq. ft.
Total living area: (Not counting basement or garage)	908 sq. ft.

Blueprint Price Code A

Plan H-15-1

TO ORDER THIS BLUEPRINT, CALL TOLL-FREE 1-800-547-5570

PRICES AND DETAILS ON PAGES 12-15

Raised Interest

- The raised living and deck areas of this design take full advantage of surrounding views. A sloping lot can be accommodated with the shown lower level retaining wall.
- The lower level foyer feels high and is bright with a two-and-a-half-story opening lighting the stairwell.
- A two-car tuck-under garage and two bedroom suites complete the lower level.
- At the top of the stairs, guests are wowed with a view into the Grand Room, with high vaulted ceiling, fireplace and atrium doors and windows overlooking the main deck.
- The kitchen incorporates a sunny good morning room.
- The master suite dazzles with a vaulted ceiling, plant shelves, a private deck and a splashy master bath.

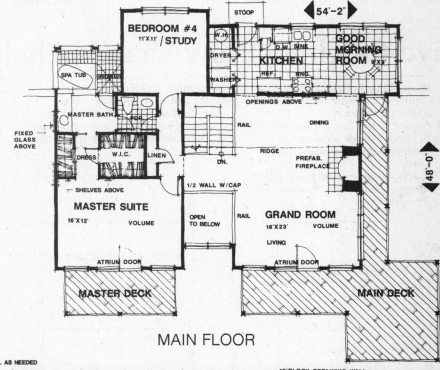

MAIN FLOOR

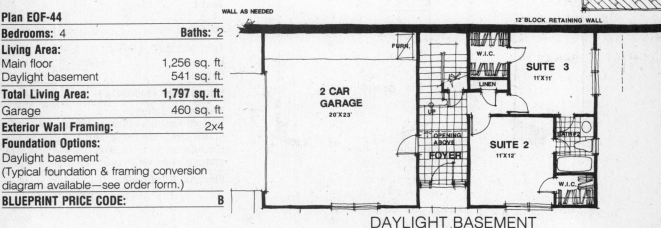

DAYLIGHT BASEMENT

Plan EOF-44

Bedrooms: 4	**Baths:** 2

Living Area:

Main floor	1,256 sq. ft.
Daylight basement	541 sq. ft.
Total Living Area:	**1,797 sq. ft.**
Garage	460 sq. ft.
Exterior Wall Framing:	2x4

Foundation Options:

Daylight basement
(Typical foundation & framing conversion diagram available—see order form.)

BLUEPRINT PRICE CODE:	**B**

Eye-Catching Prow-Shaped Chalet

- Steep pitched roof lines and wide cornices give this chalet a distinct alpine appearance.
- Prowed shape, large windows, and 10' deck provide view and enhancement of indoor/outdoor living.
- Functional division of living and sleeping areas by hallway and first floor full bath.
- Laundry facilities conveniently located near bedroom wing.
- U-shaped kitchen and spacious dining/living areas make the main floor perfect for entertaining.

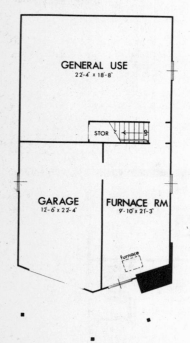

BASEMENT

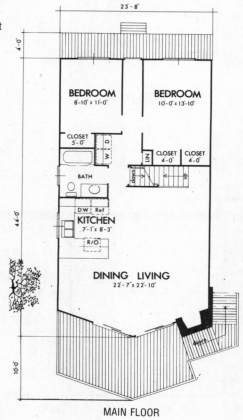

MAIN FLOOR

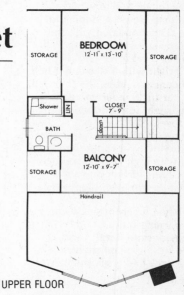

UPPER FLOOR

Plans H-886-3 & -3A

Bedrooms: 3	Baths: 2

Space:	
Upper floor:	486 sq. ft.
Main floor:	994 sq. ft.

Total without basement:	1,480 sq. ft.
Basement:	approx. 715 sq. ft.
Garage:	279 sq. ft.

Exterior Wall Framing:	2x6

Foundation options:
Daylight basement (Plan H-886-3).
Crawlspace (Plan H-886-3A).
(Foundation & framing conversion diagram available — see order form.)

Blueprint Price Code:	A

TO ORDER THIS BLUEPRINT, CALL TOLL-FREE 1-800-547-5570

Plans H-886-3 & -3A

PRICES AND DETAILS ON PAGES 12-15

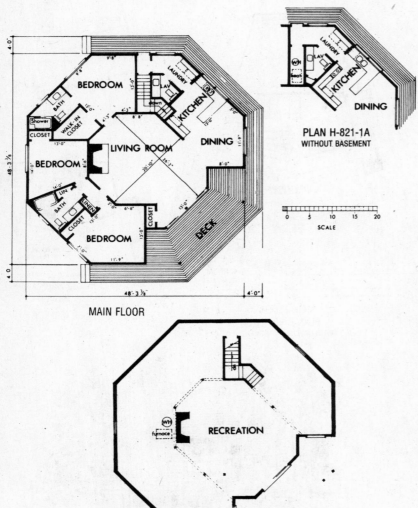

MAIN FLOOR

PLAN H-821-1A
WITHOUT BASEMENT

SCALE
0 5 10 15 20

BASEMENT

Versatile Octagon

- Popular octagonal design features a secondary raised roof to allow light into the 500 sq. ft. living room.
- Unique framing design allows you to divide the living space any way you choose: left open, with 3 or more bedrooms, a den, library or other options.
- Large, winding deck can accommodate outdoor parties and guests.
- Optional basement expands recreational opportunities.

Plans H-821-1 & -1A

Bedrooms: 3	Baths: 2½
Space: Main floor:	1,699 sq. ft.
Total living area:	1,699 sq. ft.
Basement:	approx. 1,699 sq. ft.
Exterior Wall Framing:	2x4

Foundation options:
Daylight basement (Plan H-821-1).
Crawlspace (Plan H-821-1A).
(Foundation & framing conversion diagram available — see order form.)

Blueprint Price Code:

Without basement	B
With basement	E

Proven Plan Features Passive Sun Room

- A passive sun room, energy-efficient wood stove, and a panorama of windows make this design highly economical.
- Open living/dining room features attractive balcony railing, stone hearth, and adjoining sun room with durable stone floor.
- Well-equipped kitchen is separated from dining area by a convenient breakfast bar.
- Second level sleeping areas border a hallway and balcony.
- Optional basement plan provides extra space for entertaining or work.

Plans H-855-3A & -3B

Bedrooms: 3	Baths: 2-3

Space:	
Upper floor:	586 sq. ft.
Main floor:	1,192 sq. ft.
Sun room:	132 sq. ft.

Total living area:	1,910 sq. ft.
Basement:	approx. 1,192 sq. ft.
Garage:	520 sq. ft.

Exterior Wall Framing:	2x6

Foundation options:
Daylight basement (Plan H-855-3B).
Crawlspace (Plan H-855-3A).
(Foundation & framing conversion diagram available — see order form.)

Blueprint Price Code:
Without basement	B
With basement	E

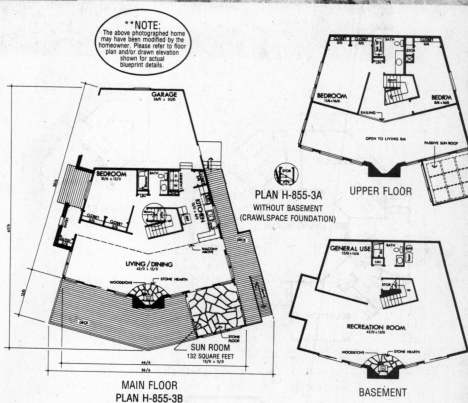

NOTE: The above photographed home may have been modified by the homeowner. Please refer to floor plan and/or drawn elevation shown for actual blueprint details.

PLAN H-855-3A
WITHOUT BASEMENT
(CRAWLSPACE FOUNDATION)

UPPER FLOOR

MAIN FLOOR
PLAN H-855-3B
WITH DAYLIGHT BASEMENT

BASEMENT

Small Home Generous with Living Comforts

- Open, space-saving Great Room with vaulted ceilings and stone fireplace; expansive front adjoining deck.
- Open staircase and balcony overlook living area below.
- U-shaped kitchen with pantry and snack bar.
- All three bedrooms feature private access to rear decks.

Plan H-5

Bedrooms: 3	Baths: 1

Space:	
Upper floor:	332 sq. ft.
Main floor:	660 sq. ft.
Total living area:	**992 sq. ft.**
Exterior Wall Framing:	**2x4**

Foundation options:
Crawlspace only.
(Foundation & framing conversion diagram available — see order form.)

Blueprint Price Code:	A

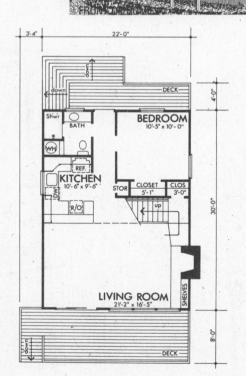

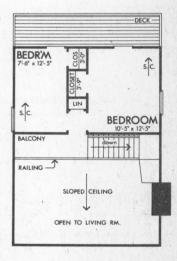

MAIN FLOOR

UPPER FLOOR

Weekend Retreat

For those whose goal is a small, affordable retreat at the shore or in the mountains, this plan may be the answer. Although it measures less than 400 sq. ft. of living space on the main floor, it lacks nothing in comfort and convenience. A sizeable living room boasts a masonry hearth on which to mount your choice of a wood stove or a pre-fab fireplace. There is plenty of room for furniture, including a dining table.

The galley-type kitchen is a small marvel of compact convenience and utility, even boasting a dishwasher and space for a stackable washer and dryer. The wide open nature of the first floor guarantees that even the person working in the kitchen area will still be included in the party. On the floor plan, a dashed line across the living room indicates the limits of the balcony bedroom above. In front of this line, the A-frame shape of the living room soars from the floor boards to the ridge beam high above. Clerestory windows lend a further note of spaciousness and unity with nature's outdoors. A huge planked deck adds to the indoor-outdoor relationship.

A modest-sized bedroom on the second floor is approached by a standard stairway, not an awkward ladder or heavy pull-down stairway as is often the case in small A-frames. The view over the balcony rail to the living room below adds a note of distinction. The unique framing pattern allows a window at either end of the bedroom, improving both outlook and ventilation.

A compact bathroom serves both levels and enjoys natural daylight through a skylight window.

First floor:	391 sq. ft.
Upper level:	144 sq. ft.
Total living area:	535 sq. ft.

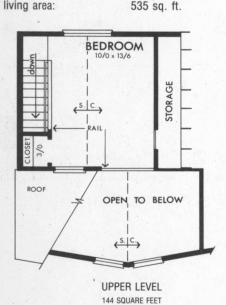

UPPER LEVEL
144 SQUARE FEET

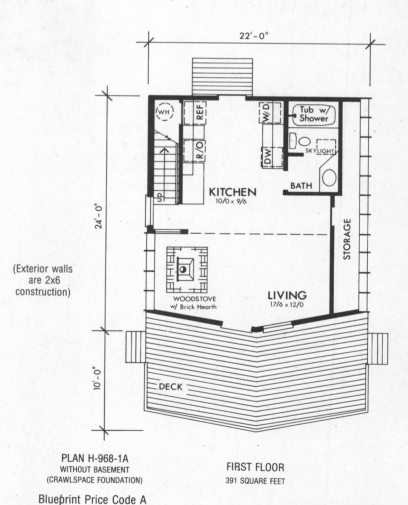

(Exterior walls are 2x6 construction)

PLAN H-968-1A
WITHOUT BASEMENT
(CRAWLSPACE FOUNDATION)

FIRST FLOOR
391 SQUARE FEET

Blueprint Price Code A

Plan H-968-1A

Every Room with a View

Unique, octagonal design allows an outdoor view from each room. Three bordering decks extend first-level living areas. Generous living room features dramatic stone fireplace and central skylight open to second floor. Second level features circular balcony connecting all bedrooms. Alternate second-floor plan replaces one bedroom with a viewing deck.

Plan H-27: 4-Bedroom Version

Bedrooms: 4	Baths: 2½

Space:

Upper floor:	1,167 sq. ft.
Main floor:	697 sq. ft.
Total living area:	**1,864 sq. ft.**
Exterior Wall Framing:	2x4

Foundation options:
Crawlspace only.
(Foundation & framing conversion diagram available — see order form.)

Blueprint Price Code:	B

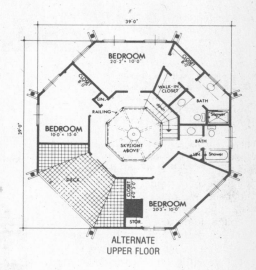

ALTERNATE
UPPER FLOOR

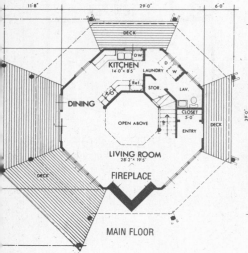

MAIN FLOOR

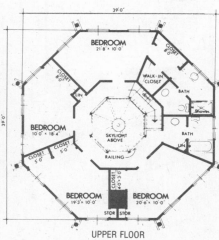

UPPER FLOOR

Plan H-27: 3-Bedroom Version

Bedrooms: 3	Baths: 2½

Space:

Upper floor:	960 sq. ft.
Main floor:	697 sq. ft.
Total living area:	**1,657 sq. ft.**
Exterior Wall Framing:	2x4

Foundation options:
Crawlspace only.
(Foundation & framing conversion diagram available — see order form.)

Blueprint Price Code:	B

Windowed Great Room

- This attractive, open design with a wonderful windowed Great Room can function as a cabin, a mountain retreat or a permanent residence.
- The main level of the home is entered via a split-landing stairway to a wraparound deck.
- The kitchen and the Great Room merge to form a huge family activity area under a soaring 22-ft. cathedral ceiling.
- Two quiet main-floor bedrooms share a hall bath.
- Upstairs, an open balcony loft offers elevated views through the massive front window wall.
- The large sleeping loft could be split into two smaller bedrooms.

Plan I-1354-B

Bedrooms: 2+	Baths: 2
Living Area:	
Upper floor	366 sq. ft.
Main floor	988 sq. ft.
Total Living Area:	**1,354 sq. ft.**
Daylight basement	658 sq. ft.
Tuck-under garage	260 sq. ft.
Exterior Wall Framing:	**2x6**

Foundation Options:

Daylight basement

(All plans can be built with your choice of foundation and framing. A generic conversion diagram is available. See order form.)

BLUEPRINT PRICE CODE:	**A**

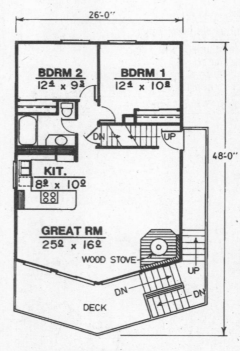

MAIN FLOOR

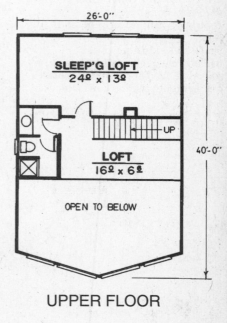

UPPER FLOOR

Plan I-1354-B

Narrow-Lot Solar Design

This design offers your choice of foundation and number of bedrooms, and it can be built on a narrow, sloping lot.

The passive-solar dining room has windows on three sides and a slate floor for heat storage. A French door leads to a rear deck.

The living room features a sloped ceiling, a woodstove in ceiling-high masonry, and sliding glass doors to the adjoining deck.

The kitchen is open to the dining room but separated from the living room by a 7½-ft.-high wall.

The upper-level variations include a choice of one or two bedrooms. Clerestory windows above the balcony railing add drama to both versions.

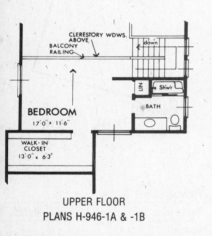

UPPER FLOOR
PLANS H-946-1A & -1B

Plans H-946-1A & -1B (Two Bedrooms)

Bedrooms: 2	Baths: 2
Living Area:	
Upper floor	381 sq. ft.
Main floor	814 sq. ft.
Total Living Area:	**1,195 sq. ft.**
Basement	approx. 814 sq. ft.
Garage	315 sq. ft.
Exterior Wall Framing:	2x6

Foundation Options:
Daylight basement (Plan H-946-1B)
Crawlspace (Plan H-946-1A)
(Typical foundation & framing conversion diagram available—see order form.)

BLUEPRINT PRICE CODE: A

MAIN FLOOR

PLANS H-946-2A & -2B

Plans H-946-2A & -2B (Three Bedrooms)

Bedrooms: 3	Baths: 2
Living Area:	
Upper floor	290 sq. ft.
Main floor	814 sq. ft.
Total Living Area:	**1,104 sq. ft.**
Basement	approx. 814 sq. ft.
Garage	315 sq. ft.
Exterior Wall Framing:	2x6

Foundation Options:
Daylight basement (Plan H-946-2B)
Crawlspace (Plan H-946-2A)
(Typical foundation & framing conversion diagram available—see order form.)

BLUEPRINT PRICE CODE: A

Panoramic View Embraces Outdoors

- This geometric design takes full advantage of scenic sites.
- Living area faces a glass-filled wall and wrap-around deck.
- Open dining/living room arrangement is complemented by vaulted ceilings, an overhead balcony, and a 5-ft-wide fireplace.
- 12' deep main deck offers generous space for outdoor dining and entertaining.

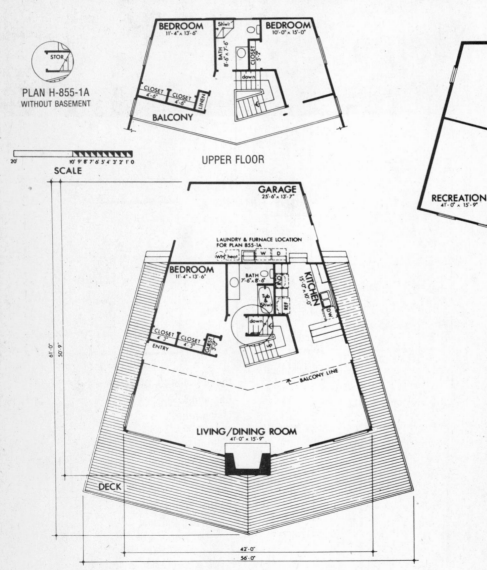

PLAN H-855-1A
WITHOUT BASEMENT

UPPER FLOOR

SCALE

MAIN FLOOR

GENERAL USE

RECREATION
41'-0" x 15'-9"

BASEMENT

Plans H-855-1 & -1A

Bedrooms: 3	Baths:
Space:	
Upper floor:	625 sq. f
Main floor:	1,108 sq. f
Total living area:	**1,733 sq. f**
Basement:	approx. 1,108 sq. f
Garage:	346 sq. f
Exterior Wall Framing:	2x

Foundation options:
Daylight basement (Plan H-855-1).
Crawlspace (Plan H-855-1A).
(Foundation & framing conversion diagram available — see order form.)

Blueprint Price Code:
Without basement
With basement

Plans H-855-1 & -1A

PRICES AND DETAILS ON PAGES 12-15

Covered Wraparound Deck Featured

- A covered deck spans this home from the main entrance to the kitchen door.
- An over-sized fireplace is the focal point of the living room, which merges into an expandable dining area.
- The kitchen is tucked into one corner, but open counter space allows visual contact with living areas beyond.
- Two good-sized main-floor bedrooms are furnished with sufficient closet space.
- The basement level adds a third bedroom in an additional 673 sq. ft. of living space.

Plan H-806-2

Bedrooms: 3	Baths: 1
Living Area:	
Main floor	952 sq. ft.
Daylight basement	673 sq. ft.
Total Living Area:	**1,625 sq. ft.**
Garage	279 sq. ft.
Exterior Wall Framing:	2x6

Foundation Options:
Daylight basement
(Typical foundation & framing conversion diagram available—see order form.)

BLUEPRINT PRICE CODE: B

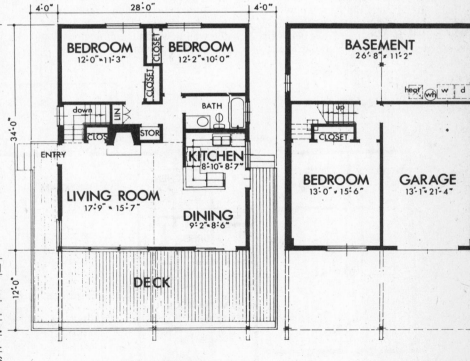

MAIN FLOOR   DAYLIGHT BASEMENT

Rustic Welcome

- This rustic design boasts an appealing exterior with a covered front porch that offers guests a friendly welcome.
- Inside, the centrally located Great Room features an 11-ft., 8-in. cathedral ceiling with exposed wood beams. A massive fireplace separates the living area from the large dining room, which offers access to a nice backyard patio.
- The galley-style kitchen flows between the formal dining room and the bayed

breakfast room, which offers a handy pantry and access to laundry facilities.
- The master suite features a walk-in closet and a compartmentalized bath.
- Across the Great Room, two additional bedrooms have extra closet space and share a second full bath.
- The side-entry garage gives the front of the home an extra-appealing and uncluttered look.
- The optional daylight basement offers expanded living space. The stairway (not shown) would be located along the wall between the dining room and the back bedroom.

Plan C-8460	
Bedrooms: 3	**Baths:** 2
Living Area:	
Main floor	1,670 sq. ft.
Total Living Area:	**1,670 sq. ft.**
Daylight basement	1,600 sq. ft.
Garage	427 sq. ft.
Exterior Wall Framing:	2x4
Foundation Options:	
Daylight basement	
Crawlspace	
Slab	

(All plans can be built with your choice of foundation and framing. A generic conversion diagram is available. See order form.)

BLUEPRINT PRICE CODE: B

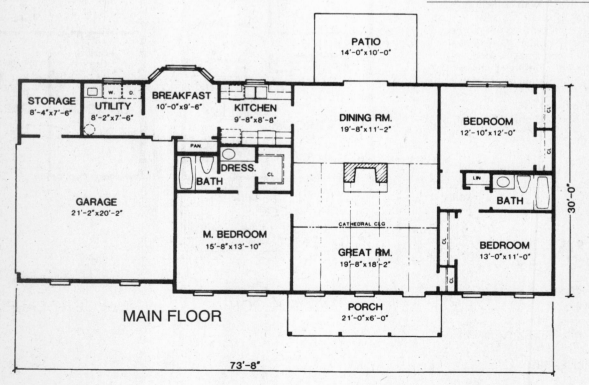

MAIN FLOOR

Plan C-8460

Unique Inside and Out

This delightful design is striking from both inside and out.

The huge "Grand Room" is flanked by two equally impressive master suites, both of which feature a vaulted ceiling, a sunny window seat, a walk-in closet and a private bath. Double doors in each of the suites open to a sun deck. The centrally located kitchen offers easy access from any part of the home, and a full bath, a laundry area and the entrance to the garage are nearby. Upstairs, two guest suites overlook the vaulted "Great Room" below.

Plan EOF-13

Bedrooms: 4	**Baths:** 3

Living Area:

Upper floor	443 sq. ft.
Main floor	1,411 sq. ft.
Total Living Area:	**1,854 sq. ft.**
Garage	264 sq. ft.
Storage	50 sq. ft.
Exterior Wall Framing:	2x6

Foundation Options:

Crawlspace

(Typical foundation & framing conversion diagram available—see order form.)

BLUEPRINT PRICE CODE:	B

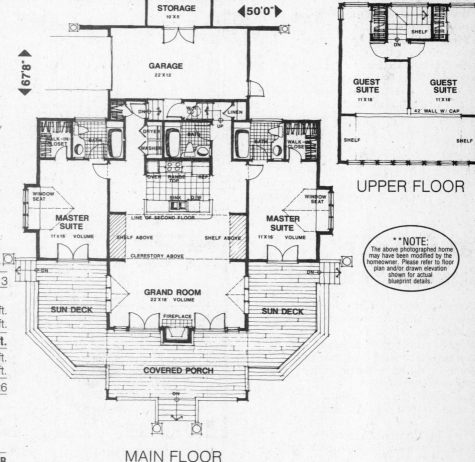

UPPER FLOOR

MAIN FLOOR

**NOTE: The above photographed home may have been modified by the homeowner. Please refer to floor plan and/or drawn elevation shown for actual blueprint details.

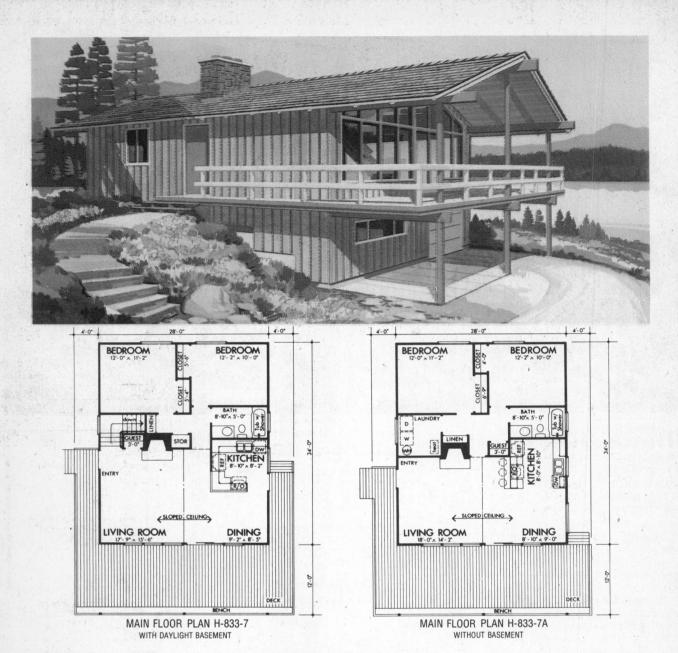

MAIN FLOOR PLAN H-833-7
WITH DAYLIGHT BASEMENT

MAIN FLOOR PLAN H-833-7A
WITHOUT BASEMENT

An Owner-Builder Special

- Everything you need for a leisure or retirement retreat is neatly packaged in just 952 square feet.
- The basic rectangular design features a unique wraparound deck, which is entirely covered by the projecting roof-line.
- Vaulted ceilings and a central fireplace visually enhance the cozy living/dining room.
- The daylight-basement option is suitable for building on a sloping lot.

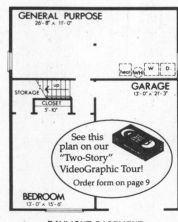

See this plan on our "Two-Story" VideoGraphic Tour! Order form on page 9

DAYLIGHT BASEMENT

Plans H-833-7 & -7A

Bedrooms: 2-3	**Baths: 1**
Living Area:	
Main floor	952 sq. ft.
Optional daylight basement	676 sq. ft.
Total Living Area:	**952/1,628 sq. ft.**
Garage	276 sq. ft.
Exterior Wall Framing:	2x6
Foundation Options:	**Plan #**
Daylight basement	H-833-7
Crawlspace	H-833-7A
(Typical foundation & framing conversion diagram available—see order form.)	
BLUEPRINT PRICE CODE:	**A/B**

See this plan on our "One-Story" VideoGraphic Tour! Order form on page 9

A Chalet for Today

- With its wraparound deck and soaring windows, this chalet-style home is ideal for recreational living and scenic sites.
- The living and dining rooms are combined to take advantage of the dramatic cathedral ceiling, the rugged stone fireplace and the view through the spectacular windows.
- A quaint balcony above adds to the warm country feeling of the living area, which extends to the expansive deck.

- The open kitchen features a bright corner sink and a nifty breakfast bar that adjoins the living area.
- The handy main-floor laundry area is close to two bedrooms and a full bath.
- The study is a feature rarely found in a home of this size and style.
- The master suite and a storage area encompass the upper floor. A cathedral ceiling, a whirlpool bath and sweeping views from the balcony give this space an elegant feel.
- The basement option includes a tuck-under garage, additional storage space and a separate utility area. A family room may be finished later.

Plan AHP-9340

Bedrooms: 3+	Baths: 2
Living Area:	
Upper floor	332 sq. ft.
Main floor	974 sq. ft.
Total Living Area:	**1,306 sq. ft.**
Basement	624 sq. ft.
Tuck-under garage	350 sq. ft.
Exterior Wall Framing:	2x4 or 2x6

Foundation Options:
Standard basement
Daylight basement
Crawlspace
Slab
(All plans can be built with your choice of foundation and framing. A generic conversion diagram is available. See order form.)

BLUEPRINT PRICE CODE:	A

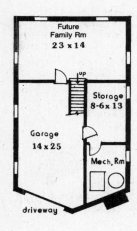

BASEMENT

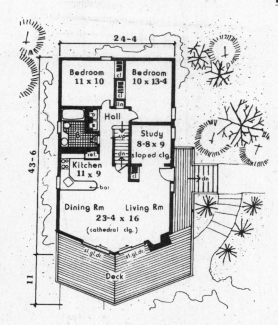

MAIN FLOOR

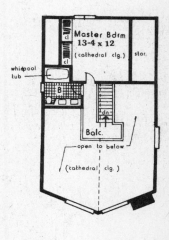

UPPER FLOOR

Appealing Farmhouse

- This appealing farmhouse design features a shady and inviting front porch with decorative railings.
- Inside, 14-ft. vaulted ceilings expand the living and dining rooms.
- This large area is brightened by bay windows and warmed by a unique two-way fireplace. Sliding glass doors lead to a sunny backyard patio.
- The functional kitchen includes a pantry closet, plenty of cabinet space and a serving bar to the dining room.
- The master bedroom boasts a mirrored dressing area, a private bath and abundant closet space.
- Two additional bedrooms share another full bath. The third bedroom includes a cozy window seat.

Plan NW-521

Bedrooms: 3	Baths: 2
Living Area:	
Main floor	1,187 sq. ft.
Total Living Area:	**1,187 sq. ft.**
Garage	448 sq. ft.
Exterior Wall Framing:	2x6

Foundation Options:

Crawlspace
(All plans can be built with your choice of foundation and framing. A generic conversion diagram is available. See order form.)

BLUEPRINT PRICE CODE:	**A**

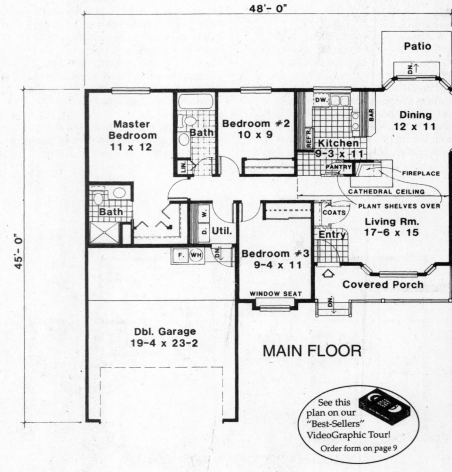

MAIN FLOOR

See this plan on our "Best-Sellers" VideoGraphic Tour! Order form on page 9

TO ORDER THIS BLUEPRINT, CALL TOLL-FREE 1-800-547-5570   Plan NW-521   **PRICES AND DETAILS ON PAGES 12-15**

Unexpected Amenities

- Surprising interior amenities are found within the casual exterior of this good-looking design.
- A dramatic fireplace warms the comfortable formal areas. The living and dining rooms share a 20-ft. cathedral ceiling and high windows that flank the fireplace. Sliding glass doors access an expansive side patio.

- The efficient walk-through kitchen provides plenty of counter space, in addition to a windowed sink and a pass-through to the living areas.
- A large bedroom, a full bath and an oversized utility room complete the main floor. The utility room offers space for a washer and dryer, plus a sink and an extra freezer.
- Upstairs, the spacious and secluded master suite boasts a walk-in closet, a private bath and lots of storage space. A railed loft area overlooks the living and dining rooms.

Plan I-1249-A	
Bedrooms: 2	**Baths:** 2
Living Area:	
Upper floor	297 sq. ft.
Main floor	952 sq. ft.
Total Living Area:	**1,249 sq. ft.**
Standard basement	952 sq. ft.
Exterior Wall Framing:	2x6
Foundation Options:	
Standard basement	
Crawlspace	

(All plans can be built with your choice of foundation and framing. A generic conversion diagram is available. See order form.)

BLUEPRINT PRICE CODE:	**A**

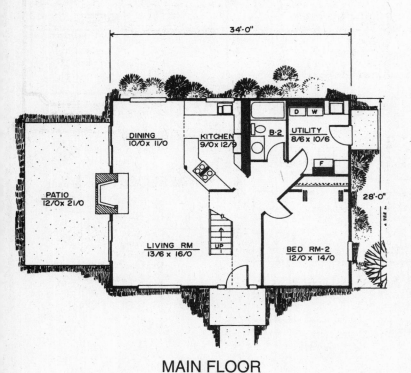

MAIN FLOOR

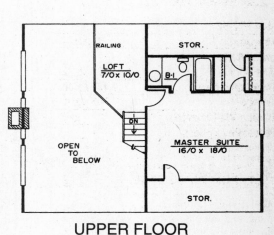

UPPER FLOOR

REAR VIEW

Bright Ideas!

- Four clerestory windows, a boxed-out window and wing walls sheltering the entry porch give this home definition.
- Inside, an open room arrangement coupled with vaulted ceilings, abundant windows and a sensational sun room make this home a definite bright spot.
- The living room features a 22-ft.-high vaulted ceiling, a warm woodstove and a glass-filled wall that offers views into the sun room. A patio door in the sun room opens to a large backyard deck.
- The adjoining dining room flows into the kitchen, which offers a versatile snack bar. A handy laundry room is just steps away, near the garage.
- Upstairs, the intimate bedroom suite includes a 14-ft.-high vaulted ceiling, a view to the living room, a walk-in closet and a private bath.
- The optional daylight basement boasts a spacious recreation room with a second woodstove, plus a fourth bedroom and a third bath. A shaded patio occupies the area under the deck.

FRONT VIEW

Plans H-877-5A & -5B

Bedrooms: 3+	Baths: 2-3
Living Area:	
Upper floor	382 sq. ft.
Main floor	1,200 sq. ft.
Sun room	162 sq. ft.
Daylight basement	1,200 sq. ft.
Total Living Area:	**1,744/2,944 sq. ft.**
Garage	457 sq. ft.
Exterior Wall Framing:	2x6
Foundation Options:	**Plan #**
Daylight basement	H-877-5B
Crawlspace	H-877-5A

(All plans can be built with your choice of foundation and framing. A generic conversion diagram is available. See order form.)

BLUEPRINT PRICE CODE:	**B/D**

UPPER FLOOR

DAYLIGHT BASEMENT

See this plan on our "Best-Sellers" VideoGraphic Tour! Order form on page 9

BASEMENT STAIRWAY LOCATION

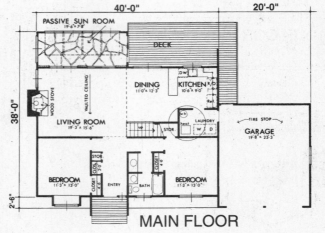

MAIN FLOOR

Plans H-877-5A & -5B

PRICES AND DETAILS ON PAGES 12-15

Large Deck Wraps Home

- A full deck and an abundance of windows surround this exciting two-level contemporary.
- The brilliant living room boasts a huge fireplace and a 14-ft.-high cathedral ceiling, plus a stunning prow-shaped window wall.

- Skywalls brighten the island kitchen and the dining room. A pantry closet and laundry facilities are nearby.
- The master bedroom offers private access to the deck. The master bath includes a dual-sink vanity, a large tub and a separate shower. A roomy hall bath serves a second bedroom.
- A generous-sized family room, another full bath and two additional bedrooms share the lower level with a two-car garage and a shop area.

Plan NW-579	
Bedrooms: 4	**Baths:** 3
Living Area:	
Main floor	1,707 sq. ft.
Daylight basement	901 sq. ft.
Total Living Area:	**2,608 sq. ft.**
Tuck-under garage	588 sq. ft.
Shop	162 sq. ft.
Exterior Wall Framing:	2x6
Foundation Options:	

Daylight basement
(All plans can be built with your choice of foundation and framing. A generic conversion diagram is available. See order form.)

BLUEPRINT PRICE CODE:	D

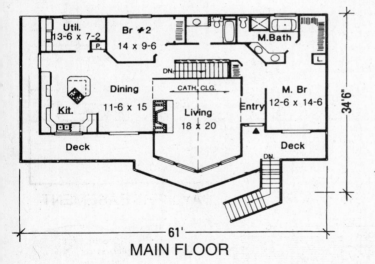

MAIN FLOOR

VIEW INTO LIVING ROOM

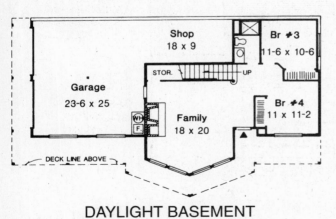

DAYLIGHT BASEMENT

Family Tradition

- This home basks in tradition, with beautiful detailing on the outside and vaulted family gathering areas inside.
- A columned front porch opens to a spacious family room, where a 16-ft. vaulted ceiling soars above a striking fireplace flanked by arched windows. The 16-ft. ceiling continues into the dining room and kitchen beyond.
- The sunny dining room opens to the backyard through a French door. The vaulted kitchen offers a bright angled sink, a snack bar and a large pantry closet topped by a plant shelf.
- The master suite boasts a 10½-ft. tray ceiling in the sleeping area and a 13½-ft. vaulted ceiling in the luxurious garden bath.
- Two secondary bedrooms share another full bath. A roomy laundry area is close to the bedrooms and the garage.
- For added spaciousness, all ceilings are 9 ft. high unless otherwise specified.

Plan FB-5115-CLAI

Bedrooms: 3	Baths: 2
Living Area:	
Main floor	1,198 sq. ft.
Total Living Area:	**1,198 sq. ft.**
Standard basement	1,198 sq. ft.
Garage	484 sq. ft.
Exterior Wall Framing:	2x4

Foundation Options:

Daylight basement
Crawlspace

(All plans can be built with your choice of foundation and framing. A generic conversion diagram is available. See order form.)

BLUEPRINT PRICE CODE: A

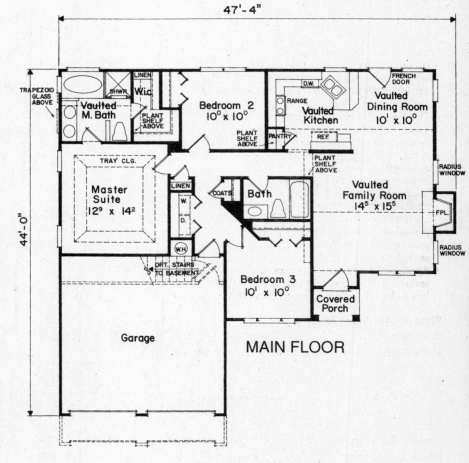

MAIN FLOOR

Instant Impact

- Bold rooflines, interesting angles and unusual window treatments give this stylish home lots of impact.
- Inside, high ceilings and an open floor plan maximize the home's square footage. At only 28 ft. wide, the home also is ideal for a narrow lot.
- A covered deck leads to the main entry, which features a sidelighted door, angled glass walls and a view of the striking open staircase.
- The Great Room is stunning, with its 16-ft. vaulted ceiling, energy-efficient woodstove and access to a large deck.
- A flat ceiling distinguishes the dining area, which shares an angled snack bar/cooktop with the step-saving kitchen. A laundry/mudroom is nearby.
- Upstairs, the master suite offers a sloped 13-ft. ceiling and a clerestory window. A walk-through closet leads to the private bath, which is enhanced by a skylighted, sloped ceiling.
- Another full bath and plenty of storage serve the other bedrooms, one of which has a sloped ceiling and a dual closet.

Plans H-1427-3A & -3B

Bedrooms: 3	Baths: 2½
Living Area:	
Upper floor	880 sq. ft.
Main floor	810 sq. ft.
Total Living Area:	**1,690 sq. ft.**
Daylight basement	810 sq. ft.
Garage	409 sq. ft.
Exterior Wall Framing:	2x4
Foundation Options:	**Plan #**
Daylight basement	H-1427-3B
Crawlspace	H-1427-3A

(All plans can be built with your choice of foundation and framing. A generic conversion diagram is available. See order form.)

BLUEPRINT PRICE CODE:	**B**

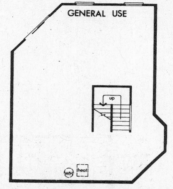

DAYLIGHT BASEMENT

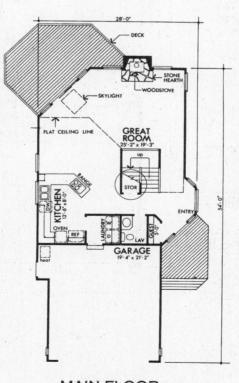

MAIN FLOOR

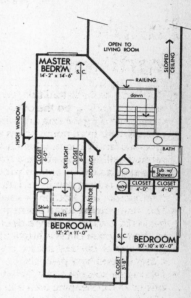

UPPER FLOOR

STAIRWAY AREA
IN CRAWLSPACE
VERSION

See this plan on our "Best-Sellers" VideoGraphic Tour! Order form on page 9

Comfortable L-Shaped Ranch

- From the covered entry to the beautiful and spacious family gathering areas, this comfortable ranch-style home puts many extras into a compact space.
- Straight off the central foyer, an inviting fireplace and a bright bay window highlight the living and dining area, while sliding glass doors open to a wide backyard terrace.
- The combination kitchen/family room features a large eating bar. The nearby mudroom offers a service entrance, laundry facilities, access to the garage and room for a half-bath.
- In the isolated sleeping wing, the master bedroom boasts a private bath and plenty of closet space. Two additional bedrooms share another full bath.

Plan K-276-R

Bedrooms: 3	**Baths:** 2+

Living Area:

Main floor	1,245 sq. ft.
Total Living Area:	**1,245 sq. ft.**
Standard basement	1,245 sq. ft.
Garage	499 sq. ft.
Exterior Wall Framing:	2x4 or 2x6

Foundation Options:

Standard basement
Crawlspace
Slab

(All plans can be built with your choice of foundation and framing. A generic conversion diagram is available. See order form.)

BLUEPRINT PRICE CODE: **A**

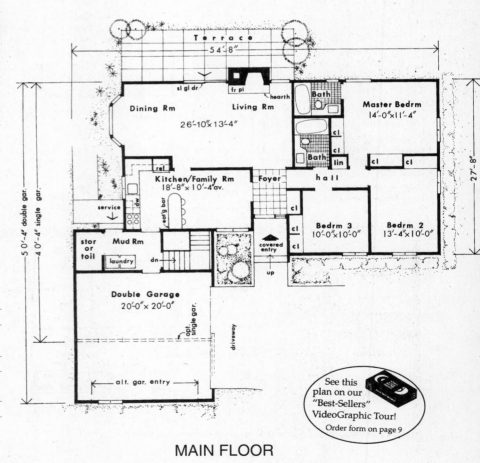

MAIN FLOOR

See this plan on our "Best-Sellers" VideoGraphic Tour! Order form on page 9

Rustic Comfort

- Rustic charm highlights the exterior of this design, while the interior is filled with all the latest comforts.
- The wide, covered porch opens to a roomy entry, where two 7-ft.-high openings with decorative railings view into the dining room.
- Straight ahead lies the sunken living room, which features a 16-ft.-high vaulted ceiling with exposed beams. The fireplace is faced with floor-to-ceiling fieldstone, adding to the rustic look. A rear door opens to a large patio with twin plant areas.

- The large U-shaped kitchen has such nice extras as a china niche with glass shelves. Other bonuses include the adjacent sewing/hobby room, the oversized utility room and the storage area and built-in workbench in the side-entry garage.
- The secluded master suite hosts a sunken sleeping area with built-in bookshelves. One step up is a cozy sitting area that is outlined by brick columns and a railed room divider. Double doors open to the deluxe bath, which offers a niche with glass shelves.
- Double doors conceal two more bedrooms and a full bath.

Plan E-1607	
Bedrooms: 3	**Baths:** 2
Living Area:	
Main floor	1,600 sq. ft.
Total Living Area:	**1,600 sq. ft.**
Standard basement	1,600 sq. ft.
Garage	484 sq. ft.
Storage	132 sq. ft.
Exterior Wall Framing:	2x6
Foundation Options:	

Standard basement
Crawlspace
Slab
(All plans can be built with your choice of foundation and framing. A generic conversion diagram is available. See order form.)

BLUEPRINT PRICE CODE: B

See this plan on our "Country & Traditional" Video Tour! Order form on page 9

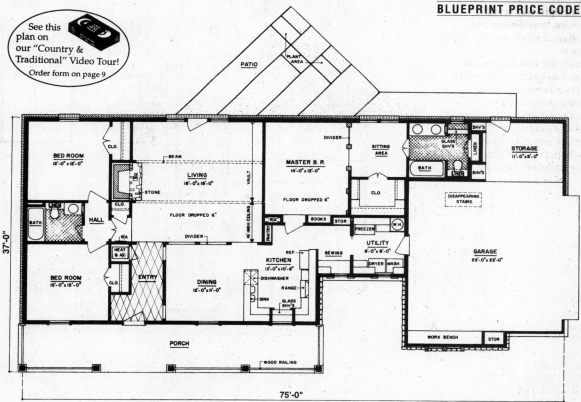

MAIN FLOOR

Stylish Exterior, Open Floor Plan

- With its simple yet stylish exterior, this modest-sized design is suitable for country or urban settings.
- A covered front porch and a gabled roof extension accent the facade while providing plenty of sheltered space for outdoor relaxation.
- Inside, the open floor plan puts available space to efficient use.
- The living room, which offers an inviting fireplace, is expanded by a cathedral ceiling. The adjoining dining area is open to the island kitchen, and all three rooms combine to create one huge gathering place.
- The master suite features a private bath and a large walk-in closet.
- Two more good-sized bedrooms share a second full bath.
- A convenient utility area leads to the carport, which incorporates extra storage space.

Plan J-86155

Bedrooms: 3	Baths: 2
Living Area:	
Main floor	1,385 sq. ft.
Total Living Area:	**1,385 sq. ft.**
Standard basement	1,385 sq. ft.
Carport	380 sq. ft.
Exterior Wall Framing:	2x4

Foundation Options:

Standard basement
Crawlspace
Slab
(All plans can be built with your choice of foundation and framing. A generic conversion diagram is available. See order form.)

BLUEPRINT PRICE CODE: A

See this plan on our "Best-Sellers" VideoGraphic Tour! Order form on page 9

CARPORT 20 x 19

STO

UTIL 9 x 5·6

w d

KITCHEN 9 x 12

DINING 12·6 x 12

60·4

MBR 15 x 12

BR 11·6 x 11·6

BR 11·6 x 11

LIVING 17·3 x 15·6

PORCH

45

MAIN FLOOR

Alluring Arches

- Massive columns, high, dramatic arches and expansive glass attract passersby to this alluring one-story home.
- Inside, 12-ft. coffered ceilings are found in the foyer and living room. A bank of windows in the living room provides a sweeping view of the covered backyard patio, creating a bright, open effect that is carried throughout the home.
- The informal, family activity areas are oriented to the back of the home as well. Spectacular window walls in the breakfast room and family room offer tremendous views. The family room's inviting corner fireplace is positioned to be enjoyed from the breakfast area and the spacious island kitchen.
- Separated from the secondary bedrooms, the superb master suite is entered through double doors and features a sitting room and a garden bath. Another full bath is across the hall from the den, which would also make a great guest room or nursery.

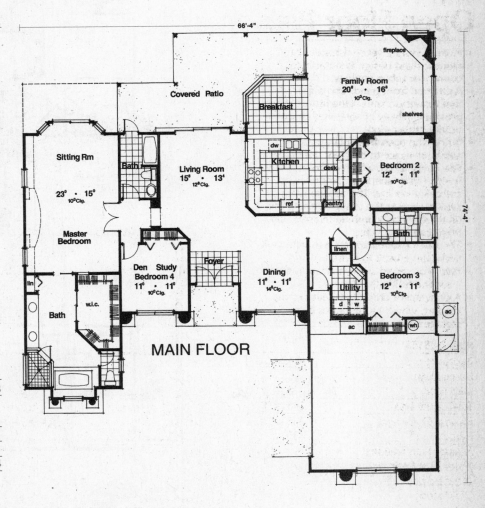

MAIN FLOOR

Plan HDS-99-179

Bedrooms: 3+	Baths: 3
Living Area:	
Main floor	2,660 sq. ft.
Total Living Area:	**2,660 sq. ft.**
Garage	527 sq. ft.
Exterior Wall Framing:	2x4

Foundation Options:

Slab
(All plans can be built with your choice of foundation and framing. A generic conversion diagram is available. See order form.)

BLUEPRINT PRICE CODE:	D

Luxurious Interior

- This luxurious home is introduced by an exciting tiled entry with a 17½-ft. vaulted ceiling and a skylight.
- The highlight of the home is the expansive Great Room and dining area, with its fireplace, planter, 17½-ft. vaulted ceiling and bay windows. The fabulous wraparound deck with a step-up hot tub is the perfect complement to this large entertainment space.
- The kitchen features lots of counter space, a large pantry and an adjoining bay-windowed breakfast nook.
- The exquisite master suite flaunts a sunken garden tub, a separate shower, a dual-sink vanity, a walk-in closet and private access to the deck area.
- The game room downstairs is perfect for casual entertaining, with its warm woodstove, oversized wet bar and patio access. Two bedrooms, a full bath and a large utility area are also included.

Plan P-6595-3D

Bedrooms: 3	**Baths:** 2½

Living Area:	
Main floor	1,530 sq. ft.
Daylight basement	1,145 sq. ft.
Total Living Area:	**2,675 sq. ft.**
Garage	462 sq. ft.
Exterior Wall Framing:	2x6

Foundation Options:
Daylight basement
(All plans can be built with your choice of foundation and framing. A generic conversion diagram is available. See order form.)

BLUEPRINT PRICE CODE: **D**

MAIN FLOOR

DAYLIGHT BASEMENT

See this plan on our "Best-Sellers" VideoGraphic Tour! Order form on page 9

Cozy, Rustic Country Home

- This cozy, rustic home offers a modern, open interior that efficiently maximizes the square footage.
- The large living room features a 13-ft. sloped ceiling accented by rustic beams and an eye-catching corner fireplace.
- The living room flows into the adjoining dining room and the efficient U-shaped kitchen for a spacious, open feel.
- The master and secondary bedrooms are separated by the activity areas. The master suite includes a private bath and a separate dressing area with a dual-sink vanity.
- The secondary bedrooms share another full bath.

Plan E-1109

Bedrooms: 3	Baths: 2
Living Area:	
Main floor	1,191 sq. ft.
Total Living Area:	**1,191 sq. ft.**
Garage	462 sq. ft.
Storage & utility	55 sq. ft.
Exterior Wall Framing:	2x6

Foundation Options:

Crawlspace
Slab
(All plans can be built with your choice of foundation and framing. A generic conversion diagram is available. See order form.)

BLUEPRINT PRICE CODE: A

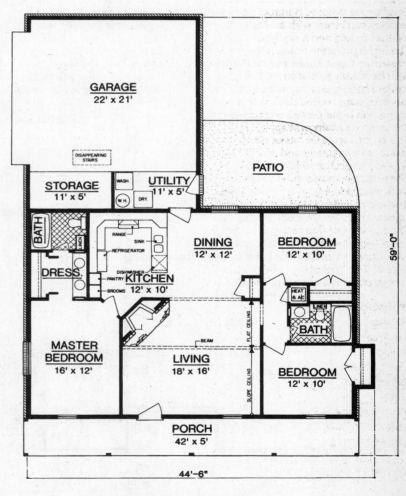

MAIN FLOOR

Classic Country-Style

- At the center of this rustic country-style home is an enormous living room with a flat beamed ceiling, a massive stone fireplace and access to a patio and a covered rear porch.
- The adjoining eating area and kitchen provide plenty of room for casual dining and meal preparation. The eating area is visually enhanced by a 14-ft. sloped ceiling with false beams. The kitchen includes a snack bar, a pantry closet and a built-in spice cabinet.
- The formal dining room gets plenty of pizzazz from the stone-faced wall and arched planter facing the living room.
- The secluded master suite has it all, including a private bath, a separate dressing area and a large walk-in closet with built-in shelves.
- The two remaining bedrooms have big closets and easy access to a full bath.

Plan E-1808

Bedrooms: 3	Baths: 2
Living Area:	
Main floor	1,800 sq. ft.
Total Living Area:	**1,800 sq. ft.**
Garage	605 sq. ft.
Exterior Wall Framing:	2x4

Foundation Options:

Crawlspace
Slab
(All plans can be built with your choice of foundation and framing. A generic conversion diagram is available. See order form.)

BLUEPRINT PRICE CODE: B

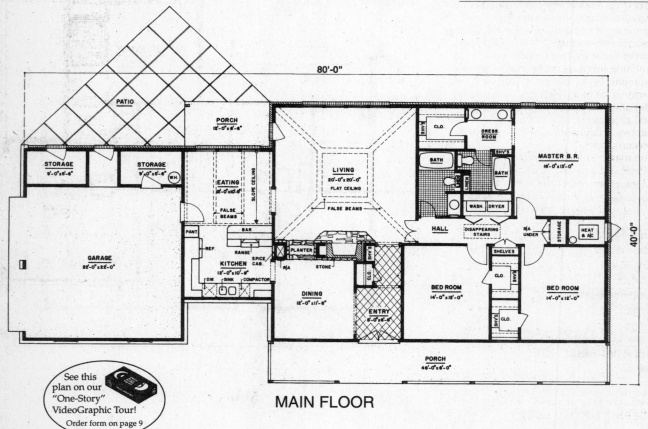

MAIN FLOOR

See this plan on our "One-Story" VideoGraphic Tour!
Order form on page 9

TO ORDER THIS BLUEPRINT, CALL TOLL-FREE 1-800-547-5570

Plan E-1808

PRICES AND DETAILS ON PAGES 12-15

Rustic Ranch-Style Design

- This ranch-style home offers a rustic facade that is warm and inviting. The railed front porch and stone accents are especially appealing.
- The interior is warm as well, with the focal point being the attractive living room. Features here include an eye-catching fireplace, patio access and a dramatic 14-ft. sloped ceiling with exposed beams.
- The open dining room lies off the foyer and adjoins the efficient U-shaped kitchen, which includes a pantry and a broom closet.
- The master suite features a large walk-in closet and a roomy master bath.
- At the other end of the home, two secondary bedrooms with abundant closet space share another full bath.

Plan E-1410

Bedrooms: 3	Baths: 2

Living Area:

Main floor	1,418 sq. ft.
Total Living Area:	**1,418 sq. ft.**
Garage	484 sq. ft.
Storage	38 sq. ft.
Exterior Wall Framing:	2x4

Foundation Options:

Crawlspace

Slab

(All plans can be built with your choice of foundation and framing. A generic conversion diagram is available. See order form.)

BLUEPRINT PRICE CODE:	A

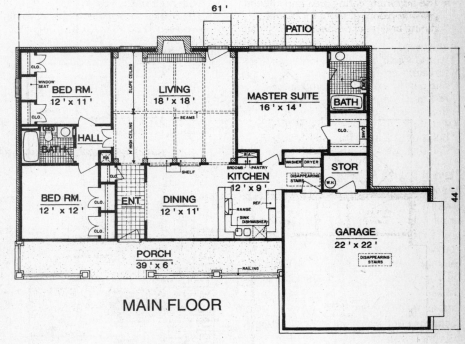

MAIN FLOOR

See this plan on our "One-Story" VideoGraphic Tour!

Order form on page 9

Deck and Spa!

- Designed for relaxation as well as for active indoor/outdoor living, this popular home offers a gigantic deck and an irresistible spa room.
- A covered porch welcomes guests into the entry hall, which flows past the central, open-railed stairway to the spectacular Great Room.
- Sliding glass doors on each side of the Great Room extend the living space to the huge V-shaped deck. The 22-ft. sloped ceiling and a woodstove add to the stunning effect.
- The master suite features a cozy window seat, a walk-in closet and private access to a full bath.
- The passive-solar spa room can be reached from the master suite as well as the backyard deck.
- The upper floor hosts two additional bedrooms, a full bath and a balcony hall that overlooks the Great Room.

REAR VIEW

Plans H-952-1A & -1B

Bedrooms: 3+	Baths: 2-3
Living Area:	
Upper floor	470 sq. ft.
Main floor	1,207 sq. ft.
Passive spa room	102 sq. ft.
Daylight basement	1,105 sq. ft.
Total Living Area:	**1,779/2,884 sq. ft.**
Garage	496 sq. ft.
Exterior Wall Framing:	2x6
Foundation Options:	**Plan #**
Daylight basement	H-952-1B
Crawlspace	H-952-1A

(All plans can be built with your choice of foundation and framing. A generic conversion diagram is available. See order form.)

BLUEPRINT PRICE CODE:	**B/D**

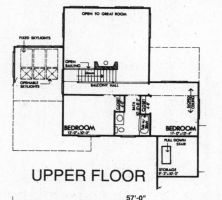

UPPER FLOOR

See this plan on our "Two-Story" VideoGraphic Tour!
Order form on page 9

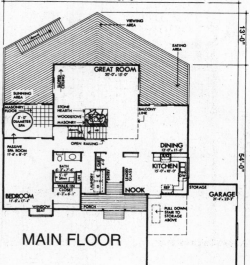

MAIN FLOOR

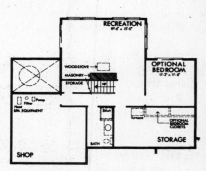

DAYLIGHT BASEMENT

TO ORDER THIS BLUEPRINT, CALL TOLL-FREE 1-800-547-5570

Plans H-952-1A & -1B

PRICES AND DETAILS ON PAGES 12-15

Active Living Made Easy

- This home is perfect for active living. Its rectangular design allows the use of truss roof framing, which makes construction easy and economical.
- The galley-style kitchen and the sunny dining area are kept open to the living room, forming one huge activity space. Two sets of sliding glass doors expand the living area to the large deck.

- The secluded master bedroom offers a private bath, while the remaining bedrooms share a hall bath.
- The two baths, the laundry facilities and the kitchen are clustered to allow common plumbing walls.
- Plan H-921-1A has a standard crawlspace foundation and an optional solar-heating system. Plan H-921-2A has a Plen-Wood system, which utilizes the sealed crawlspace as a chamber for distributing heated or cooled air. Both versions of the design call for energy-efficient 2x6 exterior walls.

Plans H-921-1A & -2A	
Bedrooms: 3	**Baths:** 2
Living Area:	
Main floor	1,164 sq. ft.
Total Living Area:	**1,164 sq. ft.**
Exterior Wall Framing:	2x6
Foundation Options:	**Plan #**
Crawlspace	H-921-1A
Plen-Wood crawlspace	H-921-2A

(All plans can be built with your choice of foundation and framing. A generic conversion diagram is available. See order form.)

BLUEPRINT PRICE CODE: A

See this plan on our "One-Story" VideoGraphic Tour! Order form on page 9

MAIN FLOOR

42'-0"   8'-0"

30'-0"

BEDROOM 11'-6" x 13'-6"

BATH

W/D LAUNDRY

DINING

CLOSET

BATH

KITCHEN 9'-7" x 8'-2"

LIVING RM 12'-0" x 23'-0"

DECK

wh

CLOS CLOS

LINEN

ENTRY

CLOS

BEDROOM 11'-6" x 10'-3"

BEDROOM 10'-9" x 10'-0"

CLOSET

Covered Porch Invites Visitors

- This nice home welcomes visitors with its covered front porch and its wide-open living areas.
- Detailed columns, railings and shutters decorate the front porch that guides guests to the central entry.
- Just off the entry, the bright living room merges with the dining room. The side wall is lined with glass, including a glass door that opens to the yard.
- The angled kitchen features a serving counter facing the dining room. A handy laundry closet and access to a storage area and the garage is nearby.
- An angled hall leads to the bedroom wing. The master suite offers a private bath, a walk-in closet and a dressing area with a vanity. Two additional bedrooms and another full bath are located down the hall.

Plan E-1217

Bedrooms: 3	Baths: 2
Living Area:	
Main floor	1,266 sq. ft.
Total Living Area:	**1,266 sq. ft.**
Garage and storage	550 sq. ft.
Exterior Wall Framing:	2x6

Foundation Options:

Crawlspace

Slab

(All plans can be built with your choice of foundation and framing. A generic conversion diagram is available. See order form.)

BLUEPRINT PRICE CODE: **A**

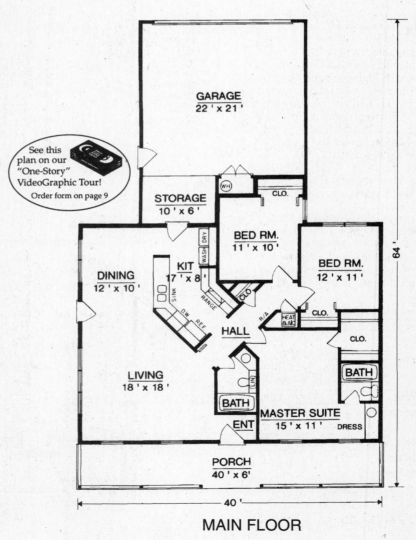

See this plan on our "One-Story" VideoGraphic Tour! Order form on page 9

MAIN FLOOR

Plan E-1217

FRONT VIEW

REAR VIEW

More for Less

- Big in function but small in square footage, this passive-solar plan can be built as a single-family home or as part of a multiple-unit complex.
- The floor plan flows visually from its open foyer to its high-ceilinged Great Room, where a high-efficiency fireplace is flanked by glass. Sliding glass doors open to a brilliant south-facing sun room that overlooks a backyard terrace.
- The eat-in kitchen has a pass-through to a bright dining area that opens to a nice side terrace.
- The master bedroom boasts a pair of tall windows, a deluxe private bath and two roomy closets.
- A handy laundry closet and a half-bath are located at the center of the floor plan, near the garage.
- Upstairs, a skylighted bath serves two more bedrooms, one with a private, rear-facing balcony.

See this plan on our "Two-Story" VideoGraphic Tour! Order form on page 9

Plan K-507-S

Bedrooms: 3	Baths: 2½
Living Area:	
Upper floor	397 sq. ft.
Main floor	915 sq. ft.
Sun room	162 sq. ft.
Total Living Area:	**1,474 sq. ft.**
Standard basement	915 sq. ft.
Garage	400 sq. ft.
Exterior Wall Framing:	2x4 or 2x6

Foundation Options:
Standard basement
Slab
(All plans can be built with your choice of foundation and framing. A generic conversion diagram is available. See order form.)

BLUEPRINT PRICE CODE:	A

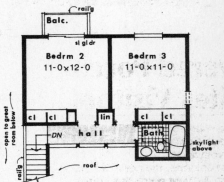

UPPER FLOOR

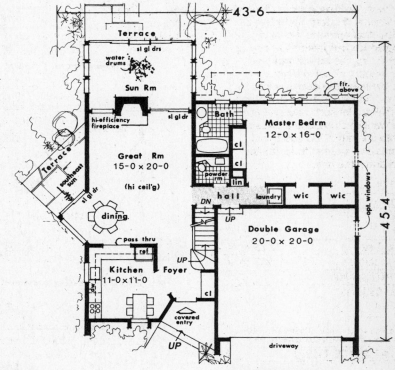

MAIN FLOOR

Hillside Design Fits Contours

- The daylight-basement version of this popular plan is perfect for a scenic, sloping lot.
- A large, wraparound deck embraces the rear-oriented living areas, accessed through sliding glass doors.
- The spectacular living room boasts a corner fireplace and a 19-ft. vaulted ceiling with three clerestory windows.
- The secluded master suite upstairs offers a walk-in closet, a private bath and sliding doors to a sun deck.
- The daylight basement (not shown) includes a fourth bedroom with a private bath and a walk-in closet, as well as a recreation room with a fireplace and access to a rear patio.
- The standard basement (not shown) includes a recreation room with a fireplace and a room for hobbies or child's play.
- Both basements also have a large unfinished area below the main-floor bedrooms.

Plans H-877-4, -4A & -4B

Bedrooms: 3+	Baths: 2-3
Living Area:	
Upper floor	333 sq. ft.
Main floor	1,200 sq. ft.
Basement (finished area)	591 sq. ft.
Total Living Area:	**1,533/2,124 sq. ft.**
Basement (unfinished area)	493 sq. ft.
Garage	480 sq. ft.
Exterior Wall Framing:	2x6
Foundation Options:	**Plan #**
Daylight basement	H-877-4B
Standard basement	H-877-4
Crawlspace	H-877-4A

(All plans can be built with your choice of foundation and framing. A generic conversion diagram is available. See order form.)

BLUEPRINT PRICE CODE:	**B/C**

REAR VIEW

UPPER FLOOR

STAIRWAY AREA IN CRAWLSPACE VERSION

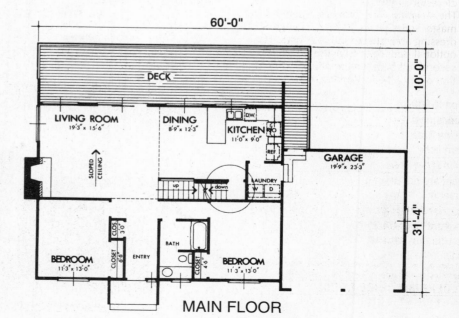

MAIN FLOOR

TO ORDER THIS BLUEPRINT, CALL TOLL-FREE 1-800-547-5570   Plans H-877-4, -4A & -4B   **PRICES AND DETAILS ON PAGES 12-15**

High-Profile Contemporary

- This design does away with wasted space, putting the emphasis on quality rather than on size.
- The angled floor plan minimizes hall space and creates smooth traffic flow while adding architectural appeal. The roof framing is square, however, to allow for economical construction.
- The spectacular living and dining rooms share a 16-ft. cathedral ceiling and a fireplace. Both rooms have lots of glass overlooking an angled rear terrace.
- The dining room includes a glass-filled alcove and sliding patio doors topped by transom windows. Tall windows frame the living room fireplace and trace the slope of the ceiling.
- A pass-through joins the dining room to the combination kitchen and family room, which features a snack bar and a clerestory window.
- The sleeping wing provides a super master suite, which boasts a skylighted dressing area and a luxurious bath. The optional den, or third bedroom, shares a second full bath with another bedroom that offers a 14-ft. sloped ceiling.

Plan K-688-D

Bedrooms: 2+	Baths: 2½
Living Area:	
Main floor	1,340 sq. ft.
Total Living Area:	**1,340 sq. ft.**
Standard basement	1,235 sq. ft.
Garage	484 sq. ft.
Exterior Wall Framing:	2x4 or 2x6

Foundation Options:

Standard basement

Slab

(All plans can be built with your choice of foundation and framing. A generic conversion diagram is available. See order form.)

BLUEPRINT PRICE CODE: A

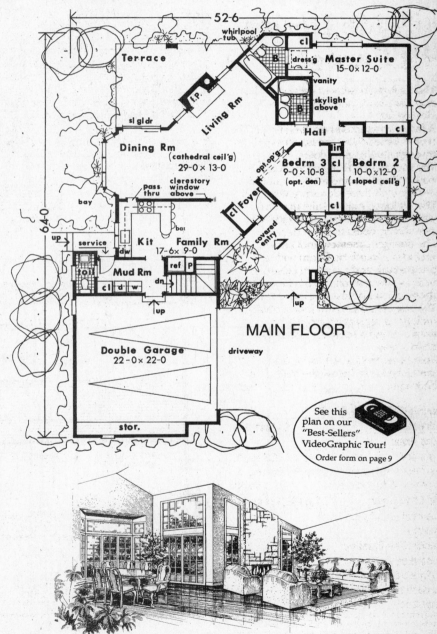

MAIN FLOOR

See this plan on our "Best-Sellers" VideoGraphic Tour! Order form on page 9

VIEW INTO DINING ROOM AND LIVING ROOM

Rustic, Relaxed Living

- The screened porch of this rustic home offers a cool place to dine on warm summer days. The covered front porch provides an inviting welcome and a place for pure relaxation.
- With its warm fireplace and surrounding windows, the home's spacious living room is ideal for unwinding indoors. The living room unfolds to a nice-sized dining area that overlooks a backyard patio and opens to the screened porch.
- The U-shaped kitchen is centrally located and features a nice windowed sink. A handy pantry and a laundry room adjoin to the right.
- Three large bedrooms make up the home's sleeping wing. The master bedroom boasts a roomy private bath with a step-up spa tub, a separate shower and two walk-in closets.
- The secondary bedrooms share a compartmentalized hall bath.

Plan C-8650	
Bedrooms: 3	**Baths: 2**
Living Area:	
Main floor	1,773 sq. ft.
Total Living Area:	**1,773 sq. ft.**
Daylight basement	1,773 sq. ft.
Garage	441 sq. ft.
Exterior Wall Framing:	2x4

Foundation Options:
Daylight basement
Crawlspace
Slab
(All plans can be built with your choice of foundation and framing. A generic conversion diagram is available. See order form.)

BLUEPRINT PRICE CODE:	**B**

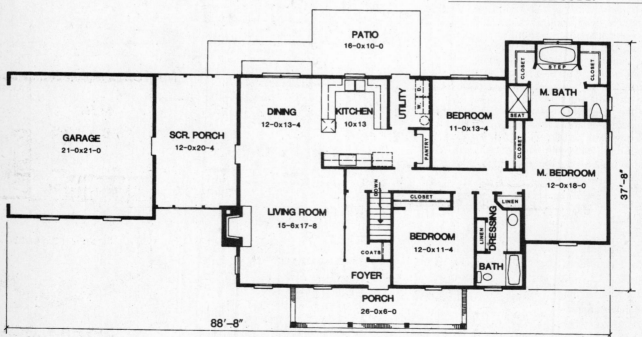

MAIN FLOOR

Plan C-8650

PRICES AND DETAILS ON PAGES 12-15

Panoramic Prow View

- This glass-filled prow gable design is almost as spectacular as the panoramic view from inside.
- French doors open from the front deck to the dining room. A stunning window wall illuminates the adjoining living room, which flaunts a 20-ft.-high cathedral ceiling.

- The open, corner kitchen is perfectly angled to service the dining room and the family room, while offering views of the front and rear decks.
- A handy utility/laundry room opens to the rear deck. Two bedrooms share a full bath, to complete the main floor.
- A dramatic, open-railed stairway leads up to the secluded master bedroom, which boasts a dressing room and a private bath with a dual-sink vanity and a separate tub and shower.

Plan NW-196	
Bedrooms: 3	**Baths: 2**
Living Area:	
Upper floor	394 sq. ft.
Main floor	1,317 sq. ft.
Total Living Area:	**1,711 sq. ft.**
Exterior Wall Framing:	2x6

Foundation Options:
Crawlspace
(All plans can be built with your choice of foundation and framing. A generic conversion diagram is available. See order form.)

BLUEPRINT PRICE CODE:	**B**

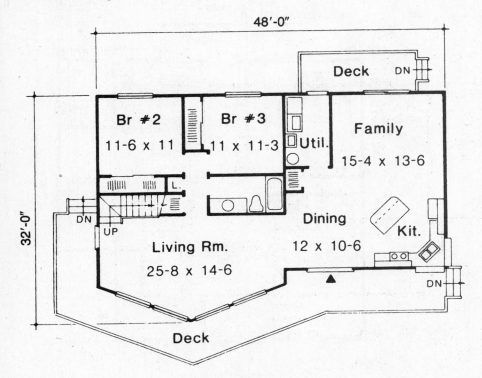

MAIN FLOOR

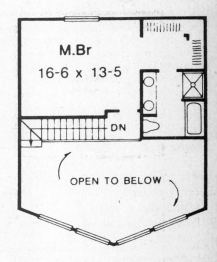

UPPER FLOOR

Cozy, Cost-Saving Retreat

- This cozy cabin is the perfect vacation retreat for that special mountain, lake or river location.
- The design is large enough to provide comfortable living quarters and small enough to fit a modest building budget.
- An 18½-ft. vaulted ceiling and expanses of glass add volume to the living and dining area. Double doors provide access to an inviting deck or patio.
- The U-shaped kitchen offers a bright sink and a convenient pass-through to the dining area.
- A quiet bedroom and a hall bath complete the main floor.
- The upper floor consists of a railed loft that provides sweeping views of the living areas below and the scenery outside. The loft could serve as an extra sleeping area or a quiet haven for reading, relaxing and other activities.

Plan I-880-A

Bedrooms: 1+	Baths: 1
Living Area:	
Upper floor	308 sq. ft.
Main floor	572 sq. ft.
Total Living Area:	**880 sq. ft.**
Exterior Wall Framing:	2x6

Foundation Options:

Crawlspace

(All plans can be built with your choice of foundation and framing. A generic conversion diagram is available. See order form.)

BLUEPRINT PRICE CODE: **A**

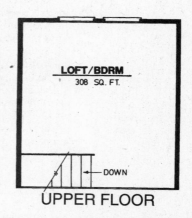

LOFT/BDRM
308 SQ. FT.

DOWN

UPPER FLOOR

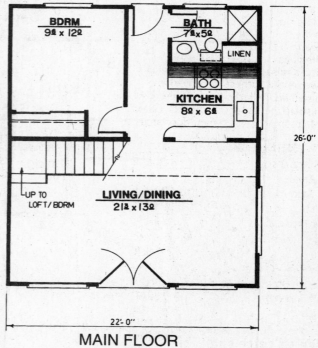

BDRM
9⁰ x 12⁰

BATH
7⁰ x 5⁰

LINEN

KITCHEN
8⁰ x 6⁰

LIVING/DINING
21⁰ x 13⁰

UP TO LOFT/BDRM

26'-0"

22'-0"

MAIN FLOOR

TO ORDER THIS BLUEPRINT, CALL TOLL-FREE 1-800-547-5570

Plan I-880-A

PRICES AND DETAILS ON PAGES 12-15

Privacy and Luxury

- This home's large roof planes and privacy fences enclose a thoroughly modern, open floor plan.
- A beautiful courtyard greets guests on their way to the secluded entrance. Inside, a two-story-high entry area leads directly into the living and dining rooms, which boast an 11-ft. vaulted ceiling, plus floor-to-ceiling windows and a fireplace with a stone hearth.
- The angular kitchen features a snack bar to the adjoining family room and a passive-solar sun room that offers natural brightness.
- A 14½-ft. vaulted ceiling presides over the family room. Sliding glass doors access a backyard patio with a sun deck and a hot tub.
- The luxurious master suite opens to both the front courtyard and the backyard hot tub area. The 11-ft.-high vaulted bath includes a dual-sink vanity, a raised garden tub, a separate shower and a corner walk-in closet.
- Two secondary bedrooms and another bath share the upper floor, which boasts commanding views of main-floor areas.

Plans P-7663-3A & -3D

Bedrooms: 3+	Baths: 3
Living Area:	
Upper floor	569 sq. ft.
Main floor	2,039 sq. ft.
Total Living Area:	**2,608 sq. ft.**
Daylight basement	2,039 sq. ft.
Garage	799 sq. ft.
Exterior Wall Framing:	2x4
Foundation Options:	**Plan #**
Daylight basement	P-7663-3D
Crawlspace	P-7663-3A

(All plans can be built with your choice of foundation and framing. A generic conversion diagram is available. See order form.)

BLUEPRINT PRICE CODE:	**D**

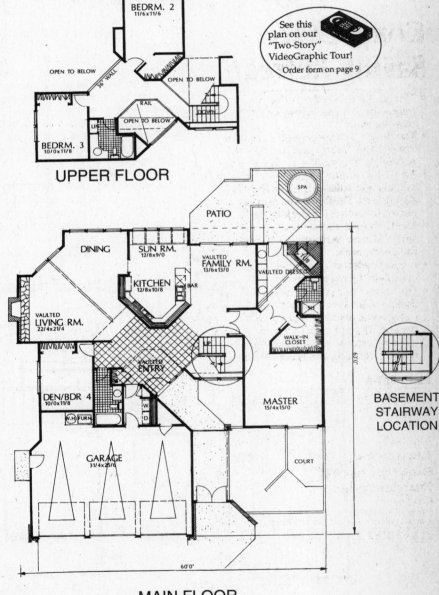

See this plan on our "Two-Story" VideoGraphic Tour!
Order form on page 9

UPPER FLOOR

MAIN FLOOR

BASEMENT STAIRWAY LOCATION

Family-Style Leisure Living

- This handsome ranch-style home features a floor plan that is great for family living and entertaining.
- In from the quaint covered porch, the spacious formal areas flow together for a dramatic impact. The living room is enhanced by a fireplace and a sloped ceiling. A patio door in the dining room extends activities to the outdoors.
- The efficient U-shaped kitchen opens to the dining room and offers a pantry, a window above the sink and abundant counter space.
- A good-sized utility room with convenient laundry facilities opens to the carport. This area also includes a large storage room and disappearing stairs to even more storage space.
- Three bedrooms and two baths occupy the sleeping wing. The master suite features a large walk-in closet and a private bath.
- The two remaining bedrooms are well proportioned and share a hall bath. Storage space is well accounted for here as well, with two linen closets and a coat closet in the bedroom hall.

Plan E-1308	
Bedrooms: 3	**Baths:** 2
Living Area:	
Main floor	1,375 sq. ft.
Total Living Area:	**1,375 sq. ft.**
Carport	430 sq. ft.
Storage	95 sq. ft.
Exterior Wall Framing:	2x4
Foundation Options:	

Crawlspace
Slab
(All plans can be built with your choice of foundation and framing. A generic conversion diagram is available. See order form.)

BLUEPRINT PRICE CODE: A

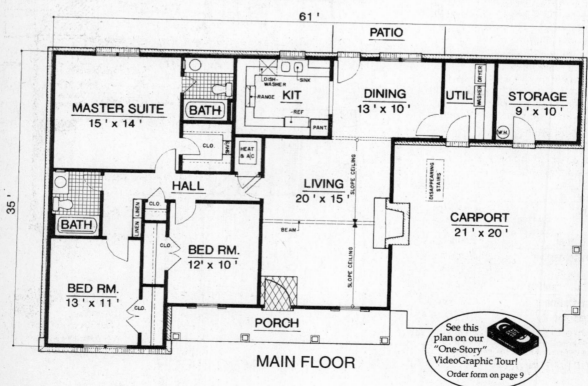

MAIN FLOOR

See this plan on our "One-Story" VideoGraphic Tour!
Order form on page 9

TO ORDER THIS BLUEPRINT, CALL TOLL-FREE 1-800-547-5570

Plan E-1308

PRICES AND DETAILS ON PAGES 12-15

Inviting Windows

- This comfortable home presents an impressive facade, with its large and inviting front window arrangement.
- A step down from the front entry, the Great Room boasts a 12-ft. vaulted ceiling with a barrel-vaulted area that outlines the half-round front window. The striking angled fireplace can be enjoyed from the adjoining dining area.
- The galley-style kitchen hosts a half-round cutout above the sink and a breakfast area that accesses a backyard deck and patio. The kitchen, breakfast area and dining area also are enhanced by 12-ft. vaulted ceilings.
- The master bedroom features a boxed-out window, a walk-in closet and a ceiling that vaults to 12 feet. The private bath includes a garden tub, a separate shower and a private toilet compartment.
- Another full bath serves the two remaining bedrooms, one of which has sliding glass doors to the deck and would make an ideal den.

Plan B-902

Bedrooms: 2+	Baths: 2
Living Area:	
Main floor	1,368 sq. ft.
Total Living Area:	**1,368 sq. ft.**
Standard basement	1,368 sq. ft.
Garage	412 sq. ft.
Exterior Wall Framing:	2x4

Foundation Options:

Standard basement

(All plans can be built with your choice of foundation and framing. A generic conversion diagram is available. See order form.)

BLUEPRINT PRICE CODE: A

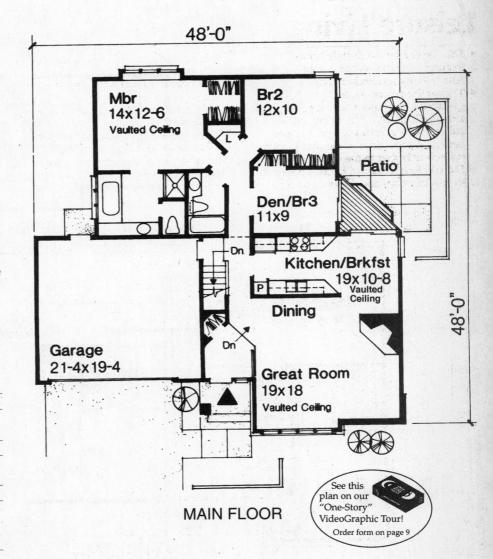

MAIN FLOOR

See this plan on our "One-Story" VideoGraphic Tour! Order form on page 9

Compact, Cozy, Inviting

- Full-width porches at the front and the rear of this home add plenty of space for outdoor living and entertaining.
- The huge, centrally located living room is the core of this three-bedroom home. The room features a corner fireplace, a 16-ft. sloped, open-beam ceiling and access to the back porch.
- The dining room combines with the kitchen to create an open, more spacious atmosphere. A long, central work island and a compact laundry closet are other space-saving features.
- The main-floor master suite offers a private bath with dual vanities and a large walk-in closet. Two additional bedrooms, a full bath and an intimate sitting area that overlooks the living room and entry are upstairs.
- A separate two-car garage is included with the blueprints.

Plan E-1421

Bedrooms: 3	Baths: 2
Living Area:	
Upper floor	561 sq. ft.
Main floor	924 sq. ft.
Total Living Area:	**1,485 sq. ft.**
Standard basement	924 sq. ft.
Exterior Wall Framing:	2x6

Foundation Options:

Standard basement
Crawlspace
Slab

(All plans can be built with your choice of foundation and framing. A generic conversion diagram is available. See order form.)

BLUEPRINT PRICE CODE: A

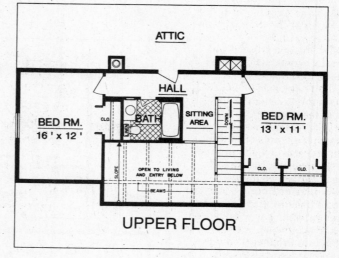

UPPER FLOOR

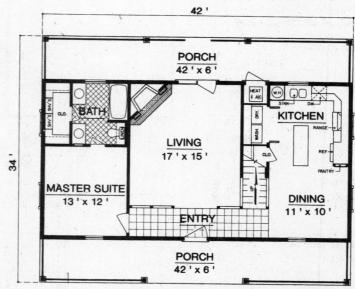

MAIN FLOOR

TO ORDER THIS BLUEPRINT, CALL TOLL-FREE 1-800-547-5570

Plan E-1421

PRICES AND DETAILS ON PAGES 12-15

Hot Tub, Deck Highlighted

See this plan on our "Two-Story" VideoGraphic Tour! Order form on page 9

- Designed for indoor/outdoor living, this home features a skylighted spa room with a hot tub and a backyard deck that spans the width of the home.
- A central hall leads to the sunny kitchen and nook, which offer corner windows, a snack bar and a pantry.
- Straight ahead, the open dining and living rooms form one huge space, further pronounced by expansive windows. The 16-ft. vaulted living room also features a fireplace and sliding glass doors to the deck.
- The master suite includes a cozy window seat, a large walk-in closet, a private bath and access to the tiled spa room. The spa may also be entered from the deck and an inner hall.
- Upstairs, two more bedrooms share a full bath and a balcony that overlooks the living room below.
- The optional daylight basement offers a deluxe sauna, a fourth bedroom, a laundry room and a wide recreation room with a fireplace. A large game room and storage are also included.

REAR VIEW

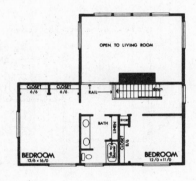

UPPER FLOOR

DAYLIGHT BASEMENT

Plans H-2114-1A & -1B

Bedrooms: 3+	Baths: 2½-3½
Living Area:	
Upper floor	732 sq. ft.
Main floor	1,682 sq. ft.
Spa room	147 sq. ft.
Daylight basement	1,386 sq. ft.
Total Living Area:	**2,561/3,947 sq. ft.**
Garage	547 sq. ft.
Exterior Wall Framing:	2x6
Foundation Options:	**Plan #**
Daylight basement	H-2114-1B
Crawlspace	H-2114-1A
(All plans can be built with your choice of foundation and framing. A generic conversion diagram is available. See order form.)	
BLUEPRINT PRICE CODE:	**D/F**

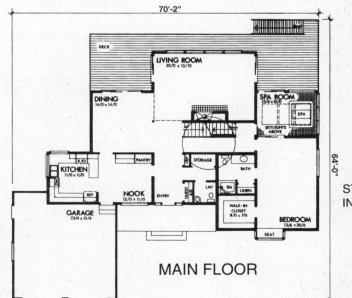

MAIN FLOOR

STAIRWAY AREA IN CRAWLSPACE VERSION

Decked-Out Chalet

- This gorgeous chalet is partially surrounded by a large and roomy deck that is great for indoor/outdoor living.
- The living and dining area shows off a fireplace with a raised hearth, plus large windows to take in the outdoor views. The area is further expanded by a 17½-ft.-high vaulted ceiling in the dining room and sliding glass doors that lead to the deck.
- The kitchen offers a breakfast bar that separates it from the dining area. A convenient laundry room is nearby.
- The main-floor master bedroom is just steps away from a linen closet and a hall bath. Two upstairs bedrooms share a second full bath.
- The highlight of the upper floor is a balcony room with a 12½-ft.-high vaulted ceiling, exposed beams and tall windows. A decorative railing provides an overlook into the dining area below.

Plans H-919-1 & -1A

Bedrooms: 3	Baths: 2
Living Area:	
Upper floor	869 sq. ft.
Main floor	1,064 sq. ft.
Daylight basement	475 sq. ft.
Total Living Area:	**1,933/2,408 sq. ft.**
Tuck-under garage	501 sq. ft.
Exterior Wall Framing:	2x6
Foundation Options:	**Plan #**
Daylight basement	H-919-1
Crawlspace	H-919-1A

(All plans can be built with your choice of foundation and framing. A generic conversion diagram is available. See order form.)

BLUEPRINT PRICE CODE:	**B/C**

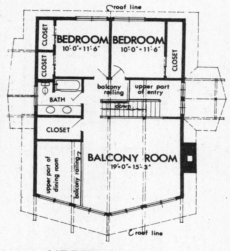

UPPER FLOOR

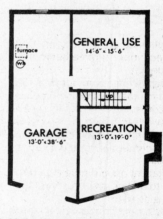

DAYLIGHT BASEMENT

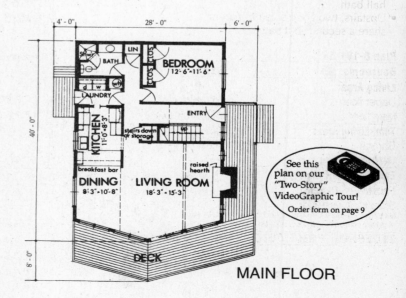

MAIN FLOOR

See this plan on our "Two-Story" VideoGraphic Tour! Order form on page 9

Plans H-919-1 & -1A

PRICES AND DETAILS ON PAGES 12-15

Compact Three-Bedroom

- Both openness and privacy are possible in this economical three-bedroom home design.
- The bright living room boasts a 17-ft. vaulted ceiling, a warming fireplace and a corner window. A high clerestory window lets in additional natural light.
- The modern, U-shaped kitchen features a handy corner pantry and a versatile snack bar.
- The adjacent open dining area provides access to a backyard deck through sliding glass doors.
- A lovely corner window brightens the secluded master bedroom, which also includes a roomy walk-in closet and private access to a compartmentalized hall bath.
- Upstairs, two good-sized bedrooms share a second split bath.

Plan B-101-8501

Bedrooms: 3	Baths: 2
Living Area:	
Upper floor	400 sq. ft.
Main floor	846 sq. ft.
Total Living Area:	**1,246 sq. ft.**
Garage	400 sq. ft.
Standard basement	846 sq. ft.
Exterior Wall Framing:	2x4

Foundation Options:

Standard basement

(All plans can be built with your choice of foundation and framing. A generic conversion diagram is available. See order form.)

BLUEPRINT PRICE CODE: A

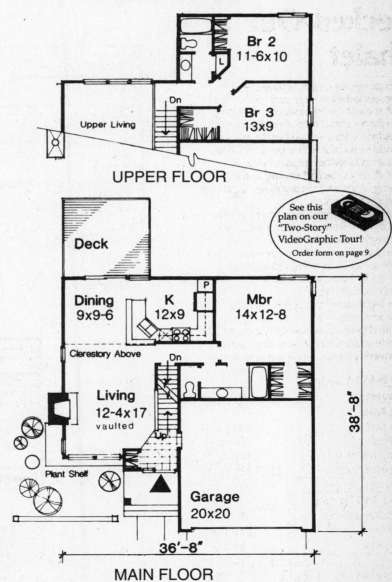

See this plan on our "Two-Story" VideoGraphic Tour! Order form on page 9

UPPER FLOOR

MAIN FLOOR

Intriguing Two-Story Home

- An unusual roofline and a rustic stone chimney grace the exterior of this intriguing two-story, four-bedroom home.
- The covered entryway opens to a reception hall that offers a strking view of the open, airy living spaces.
- The living room is enhanced by a high-efficiency fireplace and a skylighted, sloped ceiling. An upper-level balcony and a circular dining room are other eye-catching design features of the formal living areas.
- Folding doors open to the informal living areas, which consist of the family room, another circular dinette and a U-shaped kitchen. The kitchen is equipped with a snack bar, and the family room has sliding glass doors leading to an isolated terrace.
- The blueprints offer the option of reversing the locations of the kitchen and the family room.
- The secluded master bedroom suite offers many amenities, such as a private terrace, a walk-in closet and a wonderful bath with garden whirlpool tub. A main-floor laundry and a powder room are close by.
- An open stairway rises to a balcony, three additional bedrooms and a compartmentalized bath. Lots of closet space plus attic storage areas add to the efficiency of this plan.

Plan K-662-NA

Bedrooms: 4	Baths: 2 ½
Space:	
Upper floor	670 sq. ft.
Main floor	1,196 sq. ft.
Total Living Area	**1,866 sq. ft.**
Basement	1,196 sq. ft.
Garage	418 sq. ft.
Exterior Wall Framing	**2x4 or 2x6**
Foundation options:	

Standard Basement
Slab
(Foundation & framing conversion diagram available—see order form.)

Blueprint Price Code	**B**

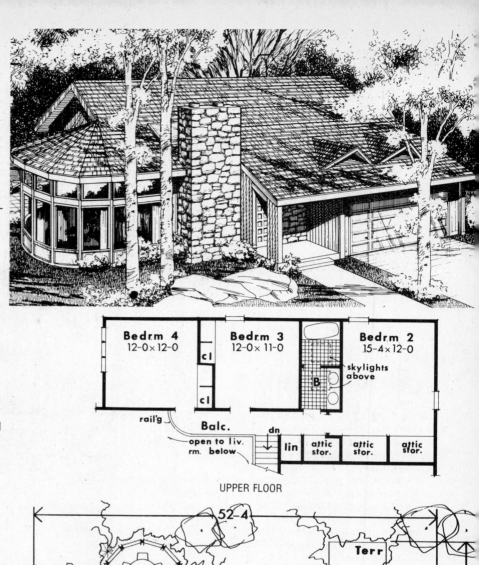

UPPER FLOOR

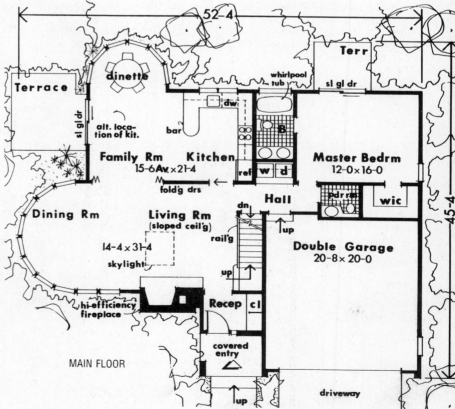

MAIN FLOOR

TO ORDER THIS BLUEPRINT, CALL TOLL-FREE 1-800-547-5570

Plan K-662-NA

PRICES AND DETAILS ON PAGES 12-15

Open Design in Compact Traditional

- An instant feeling of spaciousness and openness is created in this hospitable home with a vaulted Great Room and open-railed stairway.
- Additional appeal comes from a wood-burning fireplace, visible from the adjoining kitchen and dining area.
- The spacious kitchen has a pantry and attached walk-in laundry room.
- The main-level master bedroom is well isolated from the living areas, yet easily accessible to the children's bedrooms on the upper level.

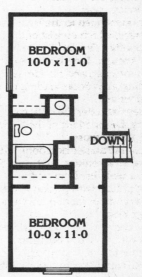

UPPER FLOOR

BEDROOM
10-0 x 11-0

DOWN

BEDROOM
10-0 x 11-0

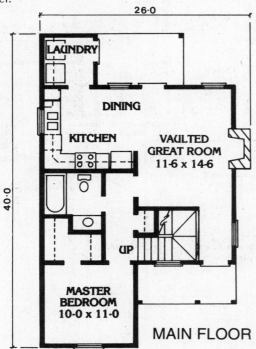

26-0

40-0

LAUNDRY

DINING

KITCHEN

VAULTED
GREAT ROOM
11-6 x 14-6

UP

MASTER
BEDROOM
10-0 x 11-0

MAIN FLOOR

Plan V-1098	
Bedrooms: 3	Baths: 2
Space:	
Upper floor	396 sq. ft.
Main floor	702 sq. ft.
Total Living Area	**1,098 sq. ft.**
Exterior Wall Framing	2x6
Foundation options:	
Crawlspace	
(Foundation & framing conversion diagram	
available—see order form.)	
Blueprint Price Code	A

REAR VIEW

FRONT VIEW

Year-Round Comfort

- Designed for the energy-conscious, this passive-solar home provides year-round comfort with much lower fuel costs.
- The open, airy interior is a delight. In the winter, sunshine penetrates deep into the living spaces. In the summer, wide overhangs shade the interior.
- The central living and dining rooms flow together, creating a bright, open space. Sliding glass doors open to a terrace and an enclosed sun spot.
- In the airy casual space, the kitchen has an eating bar and a sunny breakfast nook. The adjoining family room boasts a woodstove that warms the entire area.
- The master bedroom suite includes a private terrace, a personal bath and a walk-in closet. Two other bedrooms share another full bath.

Plan K-392-T

Bedrooms: 3	Baths: 2½
Living Area:	
Main floor	1,592 sq. ft.
Sun spot	125 sq. ft.
Total Living Area:	**1,717 sq. ft.**
Partial basement	634 sq. ft.
Garage	407 sq. ft.
Exterior Wall Framing:	2x4 or 2x6

Foundation Options:

Partial basement

Slab

(All plans can be built with your choice of foundation and framing. A generic conversion diagram is available. See order form.)

BLUEPRINT PRICE CODE: B

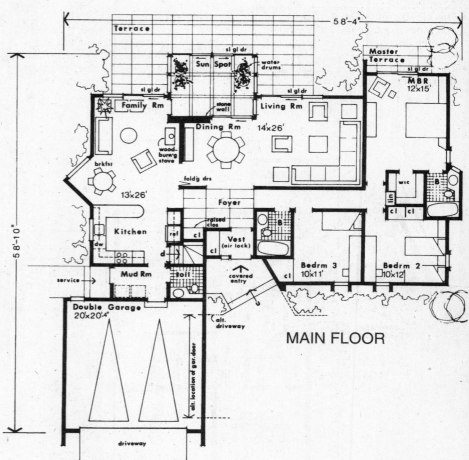

MAIN FLOOR

Plan K-392-T

Dramatic Skewed Prow

- This cleverly modified A-frame design combines a dramatic exterior with an exciting interior that offers commanding views through its many windows.
- The central foyer opens to a spacious living room and dining room combination with a soaring 23-ft. cathedral ceiling and a massive stone fireplace. Sliding glass doors open to an inviting wraparound deck.
- Directly ahead is the L-shaped kitchen, which also accesses the deck.
- Two bedrooms are located at the rear, near the laundry room and a full bath.
- A third bedroom, a second bath and a balcony loft that could sleep overnight guests are found on the upper level.

Plan HFL-1160-CW

Bedrooms: 3+	**Baths:** 2

Living Area:

Upper floor	400 sq. ft.
Main floor	1,016 sq. ft.
Total Living Area:	**1,416 sq. ft.**
Exterior Wall Framing:	2x4

Foundation Options:

Crawlspace
(All plans can be built with your choice of foundation and framing. A generic conversion diagram is available. See order form.)

BLUEPRINT PRICE CODE:	**A**

VIEW INTO LIVING ROOM

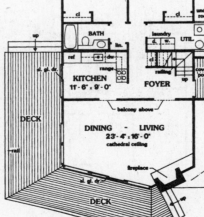

MAIN FLOOR

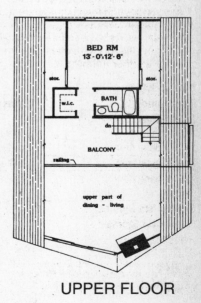

UPPER FLOOR

Comfortable Ranch Design

- This affordable ranch design offers numerous amenities and is ideally structured for comfortable living, both indoors and out.
- A tiled reception hall leads into the spacious living and dining rooms, which feature a handsome brick fireplace, an 11-ft. sloped ceiling and two sets of sliding glass doors to access a lovely backyard terrace.
- The adjacent family room, designed for privacy, showcases a large boxed-out window with a built-in seat. The kitchen features an efficient U-shaped counter, an eating bar and a pantry.
- The master suite has its own terrace and private bath with a whirlpool tub.
- Two additional bedrooms share a second full bath.
- The garage has two separate storage areas—one accessible from the interior and the other from the backyard.

Plan K-518-A

Bedrooms: 3	**Baths:** 2
Living Area:	
Main floor	1,276 sq. ft.
Total Living Area:	**1,276 sq. ft.**
Standard basement	1,247 sq. ft.
Garage and storage	579 sq. ft.
Exterior Wall Framing:	2x4 or 2x6

Foundation Options:

Standard basement
Slab
(All plans can be built with your choice of foundation and framing. A generic conversion diagram is available. See order form.)

BLUEPRINT PRICE CODE: A

VIEW INTO LIVING ROOM AND DINING ROOM

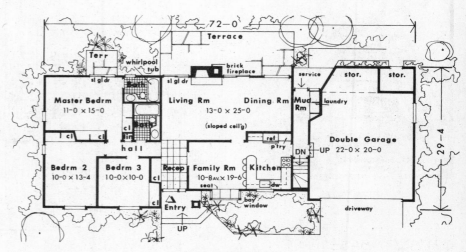

MAIN FLOOR

TO ORDER THIS BLUEPRINT, CALL TOLL-FREE 1-800-547-5570

Plan K-518-A

PRICES AND DETAILS ON PAGES 12-15

Chalet for Town or Country

- Vertical siding, spacious viewing decks with cut-out railings and exposed beams in the interior give this home the look of a mountain chalet.
- The design of the home lends itself to year-round family living as well as to part-time recreational enjoyment.
- The expansive Great Room features exposed beams and an impressive fireplace. The large wraparound deck is accessed through sliding glass doors. The dining area is expanded by an 18-ft. vaulted ceiling.
- The well-planned kitchen is open and easily accessible.
- Two main-floor bedrooms share the hall bath between them.
- The upstairs offers an adult retreat: a fine master bedroom with a private deck and bath, plus a versatile loft area. An airy 13-ft. ceiling presides over the entire upper floor.
- The daylight-basement level includes a garage and a large recreation room with a fireplace and a half-bath.

Plan P-531-2D	
Bedrooms: 3+	**Baths:** 2½
Living Area:	
Upper floor	573 sq. ft.
Main floor	1,120 sq. ft.
Daylight basement	532 sq. ft.
Total Living Area:	**2,225 sq. ft.**
Tuck-under garage	541 sq. ft.
Exterior Wall Framing:	2x6
Foundation Options:	

Daylight basement
(All plans can be built with your choice of foundation and framing. A generic conversion diagram is available. See order form.)

BLUEPRINT PRICE CODE: C

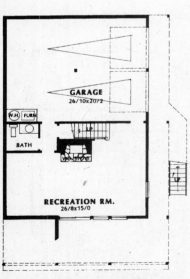

DAYLIGHT BASEMENT

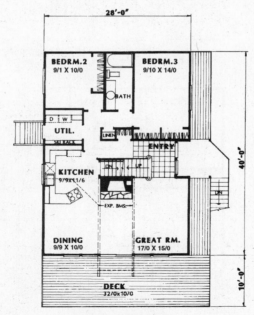

MAIN FLOOR

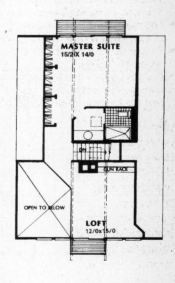

UPPER FLOOR

Romantic Retreat

- The romance and appeal of the Alpine chalet have remained constant over time. With more than 1,500 sq. ft. of living area, this chalet would make a great full-time home or vacation retreat.
- The L-shaped living room, dining room and kitchen flow together for casual living. This huge area is warmed by a freestanding fireplace and surrounded by an ornate deck, which is accessed through sliding glass doors.
- The main-level bedroom, with its twin closets and adjacent bath, could serve as a nice master suite.
- Upstairs, two large bedrooms share another full bath. One bedroom features a walk-in closet, while the other boasts its own private deck.
- The daylight basement offers laundry facilities, plenty of storage space and an extra-long garage.

Plan H-858-2	
Bedrooms: 3	**Baths:** 2
Living Area:	
Upper floor	576 sq. ft.
Main floor	960 sq. ft.
Total Living Area:	**1,536 sq. ft.**
Daylight basement	530 sq. ft.
Tuck-under garage	430 sq. ft.
Exterior Wall Framing:	2x6
Foundation Options:	

Daylight basement
(All plans can be built with your choice of foundation and framing. A generic conversion diagram is available. See order form.)

BLUEPRINT PRICE CODE:	**B**

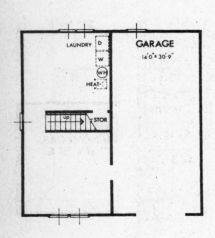

DAYLIGHT BASEMENT

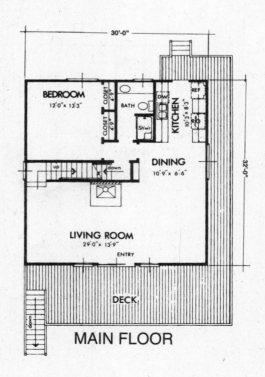

MAIN FLOOR

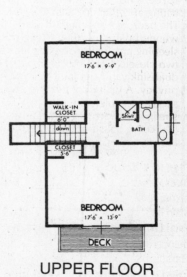

UPPER FLOOR

Plan H-858-2

PRICES AND DETAILS ON PAGES 12-15

All in One!

- This plan puts all of today's most luxurious home-design features into one attractive, economical package.
- The covered front porch and the gabled roofline, accented by an arched window and a round louver vent, give the exterior a homey yet stylish appeal.
- Just inside the front door, the ceiling rises up to 11 ft., making an impressive greeting. A skylight and French doors framing the fireplace flood the living room with light.
- The living room flows into a nice-sized dining room, also with an 11-ft. ceiling, which in turn leads to the large eat-in kitchen. Here you'll find lots of counter space, a handy laundry closet and a eating area that opens to a terrace.
- The bedroom wing includes a wonderful master suite, with a sizable sleeping area and a dressing area with two closets. Glass blocks above the dual-sink vanity let in light yet maintain privacy. A whirlpool tub and a separate shower complete the suite.
- The larger of the two remaining bedrooms boasts an 11-ft.-high ceiling and an arched window.

Plan HFL-1680-FL

Bedrooms: 3	Baths: 2

Living Area:	
Main floor	1,367 sq. ft.
Total Living Area:	**1,367 sq. ft.**
Standard basement	1,367 sq. ft.
Garage	431 sq. ft.
Exterior Wall Framing:	2x6

Foundation Options:

Standard basement

(All plans can be built with your choice of foundation and framing. A generic conversion diagram is available. See order form.)

BLUEPRINT PRICE CODE: A

VIEW INTO LIVING ROOM

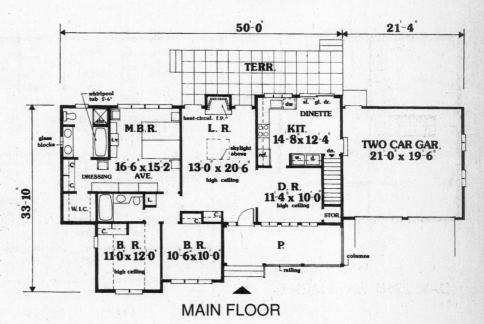

MAIN FLOOR

Shady Porches, Sunny Patio

- Designed with stylish country looks, this attractive one-story also has shady porches and a sunny patio for relaxed indoor/outdoor living.
- The inviting foyer flows into the spacious living room, which is warmed by a handsome fireplace.
- The adjoining dining room has a door to a screened-in porch, which opens to the backyard and serves as a breezeway to the nearby garage
- The U-shaped kitchen has a pantry closet and plenty of counter space. Around the corner, a space-efficient laundry/utility room exits to a big backyard patio.
- The master bedroom is brightened by windows on two sides and includes a wardrobe closet. The compartmentalized master bath offers a separate dressing area and a walk-in closet.
- Another full bath serves two additional good-sized bedrooms.

Plan C-7557	
Bedrooms: 3	**Baths:** 2
Living Area:	
Main floor	1,688 sq. ft.
Total Living Area:	**1,688 sq. ft.**
Standard basement	1,688 sq. ft.
Garage	400 sq. ft.
Exterior Wall Framing:	2x4

Foundation Options:
Standard basement
Crawlspace
Slab
(All plans can be built with your choice of foundation and framing. A generic conversion diagram is available. See order form.)

BLUEPRINT PRICE CODE:	B

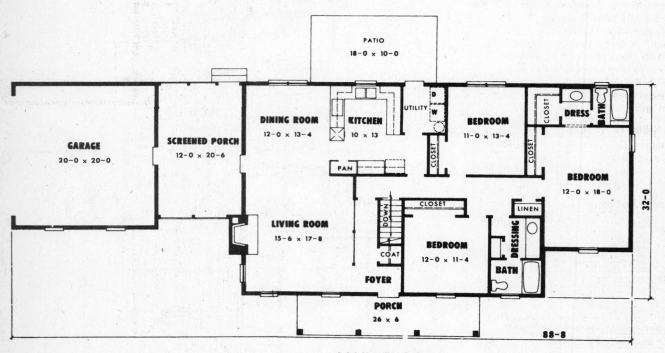

MAIN FLOOR

Plan C-7557

PRICES AND DETAILS ON PAGES 12-15

Vacation Home with Views

- The octagonal shape and window-filled walls of this home create a powerful interior packed with panoramic views.
- Straight back from the angled entry, the Great Room is brightened by expansive windows and sliding glass doors to a huge wraparound deck. An impressive spiral staircase at the center of the floor plan lends even more character.
- The walk-through kitchen offers a handy pantry. A nice storage closet and a coat closet are located between the entry and the two-car garage.
- The main-floor bedroom is conveniently located near a full bath.
- The upper-floor master suite is a sanctuary, featuring lots of glass, a walk-in closet, a private bath and access to concealed storage rooms.
- The optional daylight basement offers an extra bedroom, a full bath, a laundry area and a large recreation room.

Plans H-964-1A & -1B	
Bedrooms: 2+	**Baths:** 2-3
Living Area:	
Upper floor	346 sq. ft.
Main floor	1,067 sq. ft.
Daylight basement	1,045 sq. ft.
Total Living Area:	**1,413/2,458 sq. ft.**
Garage	512 sq. ft.
Storage (upper floor)	134 sq. ft.
Exterior Wall Framing:	2x6
Foundation Options:	**Plan #**
Daylight basement	H-964-1B
Crawlspace	H-964-1A

(All plans can be built with your choice of foundation and framing. A generic conversion diagram is available. See order form.)

BLUEPRINT PRICE CODE:	**A/C**

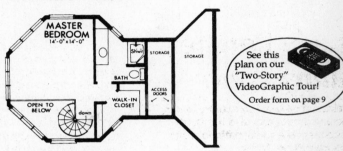

UPPER FLOOR

See this plan on our "Two-Story" VideoGraphic Tour! Order form on page 9

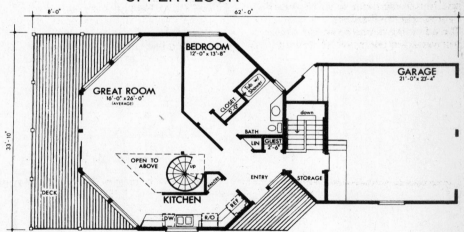

MAIN FLOOR

DAYLIGHT BASEMENT

Indoor/Outdoor Delights

- A curved porch in the front and a garden sun room in the back make this home an indoor/outdoor delight.
- Inside, a roomy kitchen is open to a five-sided, glassed-in dining room that views out to the porch.
- The living room features a fireplace along a glass wall that adjoins the gloriously sunny garden room.

- Wrapped in windows, the garden room accesses the backyard as well as a large storage area in the unobtrusive, side-entry garage.
- The master suite is no less luxurious, featuring a a sumptuous master bath with a garden spa tub, a corner shower and a walk-in closet.
- Each of the two remaining bedrooms has a boxed-out window and a walk-in closet. A full bath with a corner shower and a dual-sink vanity is close by.
- A stairway leads to the attic, which provides more potential living space.

Plan DD-1852	
Bedrooms: 3	**Baths:** 2
Living Area:	
Main floor	1,852 sq. ft.
Total Living Area:	**1,852 sq. ft.**
Standard basement	1,852 sq. ft.
Garage	528 sq. ft.
Exterior Wall Framing:	2x4
Foundation Options:	
Standard basement	
Crawlspace	
Slab	

(All plans can be built with your choice of foundation and framing. A generic conversion diagram is available. See order form.)

BLUEPRINT PRICE CODE: B

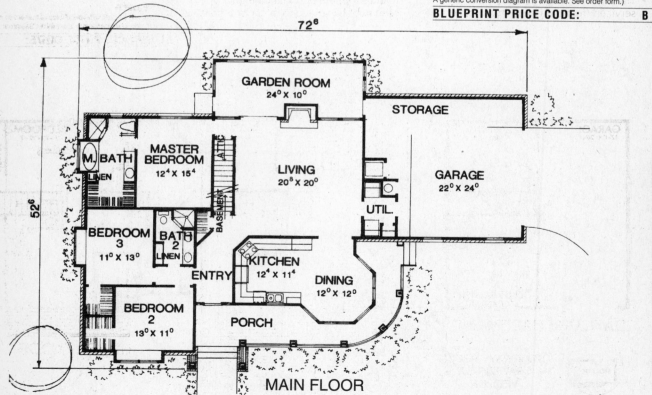

MAIN FLOOR

Super Chalet

- The charming Alpine detailing of the exterior and the open, flexible layout of the interior make this one of our most popular plans.
- In from the large front deck, the living room wraps around a central fireplace or woodstove, providing a warm and expansive multipurpose living space. Sliding glass doors open to the deck for outdoor entertaining.
- The adjoining dining room is easily serviced from the galley-style kitchen. A

convenient full bath serves a nearby bedroom and the remainder of the main floor.
- Two upper-floor bedrooms have 12-ft.-high sloped ceilings, extra closet space and access to another full bath. The larger bedroom offers sliding glass doors to a lofty deck.
- The blueprints recommend finishing the interior walls with solid lumber paneling for a rich, rustic look.
- In addition to a large general-use area and a shop, the optional daylight basement has space for a car or a boat.

Plans H-26-1 & -1A	
Bedrooms: 3	**Baths:** 2
Living Area:	
Upper floor	476 sq. ft.
Main floor	728 sq. ft.
Daylight basement	410 sq. ft.
Total Living Area:	**1,204/1,614 sq. ft.**
Tuck-under garage	318 sq. ft.
Exterior Wall Framing:	2x4
Foundation Options:	**Plan #**
Daylight basement	H-26-1
Crawlspace	H-26-1A

(All plans can be built with your choice of foundation and framing. A generic conversion diagram is available. See order form.)

BLUEPRINT PRICE CODE:	**A/B**

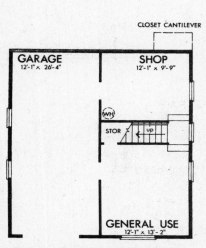

DAYLIGHT BASEMENT

STAIRWAY AREA IN CRAWLSPACE VERSION

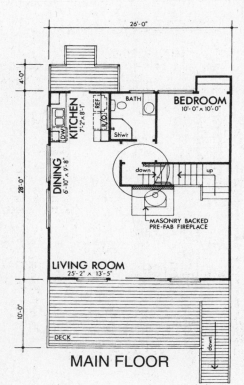

MAIN FLOOR

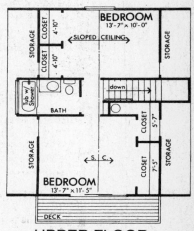

UPPER FLOOR

Comfortable, Open Plan

- This comfortable home defines function and style, with a sharp window wall to brighten the central living areas.
- In from the broad front deck, the living/family room boasts a fireplace, a cathedral ceiling and soaring views. The fireplace visually sets off the dining room, which extends to the backyard patio through sliding doors.
- The galley-style kitchen offers a bright sink and an abundance of counter space, with a laundry closet and carport access nearby.
- The secluded and spacious master bedroom features private deck access, a walk-in closet and a private bath.
- On the other side of the home, two good-sized secondary bedrooms share another full bath.

Plan C-8160	
Bedrooms: 3	**Baths:** 2
Living Area:	
Main floor	1,669 sq. ft.
Total Living Area:	**1,669 sq. ft.**
Daylight basement	1,660 sq. ft.
Carport	413 sq. ft.
Storage	85 sq. ft.
Exterior Wall Framing:	2x4

Foundation Options:
Daylight basement
Crawlspace
Slab
(All plans can be built with your choice of foundation and framing. A generic conversion diagram is available. See order form.)

BLUEPRINT PRICE CODE:	B

MAIN FLOOR

PATIO

BEDROOM
17'-3"x10'-10"

DINING
15'-10"x13'-0"

KITCHEN
18'-0"x9'-0"

W. D.

CARPORT
20'-0"x20'-8"

CLOS.

BATH

STORAGE

CLOS.

LIN.

BATH

37'-0"

CATHEDRAL CEILING

BEDROOM
14'-10"x11'-0"

COAT CLOS.

LIVING-FAMILY
15'-10"x20'-0"

BEDROOM
18'-0"x13'-4"

STORAGE

STORAGE

WOOD DECK

73'-0"

MAIN FLOOR

TO ORDER THIS BLUEPRINT, CALL TOLL-FREE 1-800-547-5570

Plan C-8160

PRICES AND DETAILS ON PAGES 12-15

Octagonal Home Has Lofty Views

- There's no better way to avoid the ordinary than to build an octagonal home and escape from conventional square corners and rigid rooms.
- The roomy main floor of this exciting home offers plenty of space for full-time family living or for comfortable second-home recreation.
- The two-story entry hall leads to the bedrooms on the right and to the Great Room around to the left.
- Warmed by a woodstove, the Great Room offers a relaxing retreat that includes a 12-ft. ceiling and a panoramic view of the outdoors.
- At the core of the main floor are two baths, one of which boasts a spa tub and private access from the adjoining master bedroom.
- A roomy kitchen and a handy utility room are also featured.
- The upper floor, surrounded by windows and topped by a 12-ft. ceiling, is designed as a recreation room, with a woodstove and a wet bar.
- The optional daylight basement adds a fourth bedroom, another bath, a garage and a large storage area.

See this plan on our "Two-Story" VideoGraphic Tour!
Order form on page 9

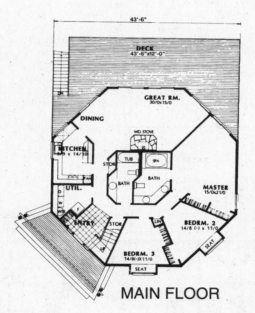

MAIN FLOOR

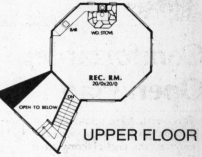

UPPER FLOOR

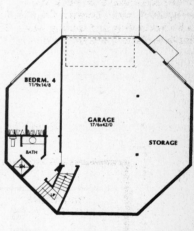

DAYLIGHT BASEMENT

Plans P-532-3A & -3D

Bedrooms: 3+	Baths: 2-3
Living Area:	
Upper floor	355 sq. ft.
Main floor	1,567 sq. ft.
Daylight basement	430 sq. ft.
Total Living Area:	**1,922/2,352 sq. ft.**
Opt. tuck-under garage/storage	1,137 sq. ft.
Exterior Wall Framing:	2x6
Foundation Options:	**Plan #**
Daylight basement	P-532-3D
Crawlspace	P-532-3A

(All plans can be built with your choice of foundation and framing. A generic conversion diagram is available. See order form.)

BLUEPRINT PRICE CODE: B/C

REAR VIEW

Plans P-532-3A & -3D

Inviting Country Porch

- A columned porch with double doors invites you into the rustic living areas of this ranch-style home.
- Inside, the entry allows views back to the expansive, central living room and the backyard beyond.
- The living room boasts an exposed-beam ceiling and a massive fireplace with a wide stone hearth, a wood box and built-in bookshelves. A sunny patio offers additional entertaining space.
- The dining room and the efficient kitchen combine for easy meal service, with a serving bar separating the two.
- The main hallway leads to the sleeping wing, which offers a large master bedroom with a walk-in closet and a private bath.
- Two additional bedrooms share another full bath, and a laundry closet is accessible to the entire bedroom wing.

Plan E-1304

Bedrooms: 3	Baths: 2

Living Area:	
Main floor	1,395 sq. ft.

Total Living Area:	**1,395 sq. ft.**
Garage & storage	481 sq. ft.

Exterior Wall Framing: 2x4

Foundation Options:

Crawlspace

Slab

(All plans can be built with your choice of foundation and framing. A generic conversion diagram is available. See order form.)

BLUEPRINT PRICE CODE: A

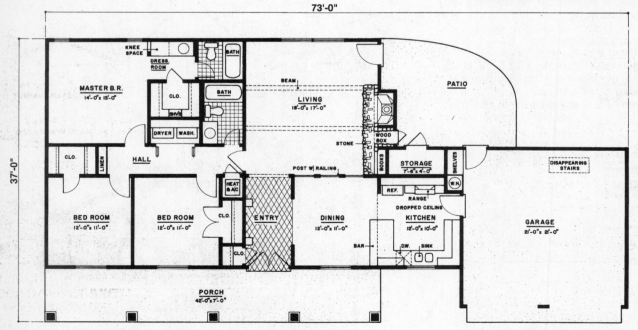

MAIN FLOOR

Plan E-1304

PRICES AND DETAILS ON PAGES 12-15

Sunny Chalet

- This captivating home is designed to maximize indoor and outdoor living. It features expansive windows, an open main floor and a large deck.
- The lower-level entry leads up a staircase to the spacious living room, which features a 12-ft. cathedral ceiling, an energy-efficient fireplace, a

railed balcony overlooking the foyer and sliding glass doors to the deck.
- The adjacent bayed dining room merges with the skylighted kitchen, which also boasts a handy serving bar.
- The lower floor features two spacious bedrooms that share a full bath, complete with a whirlpool tub.
- The quiet den could serve as a third bedroom or a guest room.

Plan K-532-L	
Bedrooms: 2+	**Baths:** 1½
Living Area:	
Main floor	492 sq. ft.
Lower floor	488 sq. ft.
Total Living Area:	**980 sq. ft.**
Exterior Wall Framing:	2x4 or 2x6

Foundation Options:

Crawlspace
(All plans can be built with your choice of foundation and framing. A generic conversion diagram is available. See order form.)

BLUEPRINT PRICE CODE: A

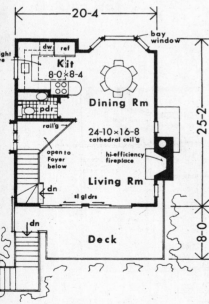

MAIN FLOOR

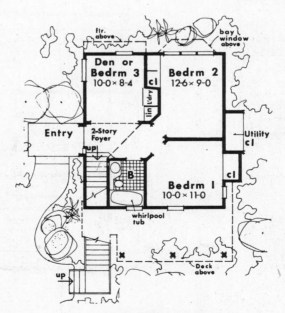

LOWER FLOOR

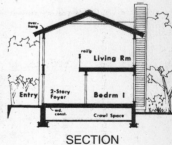

SECTION

VIEW INTO LIVING ROOM
AND DINING ROOM

Open Living for Weekend or Forever

- This cozy, 1 1/2 story home is perfect for a weekend retreat, summer home, or casual permanent residence.
- A large, open living area on the first level combines the kitchen, dining area and living room for a spacious setting; sliding doors to the front offer an outdoor relaxing or dining alternative.
- Two bedrooms and a full bath are located at the rear, both with closet space.
- The upper loft would be ideal for a private master bedroom or quiet study area.

Plan CPS-1095

Bedrooms: 2-3	Baths: 1
Space:	
Upper floor	320 sq. ft.
Main floor	784 sq. ft.
Total Living Area	**1,104 sq. ft.**
Basement	784 sq. ft.
Exterior Wall Framing	**2x6**

Foundation options:
Standard Basement
(Foundation & framing conversion diagram available—see order form.)

Blueprint Price Code	**A**

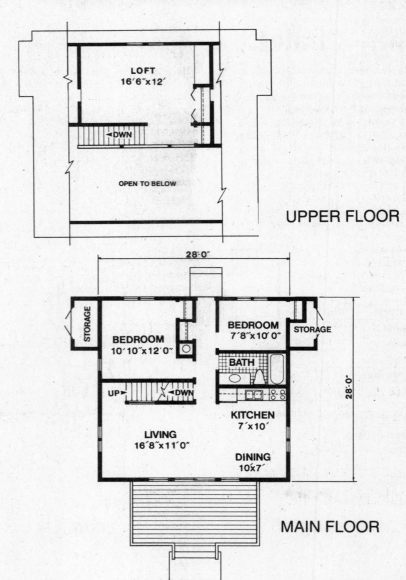

UPPER FLOOR

LOFT
16'6"x12'

DWN

OPEN TO BELOW

MAIN FLOOR

28'-0"

28'-0"

STORAGE

BEDROOM
10'10"x12'0"

BEDROOM
7'8"x10'0"

STORAGE

BATH

UP   DWN

KITCHEN
7'x10'

LIVING
16'8"x11'0"

DINING
10'x7'

Plan CPS-1095

PRICES AND DETAILS ON PAGES 12-15

Maximum Livability

- Compact and easy to build, this appealing ranch-style home is big on charm and livability.
- The entry of the home opens to a dramatic 13-ft. vaulted living room with exposed beams, a handsome fireplace and access to a backyard patio.
- Wood post dividers set off the large raised dining room, which is brightened by a stunning window wall.
- The adjoining kitchen offers a spacious snack bar and easy access to the utility room and the two-car garage. A nice storage area is also included.
- Three bedrooms and two baths occupy the sleeping wing. One of the baths is private to the master suite, which features a walk-in closet and a dressing area with a sit-down make-up table. The two remaining bedrooms also have walk-in closets.

Plan E-1305

Bedrooms: 3	**Baths:** 2

Living Area:

Main floor	1,346 sq. ft.
Total Living Area:	**1,346 sq. ft.**
Garage	441 sq. ft.
Storage	44 sq. ft.
Exterior Wall Framing:	2x4

Foundation Options:

Crawlspace

Slab

(All plans can be built with your choice of foundation and framing. A generic conversion diagram is available. See order form.)

BLUEPRINT PRICE CODE:	**A**

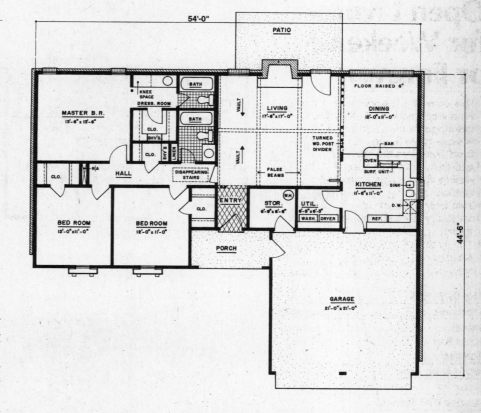

MAIN FLOOR

Contemporary Saltbox

- This contemporary two-story saltbox is compactly designed.
- Sliding glass doors and a greenhouse bay off the dining area make the rear of the home almost all enclosed in glass.
- The huge living room at the center of the floor plan features a sloped ceiling, heat-circulating fireplace and a skylight in addition to the glass wall of the greenhouse.
- A sunny dinette and open, skylit kitchen merge together with a convenient laundry room and pantry nearby.
- The main-floor master bedroom has dual closets and an adjacent full bath.
- Two nice-sized bedrooms and a second full bath share the upper level; a railing borders the balcony that overlooks the main living areas below.

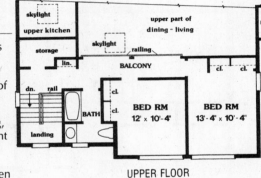

Plan HFL-1300-MS	
Bedrooms: 3	**Baths:** 2
Space:	
Upper floor	519 sq. ft
Main floor	1,042 sq. ft
Total Living Area	**1,561 sq. ft**
Basement	1,000 sq. ft
Garage	233 sq. ft
Exterior Wall Framing	2x6
Foundation options:	
Standard Basement	
Slab	
(Foundation & framing conversion diagram available—see order form.)	
Blueprint Price Code	

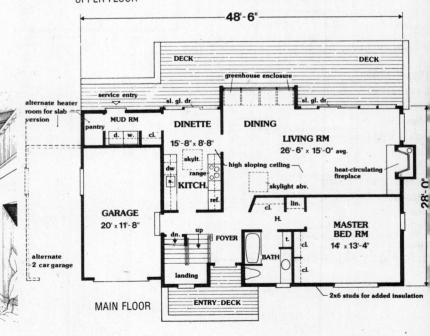

UPPER FLOOR

MAIN FLOOR

Balcony Overlooks Living Room

First floor: 1,018 sq. ft.
Second floor: 900 sq. ft.

Total living area: 1,918 sq. ft.
(Not counting garage)

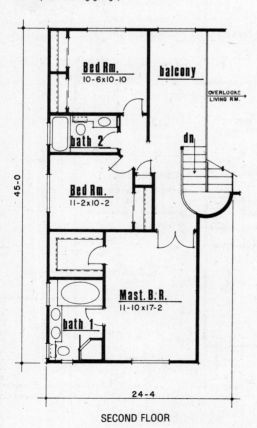

Bed Rm.
10-6x10-10

balcony

OVERLOOKS
LIVING RM.

bath 2

dn.

Bed Rm.
11-2x10-2

45-0

Mast. B.R.
11-10x17-2

bath 1

24-4

SECOND FLOOR

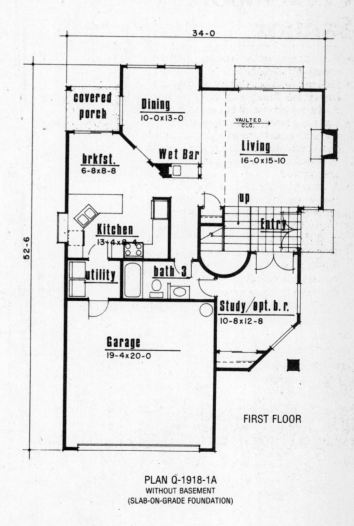

34-0

covered porch

Dining
10-0x13-0

VAULTED CLG.

brkfst.
6-8x8-8

Wet Bar

Living
16-0x15-10

52-6

Kitchen
13-4x8-4

up

Entry

utility

bath 3

Garage
19-4x20-0

Study/opt. b.r.
10-8x12-8

FIRST FLOOR

PLAN Q-1918-1A
WITHOUT BASEMENT
(SLAB-ON-GRADE FOUNDATION)

Blueprint Price Code B
Plan Q-1918-1A

New Traditional

- A lovely front porch and an open floor plan give this new traditional its modern appeal.
- The foyer opens to a fabulous living room with a 16-ft. vaulted ceiling, a fireplace and an open staircase. Railings introduce the bayed breakfast area. The efficient galley-style kitchen leads to a covered back porch.
- The sizable master suite is enhanced by a 10-ft. raised ceiling and a cozy bay window. The compartmentalized bath includes a dual-sink vanity and a walk-in closet. Another bedroom is nearby, along with a convenient laundry closet.
- Upstairs, a third bedroom has private access to a full bath. A large future area provides expansion space.

Plan J-8636

Bedrooms: 3	Baths: 3
Living Area:	
Upper floor	270 sq. ft.
Main floor	1,253 sq. ft.
Bonus room	270 sq. ft.
Total Living Area:	**1,793 sq. ft.**
Standard basement	1,287 sq. ft.
Garage	390 sq. ft.
Exterior Wall Framing:	2x4

Foundation Options:

Standard basement
Crawlspace
Slab

(All plans can be built with your choice of foundation and framing. A generic conversion diagram is available. See order form.)

BLUEPRINT PRICE CODE: B

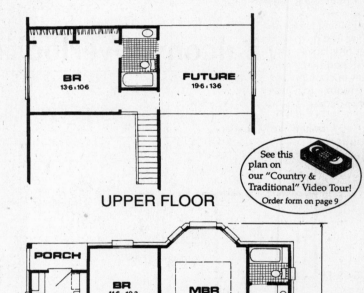

UPPER FLOOR

See this plan on our "Country & Traditional" Video Tour! Order form on page 9

MAIN FLOOR

TO ORDER THIS BLUEPRINT, CALL TOLL-FREE 1-800-547-5570   Plan J-8636   **PRICES AND DETAILS ON PAGES 12-15**

Exciting Exterior Options

Two exciting elevations are available with this striking stucco design. (Both are included with blueprint purchase.) The stately, covered front entry and elegant window treatments are just the beginning of the excitement. Inside is a huge formal living area with volume ceilings.

The adjoining family room offers built-in shelving and provisions for an optional corner fireplace or media center. Triple sliders open to the rear covered patio. The eat-in country kitchen overlooks the family room and features a handy serving counter, a pantry and a laundry closet.

Separated from the two secondary bedrooms, the master bedroom is a quiet retreat. It offers patio access and an oversized private bath with a huge walk-in closet, a big corner tub and separate vanities that flank a sitting area.

ELEVATION A

ELEVATION B

Plan HDS-99-140

Bedrooms: 3	Baths: 2

Living Area:

Main floor	1,550 sq. ft.
Total Living Area:	**1,550 sq. ft.**
Garage	475 sq. ft.
Exterior Wall Framing:	2x4

Foundation Options:

Slab

(Typical foundation & framing conversion diagram available—see order form.)

BLUEPRINT PRICE CODE: B

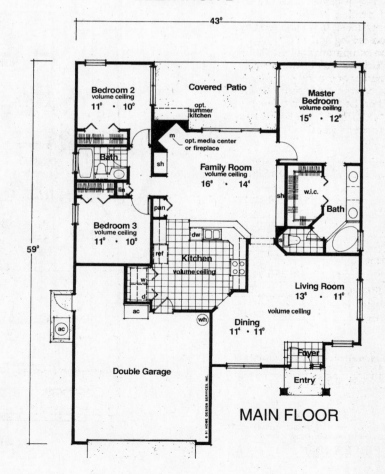

MAIN FLOOR

A Perfect Fit

- This country-style home will fit anywhere. Its charming character and narrow width make it ideal for those who value vintage styling along with plenty of yard space.
- The quaint covered front porch opens into the living room, which boasts a 12-ft., 8-in. cathedral ceiling and an inviting fireplace.
- The adjacent bay-windowed dining area features a 9-ft.-high vaulted ceiling and easy access to the efficient, galley-style kitchen.
- Off the kitchen, a handy laundry/utility room is convenient to the back entrance. The carport can accommodate two cars and includes a lockable storage area.
- The master bedroom suite offers a roomy walk-in closet, a private bath and sliding glass doors to a rear patio.
- Another full bath is centrally located for easy service to the rest of the home. Two more nice-sized bedrooms complete the plan.

Plan J-86119

Bedrooms: 3	**Baths:** 2

Living Area:	
Main floor	1,346 sq. ft.
Total Living Area:	**1,346 sq. ft.**
Standard basement	1,346 sq. ft.
Carport	400 sq. ft.
Exterior Wall Framing:	2x4

Foundation Options:

Standard basement
Crawlspace
Slab
(All plans can be built with your choice of foundation and framing. A generic conversion diagram is available. See order form.)

BLUEPRINT PRICE CODE: A

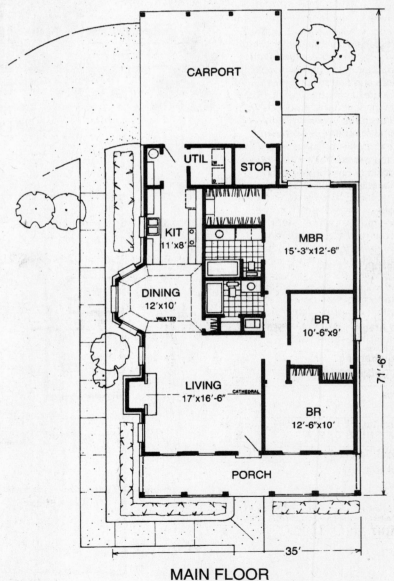

MAIN FLOOR

Plan J-86119

PRICES AND DETAILS ON PAGES 12-15

Classic Country-Style

- The classic covered front porch with decorative railings and columns make this home reminiscent of an early 20th-century farmhouse.
- Dormers give the home the appearance of a two-story, even though it is designed for single-level living.
- The huge living room features a ceiling that slopes up to 13 feet. A corner fireplace radiates warmth to both the living room and the dining room.
- The dining room overlooks a backyard patio and shares a versatile serving bar with the open kitchen. A large utility room is just steps away.
- The master bedroom boasts a roomy bath with a dual-sink vanity. The two smaller bedrooms at the other end of the home share a full bath.

Plan E-1412

Bedrooms: 3	Baths: 2

Living Area:

Main floor	1,484 sq. ft.
Total Living Area:	**1,484 sq. ft.**
Garage	440 sq. ft.
Exterior Wall Framing:	2x6

Foundation Options:

Crawlspace

Slab

(All plans can be built with your choice of foundation and framing. A generic conversion diagram is available. See order form.)

BLUEPRINT PRICE CODE: A

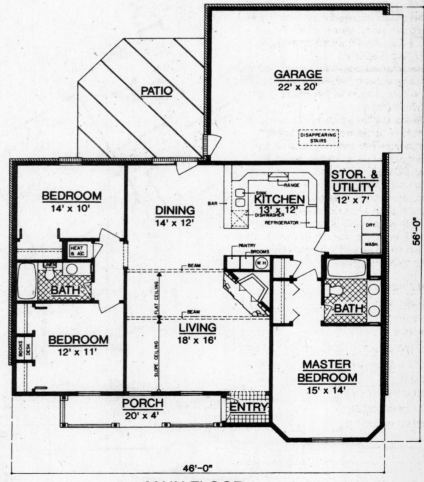

MAIN FLOOR

Passive Solar with Many Orientation Options

This angled passive solar design is planned to suit almost any plot and many orientation alternatives. Exterior siding of vertical natural wood and a high front chimney give the house an interesting appearance.

Inside, the central focus is the light-filled south-facing sun garden that greets occupants and visitors as they enter the reception hall. The large combination living room and dining room are highlighted by a dramatic sloped ceiling and a high-efficiency wood-burning fireplace. Glass around and above the fireplace contributes more light and provides a panoramic view of the rear landscaping. Sharing a second fireplace is the informal area that includes the family room and U-shaped kitchen.

Three bedrooms are located in the left wing of the house. The large master suite has a cheerful sitting area which borders on the sun garden. Living area, excluding the sun garden, is 1,574 sq. ft.; optional basement is 1,522 sq. ft.; garage is 400 sq. ft.

Total living area: 1,574 sq. ft
(Not counting basement or garage)

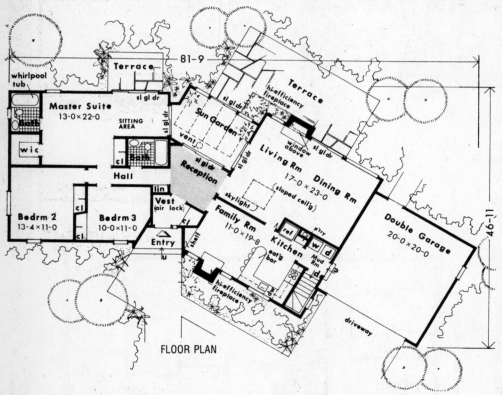

FLOOR PLAN

SECTION
PASSIVE SOLAR AT WORK

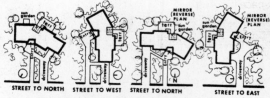

IMAGINE THE ORIENTATION POSSIBILITIES

**TO ORDER THIS BLUEPRINT,
CALL TOLL-FREE 1-800-547-5570**

Blueprint Price Code B
Plan K-526-C

*PRICES AND DETAILS
ON PAGES 12-15*

pacious
wiss Chalet

Three decks, lots of views and Swiss styling make this three-bedroom chalet the perfect design for that special site. A stone-faced fireplace is the focal point of the huge central living area. Sliding glass doors between the living room and the dining room lead to the large main-level deck. The space-saving kitchen conveniently serves the entire entertaining area.

The main-floor bedroom is close to a full bath. The oversized laundry room doubles as a mudroom.

Upstairs, each of the two bedrooms has a sloped ceiling, accessible attic storage space and a private deck.

The optional daylight basement provides space for utilities as well as the opportunity for expansion. In the crawlspace version of the design, the furnace and water heater are located in the laundry room.

Plans H-755-5E & -6E

Bedrooms: 3	Baths: 2

Living Area:

Upper floor	454 sq. ft.
Main floor	896 sq. ft.
Daylight basement	896 sq. ft.
Total Living Area:	**1,350/2,246 sq. ft.**
Exterior Wall Framing:	**2x4**

Foundation Options:	**Plan #**
Daylight basement	H-755-6E
Crawlspace	H-755-5E

(All plans can be built with your choice of foundation and framing. A generic conversion diagram is available. See order form.)

BLUEPRINT PRICE CODE:	**A/C**

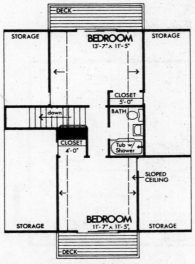

UPPER FLOOR

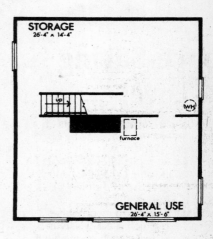

DAYLIGHT BASEMENT

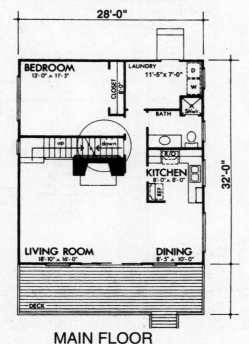

MAIN FLOOR

STAIRWAY AREA IN CRAWLSPACE VERSION

Space-Saving Tri-Level

- This clever tri-level design offers an open, airy interior while taking up a minimum of land space.
- The Great Room features a spectacular 15-ft. vaulted and skylighted ceiling, an inviting woodstove and sliding glass doors to a full-width deck.
- The Great Room also incorporates a dining area, which is easily serviced from the efficient, space-saving kitchen.
- The main-floor bedroom boasts two closets. A compact laundry closet, a guest closet and a storage area line the hallway to the spacious main bath.
- The large loft offers infinite possibilities, such as extra sleeping quarters, a home office, an art studio or a recreation room. Clerestory windows and a sloped ceiling enhance the bright, airy feeling.
- The tuck-under garage saves on building costs and lets you make the most of your lot.

Plan H-963-2A

Bedrooms: 1+	Baths: 1
Living Area:	
Upper floor	432 sq. ft.
Main floor	728 sq. ft.
Total Living Area:	**1,160 sq. ft.**
Tuck-under garage	728 sq. ft.
Exterior Wall Framing:	2x4

Foundation Options:

Slab
(All plans can be built with your choice of foundation and framing. A generic conversion diagram is available. See order form.)

BLUEPRINT PRICE CODE: **A**

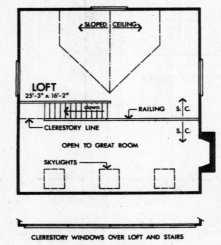

UPPER FLOOR

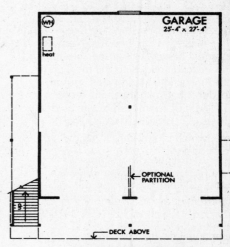

LOWER FLOOR

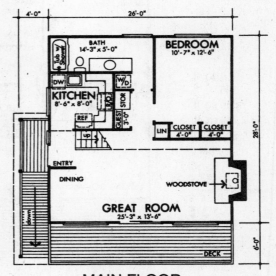

MAIN FLOOR

TO ORDER THIS BLUEPRINT, CALL TOLL-FREE 1-800-547-5570

Plan H-963-2A

PRICES AND DETAILS ON PAGES 12-15

REAR VIEW

FRONT VIEW

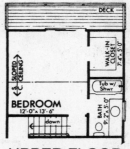

UPPER FLOOR

Easy Living

The living is easy in this affordable home, which is perfect for a scenic lot. Five steps down from the entry, the main living areas look out over an inviting wraparound deck. The living room offers a 16-ft.-high sloped ceiling, a handsome fireplace and deck access. A snack bar separates the sunny kitchen from the spacious dining area. Additional deck access is provided near the laundry area.

Two bedrooms near the main entrance share a bath and feature 13-ft. sloped ceilings.

The secluded upper-floor master suite boasts a 14-ft. vaulted ceiling, a walk-in closet, a full bath and a private deck.

Plans H-925-1 & -1A

Bedrooms: 3	Baths: 2
Living Area:	
Upper floor	288 sq. ft.
Main floor	951 sq. ft.
Total Living Area:	**1,239 sq. ft.**
Daylight basement	951 sq. ft.
Garage	266 sq. ft.
Exterior Wall Framing:	2x4
Foundation Options:	**Plan #**
Daylight basement	H-925-1
Crawlspace	H-925-1A

(All plans can be built with your choice of foundation and framing. A generic conversion diagram is available. See order form.)

BLUEPRINT PRICE CODE: **A**

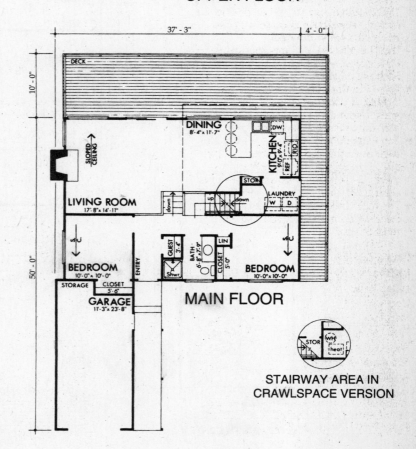

MAIN FLOOR

STAIRWAY AREA IN CRAWLSPACE VERSION

Downstairs Master Suite

- The downstairs master suite is secluded from the other bedrooms and includes a large walk-in closet.
- The living room, dining room and kitchen flow together to create plenty of space for easy family living and entertaining.
- Vaulted ceilings in the living room enhance the home's modest square footage. The fireplace can be enjoyed from both the living room and the dining room.
- Sliding glass doors in the dining room open to a large deck for extended living space.
- The bath on the second floor is compartmentalized for double duty, with the vanity separate from the toilet and bathing area.

Plan B-89031

Bedrooms: 3	Baths: 2
Space:	
Upper floor	446 sq. ft.
Main floor	857 sq. ft.
Total Living Area	**1,303 sq. ft.**
Basement	857 sq. ft.
Garage	400 sq. ft.
Exterior Wall Framing	2x4

Foundation options:

Standard Basement

(Foundation & framing conversion diagram available—see order form.)

Blueprint Price Code	**A**

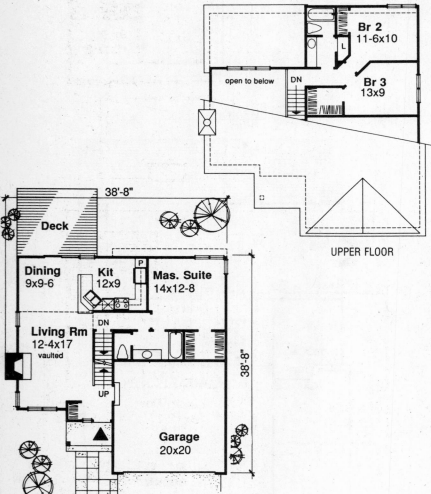

Br 2
11-6x10

open to below   DN

Br 3
13x9

UPPER FLOOR

38'-8"

Deck

Dining
9x9-6

Kit
12x9

P

Mas. Suite
14x12-8

Living Rm
12-4x17
vaulted

DN

38'-8"

UP

Garage
20x20

MAIN FLOOR

Plan B-89031

PRICES AND DETAILS
ON PAGES 12-15

Striking Stone Chimney

- With tall windows and a rustic stone chimney, the striking facade of this home demands attention.
- The sheltered entry leads into a raised foyer, which steps down to the sunny living room and its dramatic 16-ft. vaulted ceiling.
- A handsome fireplace warms the living room and the adjoining dining room, which offers access to an inviting deck.
- A cozy breakfast nook is included in the efficient, open-design kitchen. A special feature is the convenient pass-through to the dining room.
- A skylighted staircase leads upstairs to the master suite, with its private bath and large walk-in closet.
- A second bedroom shares another full bath with a loft or third bedroom.
- A dramatic balcony overlooks the living room below.

Plan B-224-8512

Bedrooms: 2+	Baths: 2½
Living Area:	
Upper floor	691 sq. ft.
Main floor	668 sq. ft.
Total Living Area:	**1,359 sq. ft.**
Standard basement	668 sq. ft.
Garage	458 sq. ft.
Exterior Wall Framing:	2x4

Foundation Options:

Standard basement

(All plans can be built with your choice of foundation and framing. A generic conversion diagram is available. See order form.)

BLUEPRINT PRICE CODE: **A**

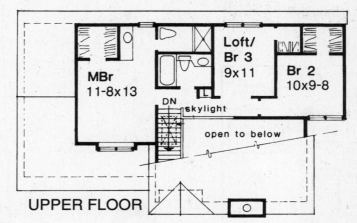

UPPER FLOOR

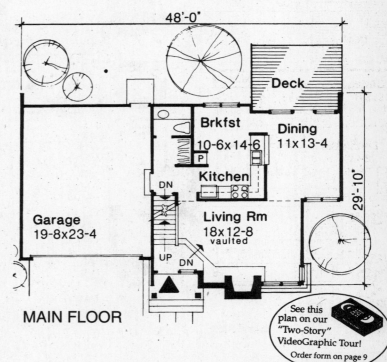

MAIN FLOOR

See this plan on our "Two-Story" VideoGraphic Tour! Order form on page 9

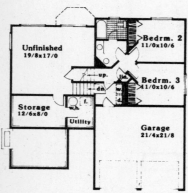

UPPER FLOOR

Plan R-4033

Bedrooms: 3	Baths: 2
Space:	
Upper two levels:	1,185 sq. ft.
Lower level:	480 sq. ft.
Total living area:	1,665 sq. ft.
Bonus area:	334 sq. ft.
Garage:	462 sq. ft.
Storage:	100 sq. ft.
Exterior Wall Framing:	2x6

Foundation options:
Daylight basement only.
(Foundation & framing conversion
diagram available — see order form.)

Blueprint Price Code:	B

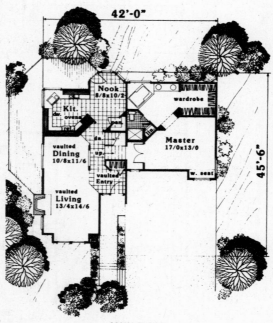

MAIN FLOOR

Exciting Design for Sloping Lot

- This design offers an exciting floor plan for a side-sloping lot.
- The vaulted foyer opens to the living room which is highlighted by a cheerful fireplace and is also vaulted.
- A half-wall with overhead arch separates the foyer and hallway from the dining room without interrupting the flow of space.
- The kitchen offers plenty of counter and cabinet space, and adjoins a brightly lit vaulted nook with a pantry in the corner.
- Separated from the rest of the household, the upper level master suite is a true haven from the day's worries, with its relaxing whirlpool tub, dual vanities and roomy closet.
- The lower level includes two bedrooms, a bath plus a large area which can be finished as a recreation room, plus a utility and storage area.

Light-Filled Interior

- A stylish contemporary exterior and an open, light-filled interior define this two-level home.
- The covered entry leads to a central gallery. The huge living room and dining room combine to generate a spacious ambience that is enhanced by a 15½-ft. cathedral ceiling and a warm fireplace with tall flanking windows.
- Oriented to the rear and overlooking a terrace and backyard landscaping are the informal spaces. The family room, the sunny semi-circular dinette and the modern kitchen share a snack bar.
- The main-floor master suite boasts a 13-ft. sloped ceiling, a private terrace, a dressing area and a personal bath with a whirlpool tub.
- Two to three extra bedrooms with 11-ft. ceilings share a skylighted bath on the upper floor.

Plan K-683-D

Bedrooms: 3+	Baths: 2½+
Living Area:	
Upper floor	491 sq. ft.
Main floor	1,475 sq. ft.
Total Living Area:	**1,966 sq. ft.**
Standard basement	1,425 sq. ft.
Garage and storage	487 sq. ft.
Exterior Wall Framing:	2x4 or 2x6
Foundation Options:	
Standard basement	
Slab	

(All plans can be built with your choice of foundation and framing. A generic conversion diagram is available. See order form.)

BLUEPRINT PRICE CODE: **B**

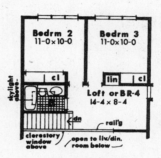

UPPER FLOOR

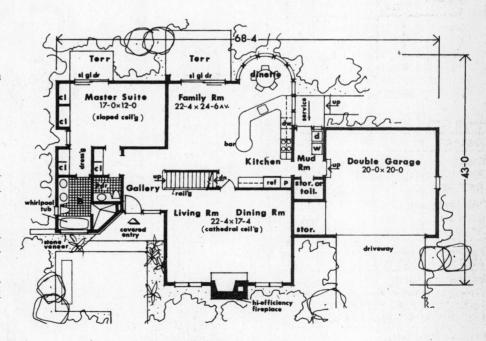

MAIN FLOOR

Garden Home

- This thoroughly modern plan exhibits beautiful traditional touches in its exterior design.
- A garden area leads visitors to a side door with a vaulted entry.
- A delightful kitchen/nook area is just to the right of the entry, and includes a convenient snack bar, a pantry and a nearby laundry room. The bayed breakfast nook overlooks the front yard.
- The living and dining areas share a 12½-ft.-high vaulted ceiling, making an impressive space for entertaining and family living. The stone fireplace and patio view add to the dramatic atmosphere.
- The master suite boasts a large closet and a private bath.
- Two more bedrooms share another bath off the hall.

Plans P-6598-2A & -2D

Bedrooms: 3	Baths: 2
Living Area:	
Main floor (with crawlspace)	1,375 sq. ft.
Main floor (with basement)	1,470 sq. ft.
Total Living Area:	**1,375/1,470 sq. ft.**
Daylight basement	1,470 sq. ft.
Garage	435 sq. ft.
Exterior Wall Framing:	2x4
Foundation Options:	**Plan #**
Daylight basement	P-6598-2D
Crawlspace	P-6598-2A

(All plans can be built with your choice of foundation and framing. A generic conversion diagram is available. See order form.)

BLUEPRINT PRICE CODE:	**A**

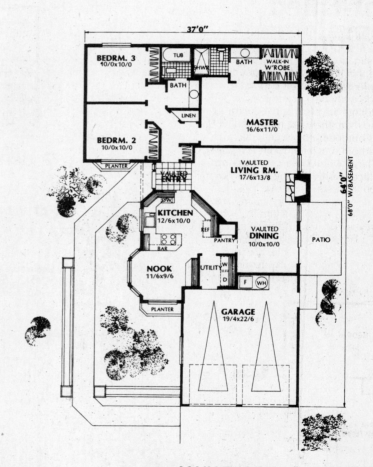

MAIN FLOOR

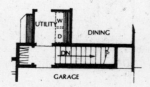

BASEMENT STAIRWAY LOCATION

Plans P-6598-2A & -2D

PRICES AND DETAILS ON PAGES 12-15

REAR VIEW

A Natural Complement

- Its rustic facade and woodsy appeal make this home a wonderful complement to nature's backdrop.
- A wide entry deck leads past a handy ski storage area to the 17-ft.-high foyer.
- To the right, the walk-through kitchen offers outdoor access.
- The adjoining dining room is brightened by a large window. A handsome fireplace warms the enormous living

room, where two sets of sliding glass doors open to a sprawling deck in the backyard.
- Two large bedrooms down the hall share a full bath.
- On the upper floor, the luxurious master bedroom boasts sliding glass doors to a romantic balcony.
- Past a dressing area, the master bath is enhanced by a refreshing whirlpool tub and a separate shower. A balcony offers beautiful morning views.
- An unfinished attic space flaunts lots of natural light and could be used as a future bedroom, if desired.

Plan AX-8382

Bedrooms: 3+		**Baths:** 2
Living Area:		
Upper floor		419 sq. ft.
Main floor		1,144 sq. ft.
Total Living Area:		**1,563 sq. ft.**
Unfinished attic (future bedroom)		235 sq. ft.
Standard basement		1,144 sq. ft.
Exterior Wall Framing:		2x4

Foundation Options:
Standard basement
Crawlspace
Slab
(All plans can be built with your choice of foundation and framing. A generic conversion diagram is available. See order form.)

BLUEPRINT PRICE CODE:	**B**

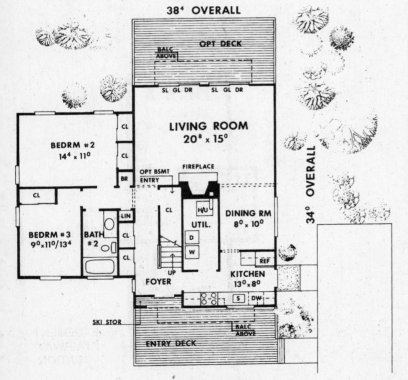

MAIN FLOOR

38⁴ OVERALL — OPT DECK — BALC ABOVE — SL GL DR — SL GL DR — LIVING ROOM 20⁸ x 15⁰ — CL — CL — BR — BEDRM #2 14⁴ x 11⁰ — CL — OPT BSMT ENTRY — FIREPLACE — H/U — CL — UTIL. — D — W — DINING RM 8⁰ x 10⁰ — LIN — CL — CL — BATH #2 — BEDRM #3 9⁰ x 11⁰/13⁴ — CL — UP — FOYER — REF — KITCHEN 13⁰ x 8⁰ — S — DW — SKI STOR — BALC ABOVE — ENTRY DECK — 34⁰ OVERALL

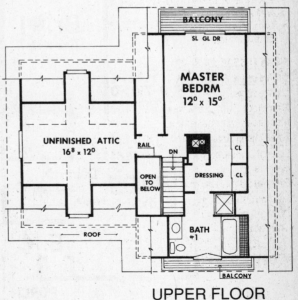

UPPER FLOOR

BALCONY — SL GL DR — MASTER BEDRM 12⁰ x 15⁰ — UNFINISHED ATTIC 16⁸ x 12⁰ — RAIL — DN — CL — DRESSING — CL — OPEN TO BELOW — BATH #1 — ROOF — BALCONY

Efficient and Affordable

- An efficient and affordable floor plan comes to life in this cozy two-story.
- A quaint covered porch framed by lovely detailing and latticework sets off the facade.
- Inside, the entry opens directly into the living/dining room, which is brightened by large front windows and offers a great open space for entertaining.
- Easy access to a covered backyard porch highlights the walk-through kitchen, which also boasts a nifty snack bar for speedy informal meals.
- Around the corner, the charming master bedroom is a perfect retreat. A full bath and basement access are just steps away.
- Upstairs, two more bedrooms share a spacious hall bath.

Plan HDG-94009	
Bedrooms: 3	**Baths:** 2
Living Area:	
Upper floor	394 sq. ft.
Main floor	638 sq. ft.
Total Living Area:	**1,032 sq. ft.**
Standard basement	608 sq. ft.
Exterior Wall Framing:	2x4
Foundation Options:	

Standard basement
(All plans can be built with your choice of foundation and framing. A generic conversion diagram is available. See order form.)

BLUEPRINT PRICE CODE:	**A**

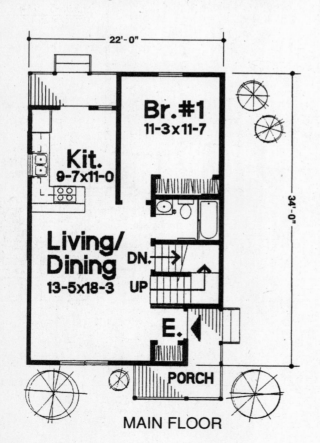

MAIN FLOOR

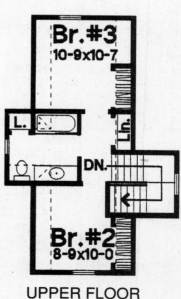

UPPER FLOOR

TO ORDER THIS BLUEPRINT, CALL TOLL-FREE 1-800-547-5570

Plan HDG-94009

PRICES AND DETAILS ON PAGES 12-15

Lush Courtyard Graces Entry

- A lush, private courtyard graces the entry of this attractive one-story.
- The skylighted foyer leads to the formal dining room, which features corner china shelves and a cozy shape for special meals.
- Easily accessed from the dining room, the open, skylighted kitchen is enhanced by a cheery, bayed breakfast nook. A French door in the nook opens to the courtyard.
- Beyond the dining room, the spacious living room boasts a handsome fireplace. Sliding glass doors access a large backyard deck that is perfect for warm-weather entertaining.
- On the other side of the home, the master bedroom enjoys a large walk-in closet and a skylighted bath.
- Two good-sized secondary bedrooms share a second skylighted bath, with laundry facilities and garage access just steps away.

Plan LMB-3714-T

Bedrooms: 3	**Baths:** 2

Living Area:	
Main floor	1,288 sq. ft.
Total Living Area:	**1,288 sq. ft.**
Garage	420 sq. ft.
Exterior Wall Framing:	2x6

Foundation Options:

Crawlspace
(All plans can be built with your choice of foundation and framing. A generic conversion diagram is available. See order form.)

BLUEPRINT PRICE CODE:	**A**

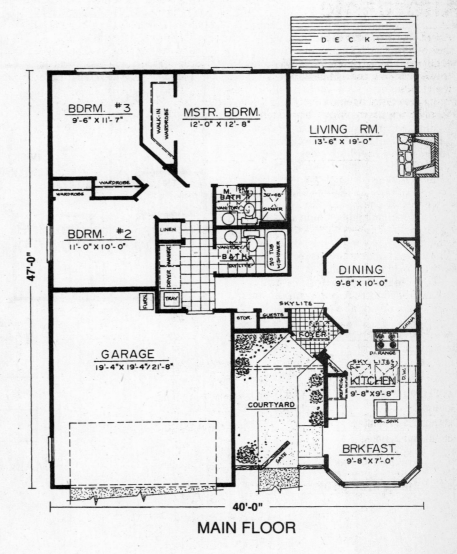

MAIN FLOOR

Comfort Weds Economy

- A simple design with comfort in mind lends this delightful home a cozy, welcoming atmosphere.
- The rustic cedar facade gives way to the foyer, which is heightened and brightened by a 12-ft. vaulted ceiling and a cheery sidelight.
- Straight ahead, the living room and the dining area are warmed by an energy-efficient fireplace. A 13-ft. vaulted ceiling soars over both areas.
- From the dining space, sliding glass doors offer easy access to a nice covered patio.
- The open kitchen features a long countertop facing the dining area for ease in serving.
- In the sleeping wing of the home, the master bedroom enjoys its own walk-in closet and private bath.
- Two more bedrooms across the hall share a second bath; one bedroom may serve as a den or a study.

Plan B-806

Bedrooms: 2+	**Baths:** 2

Living Area:	
Main floor	1,081 sq. ft.
Total Living Area:	**1,081 sq. ft.**
Garage	420 sq. ft.
Exterior Wall Framing:	2x4

Foundation Options:
Slab
(All plans can be built with your choice of foundation and framing. A generic conversion diagram is available. See order form.)

BLUEPRINT PRICE CODE: **A**

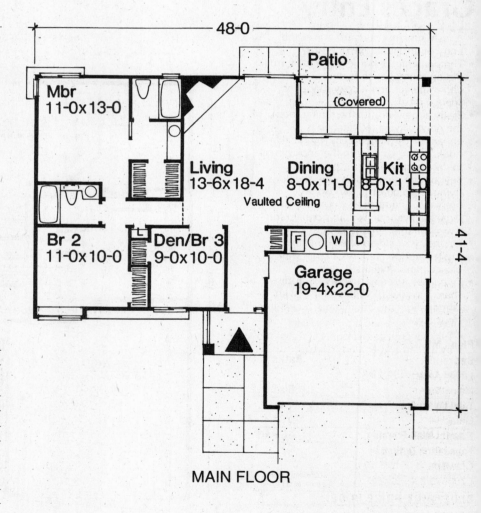

MAIN FLOOR

 Plan B-806

Windows Add Brightness

- An attractive octagonal window, an inviting bay window and a sunny skylight brighten this home's facade.
- A quiet covered porch shelters a sidelighted front door that opens into the skylighted foyer.
- Straight ahead, the living room boasts an 11-ft., 10-in. vaulted ceiling and unique angled walls. In the adjacent formal dining room, sliding glass doors introduce an inviting backyard patio.
- A neat galley design maximizes efficiency in the gourmet kitchen, which includes a double sink and a pantry closet. The kitchen extends to a cheerful bayed breakfast nook that you and your family will enjoy on relaxing weekend mornings.
- On the other side of the home, a 10-ft., 10-in. vaulted ceiling soars over the master bedroom, which boasts a handy dressing area and a private bath.
- Two secondary bedrooms are serviced by a centrally located hall bath.

Plan LMB-2204-CDA

Bedrooms: 3	Baths: 2
Living Area:	
Main floor	1,298 sq. ft.
Total Living Area:	**1,298 sq. ft.**
Garage and storage	451 sq. ft.
Exterior Wall Framing:	2x4

Foundation Options:

Crawlspace
(All plans can be built with your choice of foundation and framing. A generic conversion diagram is available. See order form.)

BLUEPRINT PRICE CODE:	**A**

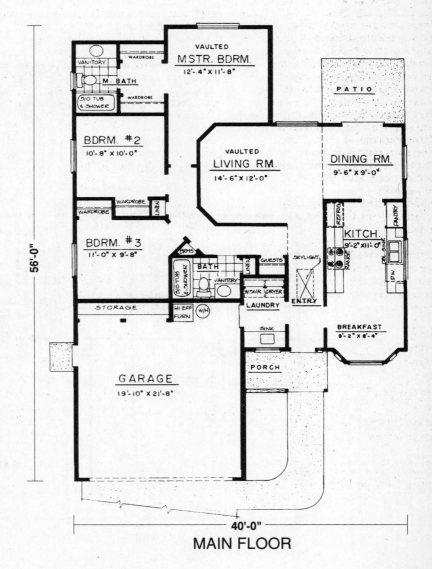

MAIN FLOOR

Striking Windows

- A dramatic covered entry with a tall, striking window arrangement draws attention to this modest-sized home.
- A bright French door opens directly into the spacious family room, which features a soaring 11½-ft. vaulted ceiling and a cozy fireplace for winter nights. A hardwood floor adds a beautiful touch at the front of the room.
- To the right of the family room, the inviting dining area offers two options

—a sunny bay window or sliding glass doors that open to the backyard.
- The efficient galley-style kitchen boasts enclosed laundry facilities and convenient access to the dining area. The kitchen's handy garage access will make unloading groceries a snap.
- The spacious master bedroom boasts a huge walk-in closet and a private bath with an airy 13½-ft. vaulted ceiling. The bath includes an inviting garden tub, a separate shower and a dual-sink vanity.
- A hall bath, which is centrally located for added convenience, serves two secondary bedrooms nearby. Both rooms include good-sized closets.

Plan APS-1003

Bedrooms: 3	Baths: 2
Living Area:	
Main floor (slab version)	1,093 sq. ft.
Main floor (basement version)	1,188 sq. ft.
Total Living Area:	**1,093/1,188 sq. ft.**
Standard basement	1,188 sq. ft.
Garage	364 sq. ft.
Exterior Wall Framing:	2x4

Foundation Options:

Standard basement
Slab
(All plans can be built with your choice of foundation and framing. A generic conversion diagram is available. See order form.)

BLUEPRINT PRICE CODE: A

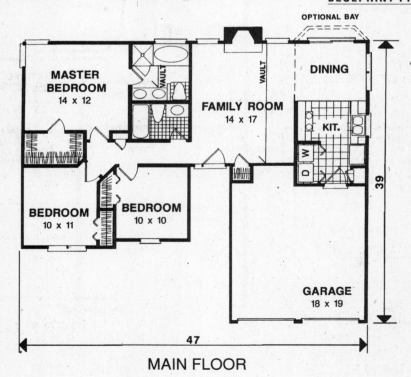

MAIN FLOOR

Plan APS-1003

PRICES AND DETAILS ON PAGES 12-15

Fun Retreat

- A huge deck, a tall stone chimney and magnificent windows make this rustic home a fun, peaceful retreat.
- On the left side of the home, the main entry opens into a welcoming vestibule, which includes a huge storage space for skis, skates and other outdoor gear.
- To the right, a dramatic 23-ft. cathedral ceiling soars above the combined living and dining rooms. A cozy fireplace with a neat built-in storage cabinet for logs warms the room on winter nights. A two-story wall of windows allows extraordinary views.

- The dining room shares a handy eating counter with the efficient kitchen. The adjacent laundry room boasts a pantry, a coat closet and outdoor access.
- At the back of the home, the restful master suite boasts two closets and a great bath with a whirlpool tub to soothe sore muscles after an active day.
- Nearby, a spacious secondary bedroom is located close to a hall bath.
- A skylighted stairway leads up to a great balcony that looks out over the living and dining rooms.
- A secluded third bedroom, which could also serve as a studio, and a full bath complete the upper floor.

Plan HFL-1750-IR

Bedrooms: 2+	Baths: 3
Living Area:	
Upper floor	368 sq. ft.
Main floor	1,292 sq. ft.
Total Living Area:	**1,660 sq. ft.**
Partial basement	694 sq. ft.
Exterior Wall Framing:	2x6

Foundation Options:
Partial basement
Slab
(All plans can be built with your choice of foundation and framing. A generic conversion diagram is available. See order form.)

BLUEPRINT PRICE CODE:	B

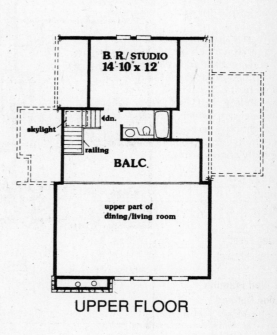

MAIN FLOOR

UPPER FLOOR

TO ORDER THIS BLUEPRINT,
CALL TOLL-FREE 1-800-547-5570

Plan HFL-1750-IR

PRICES AND DETAILS
ON PAGES 12-15

103

Affordable Comfort

- This cozy home makes comfortable living available at an affordable price.
- Nestled into a cozy covered porch, the bright, sidelighted front door opens into a welcoming tiled foyer.
- To the left of the foyer, a striking 11-ft. cathedral ceiling soars over the inviting living room, where your family will enjoy countless fun-filled nights. The living room features a warm fireplace.
- Nearby, two bright skylights cheer up the combined kitchen and dining area. The spacious eating area boasts sliding glass doors that open to an expansive backyard deck.
- In the master suite, a great 9-ft. tray ceiling lends a touch of style, while the handy private bath adds convenience.
- A second bedroom across the hall is serviced by a full hall bath.
- A bay window adds a splash of sunlight to the quiet den, which may also serve as an additional bedroom.
- The centrally located laundry facilities make daily chores a snap.

Plan GL-1226

Bedrooms: 2+	Baths: 2
Living Area:	
Main floor	1,226 sq. ft.
Total Living Area:	**1,226 sq. ft.**
Standard basement	1,204 sq. ft.
Garage	450 sq. ft.
Exterior Wall Framing:	2x4

Foundation Options:

Standard basement

(All plans can be built with your choice of foundation and framing. A generic conversion diagram is available. See order form.)

BLUEPRINT PRICE CODE: A

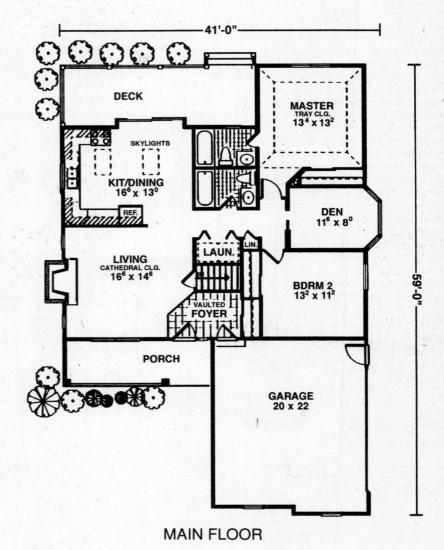

MAIN FLOOR

Plan GL-1226

PRICES AND DETAILS ON PAGES 12-15

Welcoming Facade

- The warm cedar and brick facade of this charming one-story will be a welcome sight at the end of the day.
- An inviting, sidelighted foyer opens directly to the living room, which is warmed by a central fireplace. A stunning 11-ft. cathedral ceiling rises over the living room and the foyer.
- Around an open corner, the kitchen boasts a cheery bayed eating nook with sliding glass doors to a wide, covered porch overlooking the backyard.
- The master bedroom is graced by an elegant 9-ft. tray ceiling and private porch access.
- Down the hall, a large secondary bedroom is serviced by a hall bath that is just steps away.
- A cozy den between the two bedrooms is the perfect prescription for stressful days. A delightful bayed window offers comforting views of the side yard.

Plan GL-1239

Bedrooms: 2+	**Baths: 2**

Living Area:

Main floor	1,239 sq. ft.
Total Living Area:	**1,239 sq. ft.**
Standard basement	1,203 sq. ft.
Garage	440 sq. ft.
Exterior Wall Framing:	2x4

Foundation Options:

Standard basement

(All plans can be built with your choice of foundation and framing. A generic conversion diagram is available. See order form.)

BLUEPRINT PRICE CODE: A

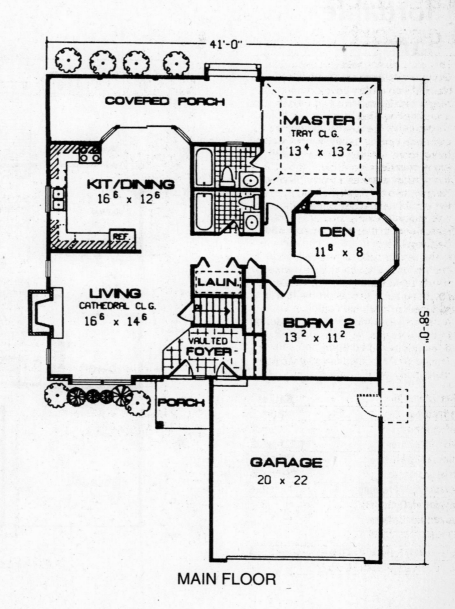

MAIN FLOOR

Affordable Charm

- An inviting columned porch introduces this affordable home.
- Inside, soaring ceilings and attention to detail highlight the efficient floor plan.
- The foyer leads to an eat-in kitchen, which includes a handy built-in pantry. A great 10-ft. ceiling enhances this sunny space.
- A convenient serving counter connects the kitchen to the open dining room. A beautiful bay window is topped by a half-round transom.
- The adjacent living room features an energy-efficient fireplace and French-door access to an inviting rear deck.
- A dramatic 14-ft. vaulted ceiling soars above the living and dining rooms.
- The spacious master bedroom boasts a striking 11-ft. vaulted ceiling, a large walk-in closet and private access to the hall bath.
- Two additional bedrooms and a linen closet round out the floor plan.

Plan B-93015

Bedrooms: 3	Baths: 1
Living Area:	
Main floor	1,227 sq. ft.
Total Living Area:	**1,227 sq. ft.**
Standard basement	1,217 sq. ft.
Garage	385 sq. ft.
Exterior Wall Framing:	2x6

Foundation Options:

Standard basement

(All plans can be built with your choice of foundation and framing. A generic conversion diagram is available. See order form.)

BLUEPRINT PRICE CODE:	**A**

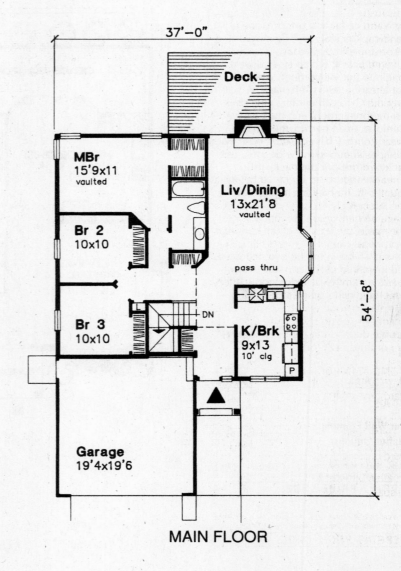

MAIN FLOOR

Plan B-93015

PRICES AND DETAILS ON PAGES 12-15

Rustic and Accessible

- This rustic cedar home features great style and comfort, in addition to a handicap-accessible design.
- A convenient ramp leads up to the covered porch, which opens into a spacious and welcoming entry.
- Just ahead, a 13-ft., 8-in. ceiling soars over the Great Room, the adjacent dining room and the efficient kitchen.
- A unique angled wall between the Great Room and the sunny dining room provides French-door access to a fun backyard deck or patio.
- A neat island in the kitchen includes a counter that serves the dining room. The kitchen also boasts ample counter space and a window above the sink.
- The master suite features French doors to a private deck and two designs for the bath—one includes a dressing area and a walk-in closet, while the other boasts a tub with a bench, a dual-sink vanity and extra space to maneuver.
- Another bedroom nearby is serviced by a centrally located hall bath.
- Double doors off the entry open to a den or third bedroom.

Plan LMB-3716-CD

Bedrooms: 2+	Baths: 2
Living Area:	
Main floor	1,345 sq. ft.
Total Living Area:	**1,345 sq. ft.**
Carport and storage	480 sq. ft.
Exterior Wall Framing:	2x4

Foundation Options:

Crawlspace

Slab

(All plans can be built with your choice of foundation and framing. A generic conversion diagram is available. See order form.)

BLUEPRINT PRICE CODE: A

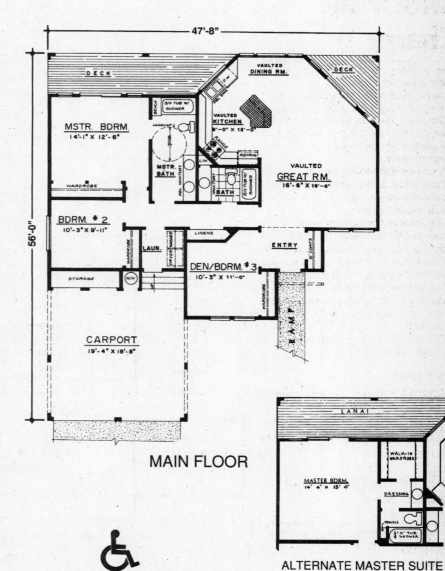

MAIN FLOOR

ALTERNATE MASTER SUITE

Classic Country

- This country home features a classic exterior and a luxurious interior design in an economical floor plan.
- A covered front porch leads through a sidelighted entry directly to the living room. A coat closet is close by.
- Stylish windows brighten the spacious living room, where a handsome recessed fireplace crackles. A marvelous 12-ft., 3-in. vaulted ceiling soars overhead and extends to the dining room and kitchen.

- Stately columns set off the entry to the dining room, which offers French-door access to a backyard terrace that is perfect for summertime entertainment.
- The dining room and the efficient kitchen share a stylish serving bar.
- The secluded master suite is graced by a 12-ft. cathedral ceiling. A French door opens to a private terrace.
- The master bath flaunts a refreshing whirlpool tub and a separate shower.
- Lovely windows bring natural light into two more bedrooms. A hall bath easily services both rooms.

Plan AHP-9507	
Bedrooms: 3	**Baths:** 2
Living Area:	
Main floor	1,232 sq. ft.
Total Living Area:	**1,232 sq. ft.**
Standard basement	1,183 sq. ft.
Garage and storage	324 sq. ft.
Exterior Wall Framing:	2x4 or 2x6

Foundation Options:
Standard basement
Crawlspace
Slab
(All plans can be built with your choice of foundation and framing. A generic conversion diagram is available. See order form.)

BLUEPRINT PRICE CODE:	A

60'-4"

35'-2"

TERRACE

TERRACE

shr.

whirlpool tub

bar   dw

d

MASTER SUITE
15 x 12'
high ceiling

w.i.c.

cl.   shr

DINING
19' x 11'
high ceiling

KITCH

MUD RM

w

STORAGE

ref. ptr.

dn.

GARAGE
11'-8" x 23'-8"

HALL

lin

high ceiling

BED RM
10' x 10'

cl.

BED RM
12'-4" x 10'

cl.

LIVING RM
19' x 13'-4"
fireplace

cl.

cl.

PORCH

railing

MAIN FLOOR

Warm Welcome

A vaulted, covered porch adds warmth to the brick and cedar shingle facade of this cozy home.

An inviting foyer opens into the living room, which boasts a 17-ft. vaulted ceiling and shares a see-through fireplace with the formal dining room. Sliding glass doors open to a spacious backyard deck.

The gourmet kitchen wraps around a sunny breakfast nook. An angled serving counter facilitates entertaining. Just a few steps away, the master bedroom sports a walk-in closet and private bath access.

Upstairs, a charming balcony leads to two secondary bedrooms, which are enhanced by roomy walk-in closets and share a full bath.

An open loft area with built-ins may be used as an entertainment room or a third bedroom, if desired.

Plan B-93033

Bedrooms: 3+	Baths: 2
Living Area:	
Upper floor	645 sq. ft.
Main floor	1,042 sq. ft.
Total Living Area:	**1,687 sq. ft.**
Standard basement	1,042 sq. ft.
Garage	385 sq. ft.
Exterior Wall Framing:	2x4

Foundation Options:

Standard basement

(All plans can be built with your choice of foundation and framing. A generic conversion diagram is available. See order form.)

BLUEPRINT PRICE CODE:	B

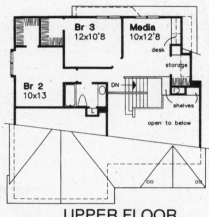

UPPER FLOOR

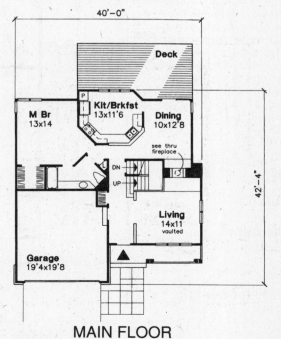

MAIN FLOOR

Attainable and Comfortable

- This home's modest size makes comfortable living attainable.
- The protective covered porch opens into the inviting tiled foyer. To the right, the enormous living room welcomes visitors for formal affairs.
- Located just across the foyer, the home's casual living areas include the efficient U-shaped kitchen, the cheery eating nook and a great family room.
- A convenient serving bar joins the kitchen to the family room, where a striking corner fireplace with a stone hearth will add a warm glow on winter nights. Bright sliding glass doors open to a good-sized backyard patio.
- At the rear of the home, the master suite features private access to the patio, plus a walk-in closet and a private bath.
- Nearby, two secondary bedrooms with good-sized closets share a full hall bath.
- For added convenience, the home's laundry facilities are located in close proximity to all three bedrooms.

Plan LMB-3703-EA

Bedrooms: 3	Baths: 2
Living Area:	
Main floor	1,316 sq. ft.
Total Living Area:	**1,316 sq. ft.**
Garage	419 sq. ft.
Exterior Wall Framing:	2x4

Foundation Options:

Crawlspace
(All plans can be built with your choice of foundation and framing. A generic conversion diagram is available. See order form.)

BLUEPRINT PRICE CODE: **A**

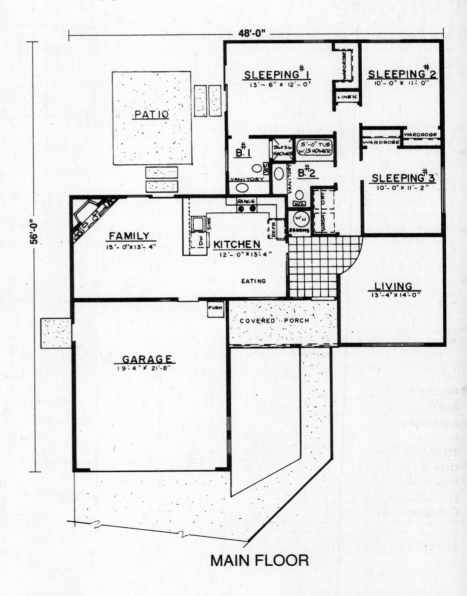

MAIN FLOOR

Plan LMB-3703-EA

PRICES AND DETAILS ON PAGES 12-15

Picture a Bright Facade

- A great picture window brightens the facade of this cozy, affordable home.
- A serene covered porch opens into a spacious tiled foyer. To the right of the foyer, the inviting living room is a great space to entertain guests.
- Across the hall, the efficient U-shaped kitchen, the cheery eating nook and a great family room will serve as the focal point of family activities.
- A neat serving bar joins the kitchen to the family room, where an attractive corner fireplace adds warmth on winter nights. Bright sliding glass doors along one wall open to a fun backyard patio.
- At the rear of the home, the master suite features private access to the patio, plus a surprisingly large walk-in closet and a convenient private bath.
- Across the hall, two more bedrooms share a full hall bath. Both bedrooms include spacious closets.
- For added convenience, the home's laundry facilities are located in close proximity to all three bedrooms.

Plan LMB-3703-EB

Bedrooms: 3	Baths: 2
Living Area:	
Main floor	1,316 sq. ft.
Total Living Area:	**1,316 sq. ft.**
Garage	419 sq. ft.
Exterior Wall Framing:	2x4

Foundation Options:

Crawlspace
(All plans can be built with your choice of foundation and framing. A generic conversion diagram is available. See order form.)

BLUEPRINT PRICE CODE: A

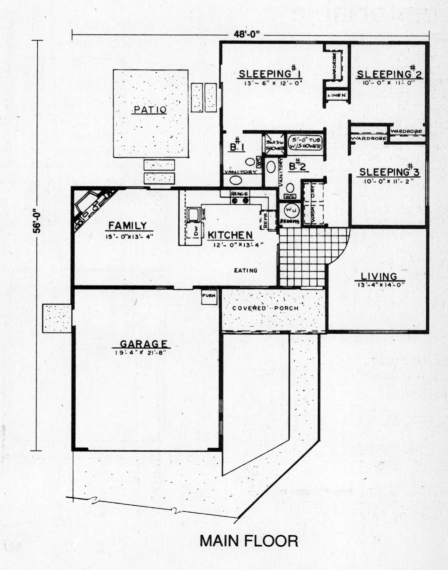

MAIN FLOOR

Peaceful Refuge

- This modest home will serve perfectly as a peaceful refuge from today's families' hectic lifestyles.
- An inviting recessed porch leads into the tiled foyer. To the right of the foyer, the enormous living room welcomes you home after a busy day.
- To the left of the foyer, the efficient U-shaped kitchen, the cheery eating nook and a great family room make up the home's casual living areas.
- A serving bar between the kitchen and the family room will make entertaining a cinch. In the family room, an attractive corner fireplace will warm the space on winter nights, and sliding glass doors open to a backyard patio. The patio is ideal for a summer barbecue.
- At the rear of the home, the master bedroom features private access to the patio, plus a large walk-in closet and a convenient private bath.
- Nearby, two secondary bedrooms with good-sized closets share a full hall bath.
- The laundry facilities are located near the bedrooms to make chores a snap.

Plan LMB-3703-EC

Bedrooms: 3	Baths: 2
Living Area:	
Main floor	1,316 sq. ft.
Total Living Area:	**1,316 sq. ft.**
Garage	419 sq. ft.
Exterior Wall Framing:	2x4

Foundation Options:

Crawlspace
(All plans can be built with your choice of foundation and framing. A generic conversion diagram is available. See order form.)

BLUEPRINT PRICE CODE: A

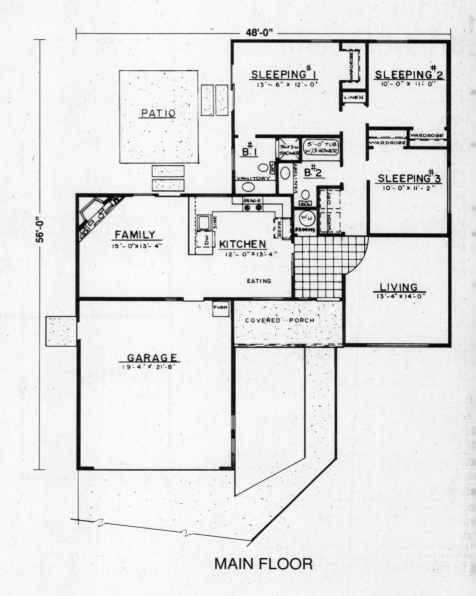

MAIN FLOOR

Plan LMB-3703-EC

PRICES AND DETAILS ON PAGES 12-15

Farmhouse for the Family

This farmhouse design's covered porch, backyard deck and spacious family room promote warm family closeness. The front entry opens directly into the family room, which is warmed by a delightful corner fireplace and features a 10-ft. ceiling.

The roomy island kitchen flaunts a 12-ft. vaulted ceiling and a lovely arched window arrangement. A cozy, informal dining area offers a nice view of the backyard deck.

A covered walkway provides easy access to the two-car garage.

Down the skylighted hall from the family room, two secondary bedrooms boast ample walk-in closets and share a full bath.

The quietly isolated master bedroom is enhanced by a large walk-in closet and a private bath with a dual-sink vanity. An alternate master bath plan adds more space and the convenience of a separate shower.

Unless otherwise noted, all rooms have 9-ft. ceilings.

Plan GMA-1475

Bedrooms: 3	**Baths:** 2

Living Area:

Main floor	1,475 sq. ft.
Total Living Area:	**1,475 sq. ft.**
Garage	455 sq. ft.
Exterior Wall Framing:	2x4

Foundation Options:

Crawlspace

Slab

(All plans can be built with your choice of foundation and framing. A generic conversion diagram is available. See order form.)

BLUEPRINT PRICE CODE: A

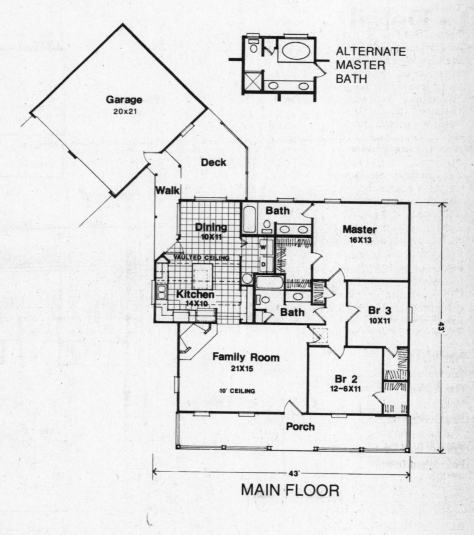

ALTERNATE MASTER BATH

Garage 20x21

Deck

Walk

Dining 10X11

VAULTED CEILING

Bath

Master 16X13

Kitchen 14X10

Bath

Br 3 10X11

Family Room 21X15

10' CEILING

Br 2 12-6X11

Porch

43'

43'

MAIN FLOOR

Attention to Detail

- Attention to detail allows this modest-sized, affordable home to maintain an open, roomy feel.
- A peaceful covered porch opens into the inviting tiled foyer. To the left, the huge living room features a soaring 10-ft., 3-in. ceiling. A cozy fireplace warms the room on winter nights.
- The living room embraces the versatile dining room, which serves well for both formal and casual meals. A beautiful French door opens to a covered backyard porch.
- The family cook will love the well-planned kitchen. The adjacent utility room provides access to a two-car garage with a storage area.
- Beyond the living room, the master suite features a walk-in closet and a private bath with a dual-sink vanity.
- Two secluded secondary bedrooms with good-sized closets share a centrally located hall bath.

Plan VL-1372

Bedrooms: 3	**Baths:** 2
Living Area:	
Main floor	1,372 sq. ft.
Total Living Area:	**1,372 sq. ft.**
Garage and storage	465 sq. ft.
Exterior Wall Framing:	2x4

Foundation Options:
Crawlspace
Slab
(All plans can be built with your choice of foundation and framing. A generic conversion diagram is available. See order form.)

BLUEPRINT PRICE CODE: A

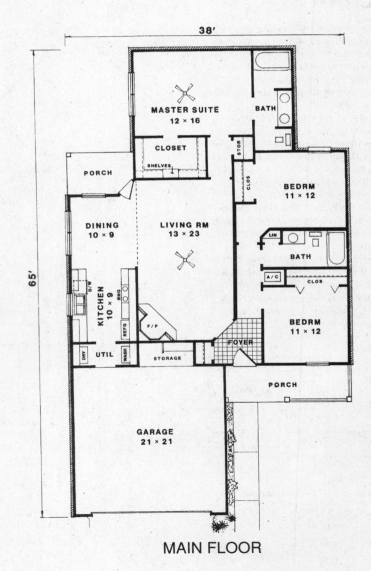

MAIN FLOOR

Epitome of Efficiency

- An efficient design makes use of every square foot in this modest ranch home.
- Charming shutters and a gable graced by a louvered vent frame the front entry.
- A short hall leads from the sidelighted foyer to the dining area, which is set off from the living room by a classy divider.
- The adjoining kitchen has efficiency in mind, with laundry facilities placed neatly at the far end.
- A 15-ft. vaulted ceiling crowns the living room, where bright windows provide natural light. A handsome corner fireplace adds warmth; during the summer months, a covered backyard porch is accessed through French doors.
- Secluded from the rest of the home, the master suite pampers you with its porch access and private bath. The walk-in closet is enhanced by built-in shelves that define two wardrobe areas. Two good-sized secondary bedrooms share a hall bath with a convenient linen closet.

Plan VL-1404

Bedrooms: 3	Baths: 2

Living Area:

Main floor	1,404 sq. ft.
Total Living Area:	**1,404 sq. ft.**
Garage	462 sq. ft.
Exterior Wall Framing:	2x4

Foundation Options:

Crawlspace
Slab

All plans can be built with your choice of foundation and framing. A generic conversion diagram is available. See order form.)

BLUEPRINT PRICE CODE: **A**

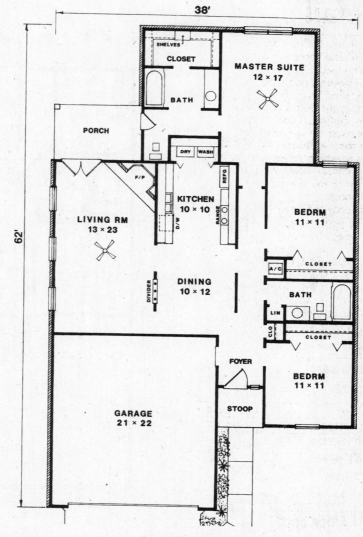

MAIN FLOOR

Free-Flowing Floor Plan

- An open floor plan highlights the interior of this airy one-story home, while a striking bay window enhances the facade.
- A low partition separates the 11-ft., 10-in.-high vaulted entry from the living and dining rooms. The bay window lets in natural light and a handsome fireplace crackles cheerfully. Above the dining room, an 11-ft., 10-in. vaulted ceiling soars.
- The open kitchen flaunts a breakfast bar, corner windows and a 10-ft., 5-in. vaulted ceiling.
- Adjoining the kitchen, the family room is a wonderful space for evening get-togethers. A French door leads to a backyard porch. Above, an impressive 11-ft., 10-in. vaulted ceiling rises.
- The secluded master suite sports private French-door porch access. The skylighted master bath offers two sinks and a good-sized walk-in closet.
- Two bedrooms around the corner share a skylighted bath. One bedroom enjoys a quiet study alcove.

Plan LMB-4119-CDA

Bedrooms: 3	Baths: 2
Living Area:	
Main floor	1,477 sq. ft.
Total Living Area:	**1,477 sq. ft.**
Garage	400 sq. ft.
Exterior Wall Framing:	2x4

Foundation Options:

Crawlspace

(All plans can be built with your choice of foundation and framing. A generic conversion diagram is available. See order form.)

BLUEPRINT PRICE CODE:	**A**

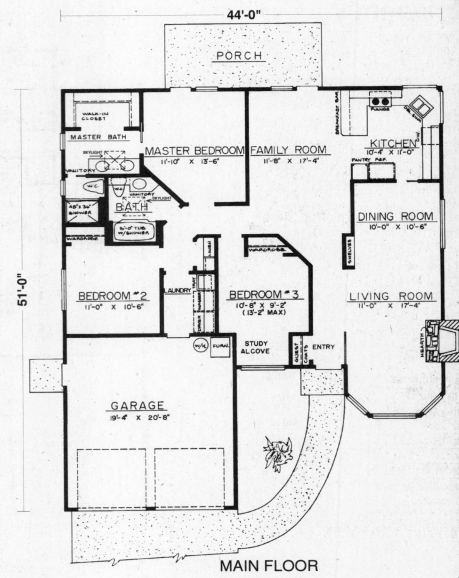

MAIN FLOOR

TO ORDER THIS BLUEPRINT, CALL TOLL-FREE 1-800-547-5570

Plan LMB-4119-CDA

PRICES AND DETAILS ON PAGES 12-15

Clever Touches

This attractive one-story was designed for comfortable living, with many clever interior touches.

Just beyond the 11-ft., 10-in. vaulted entry, the living room is warmed by a rustic fireplace. A gorgeous round-top window arrangement is set into a boxed-out area with a 10-ft. sloped ceiling.

The dining room offers an 11-ft., 10-in. vaulted ceiling and built-in shelves. Easily accessed from the dining room, the walk-through kitchen is topped by a 10-ft., 5-in. vaulted ceiling and boasts a cute breakfast bar and corner windows. The adjoining family room suits large gatherings well and offers French-door access to a backyard porch. An 11-ft., 10-in. vaulted ceiling rises overhead.

In a secluded corner, the master suite boasts private porch access through a French door. The skylighted master bath flaunts a dual-sink vanity and a spacious walk-in closet.

Two more bedrooms across the hall share a skylighted bath. One bedroom sports a bright study alcove for reading or homework.

Plan LMB-4119-CDB

Bedrooms: 3	**Baths:** 2

Living Area:

Main floor	1,477 sq. ft.
Total Living Area:	**1,477 sq. ft.**
Garage	400 sq. ft.
Exterior Wall Framing:	2x4

Foundation Options:

Crawlspace
(All plans can be built with your choice of foundation and framing. A generic conversion diagram is available. See order form.)

BLUEPRINT PRICE CODE: A

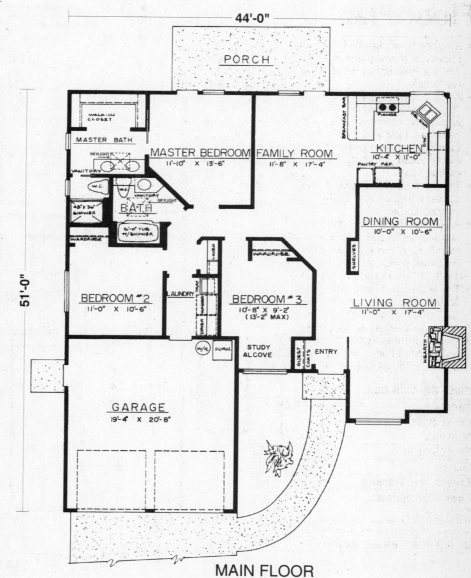

MAIN FLOOR

TO ORDER THIS BLUEPRINT,
CALL TOLL-FREE 1-800-547-5570

Plan LMB-4119-CDB

PRICES AND DETAILS
ON PAGES 12-15

117

Masterful Suite

- The entire second floor of this home belongs to the luxurious master suite!
- Stairs to the left of the home lead to a deck, which introduces the sidelighted, 12-ft., 11-in.-high vaulted entry.
- Natural light drenches the living room, with its rustic fireplace and 17-ft., 5-in. vaulted ceiling. A bay window beautifies the adjoining dining room, which offers French-door access to a second deck.
- The gourmet kitchen boasts tremendous space. Its island hosts an informal breakfast bar and a vegetable sink.
- Down the skylighted hallway, two bedrooms share a skylighted bath. One bedroom flaunts private deck access, while the other has a cute window seat.
- Upstairs, the master bedroom enjoys a cozy fireplace under a 12½-ft. vaulted ceiling. To the right of the fireplace, a French door opens to a private deck. A bayed sitting room offers serenity beneath a 10-ft., 4-in. vaulted ceiling.
- The master bath boasts a skylighted garden tub and a separate shower.
- A wood-carving room with a garden window adjoins the master suite.

Plan LMB-9600

Bedrooms: 3	Baths: 2½
Living Area:	
Upper floor	763 sq. ft.
Main floor	1,338 sq. ft.
Daylight basement	68 sq. ft.
Total Living Area:	**2,169 sq. ft.**
Tuck-under garage and storage	780 sq. ft.
Exterior Wall Framing:	2x6

Foundation Options:

Daylight basement
(All plans can be built with your choice of foundation and framing. A generic conversion diagram is available. See order form.)

BLUEPRINT PRICE CODE: C

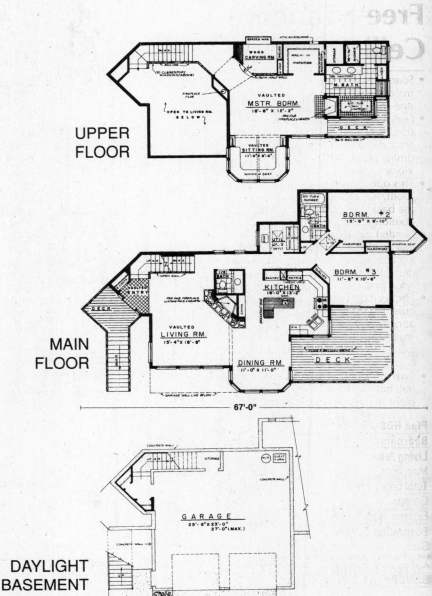

UPPER FLOOR

MAIN FLOOR

67'-0"

DAYLIGHT BASEMENT

*TO ORDER THIS BLUEPRINT,
CALL TOLL-FREE 1-800-547-5570*

Plan LMB-9600

*PRICES AND DETAILS
ON PAGES 12-15*

Free-Soaring Ceilings

- Soaring vaulted ceilings lend an air of freedom to every room in this appealing one-story home.
- French doors open from the covered front porch to the foyer, which flows smoothly into the formal living and dining areas. A high plant shelf adds vibrant color.
- This open space gives way to the family room, where sliding glass doors access the backyard. A warm fireplace exudes comfort and cheer.
- Nestled between the family and living rooms, the wonderful walk-through kitchen features a serving bar and a delightful plant shelf. A spacious bayed nook promises cheery breakfasts.
- The secluded master bedroom sports a quiet bayed sitting area and an attractive plant shelf. The sumptuous master bath is enhanced by a garden tub, a separate shower and a 12-ft., 8-in. ceiling.
- Two more good-sized bedrooms share a hall bath with an 11-ft. ceiling. Exotic plant shelves adorn each room.

Plan HDS-99-223

Bedrooms: 3	**Baths:** 2

Living Area:	
Main floor	1,571 sq. ft.
Total Living Area:	**1,571 sq. ft.**
Garage	381 sq. ft.
Exterior Wall Framing:	2x4

Foundation Options:
Slab
(All plans can be built with your choice of foundation and framing. A generic conversion diagram is available. See order form.)

BLUEPRINT PRICE CODE: B

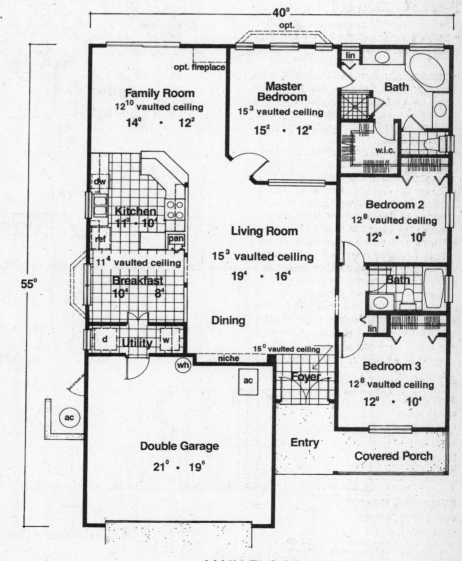

MAIN FLOOR

TO ORDER THIS BLUEPRINT,
CALL TOLL-FREE 1-800-547-5570

Plan HDS-99-223

PRICES AND DETAILS
ON PAGES 12-15

119

Affordable Family Home

- A cozy front porch accented by columns and a charming railing introduces this affordable family home.
- The inviting foyer opens to the sun-drenched living room, which is suited for both family nights at home and for more elegant entertaining.
- The living room leads to the large dining room nearby. Sliding glass doors bathe the dining room in sunlight and lead to the backyard.

- A handy snack bar connects the formal dining room to the open kitchen. Ample counter space and a large pantry allow plenty of room to work.
- A nearby mudroom serves as a great storage area for wet boots and gloves. The mudroom leads to the spacious two-car garage and the efficient laundry room.
- On the other side of the home, shuttered windows brighten the spacious master bedroom, which offers a private bath and a wall-length closet.
- Across the hall, two good-sized bedrooms share a large bath that includes a handy linen closet.

Plan GL-1465	
Bedrooms: 3	**Baths:** 2
Living Area:	
Main floor	1,465 sq. ft.
Total Living Area:	**1,465 sq. ft.**
Standard basement	1,455 sq. ft.
Garage	433 sq. ft.
Exterior Wall Framing:	2x6
Foundation Options:	
Standard basement	

(All plans can be built with your choice of foundation and framing. A generic conversion diagram is available. See order form.)

BLUEPRINT PRICE CODE:	A

MAIN FLOOR

63'-0"

34'-0"

BDRM 3 13⁴ x 9⁶

BDRM 2 11 x 11⁴

DINING 14⁴ x 11⁴

KITCHEN 12⁶ x 11⁴

LAUN

MUD ENTRY

REF. pan.

B

M. BDRM 13⁴ x 11¹⁰

B.

LIVING 13² x 15⁴

GARAGE 20 x 21⁸

PORCH

Plan GL-1465

PRICES AND DETAILS ON PAGES 12-15

Breezy Beauty

- A nostalgic covered front porch, a backyard deck and a sprawling screened porch combine to make this beautiful one-story home a breezy delight.
- The front entry opens into the Great Room, which is crowned by a soaring 12-ft.-high cathedral ceiling. A handsome fireplace is flanked by built-in bookshelves and cabinets.
- The large, bayed dining room offers a 9-ft. tray ceiling and deck access through French doors.

- The adjoining kitchen boasts plenty of counter space and a handy built-in recipe desk.
- From the kitchen, a side door leads to the screened porch. A wood floor and deck access highlight this cheery room.
- A quiet hall leads past a convenient utility room to the sleeping quarters.
- The secluded master bedroom is enhanced by a spacious walk-in closet. The private master bath includes a lovely garden tub, a separate shower and dual vanities.
- Two more bedrooms with walk-in closets share a hall bath.

Plan C-8905

Bedrooms: 3	**Baths:** 2

Living Area:	
Main floor	1,811 sq. ft.
Total Living Area:	**1,811 sq. ft.**
Screened porch	240 sq. ft.
Daylight basement	1,811 sq. ft.
Garage	484 sq. ft.
Exterior Wall Framing:	2x4

Foundation Options:
Daylight basement
Crawlspace
(All plans can be built with your choice of foundation and framing. A generic conversion diagram is available. See order form.)

BLUEPRINT PRICE CODE:	B

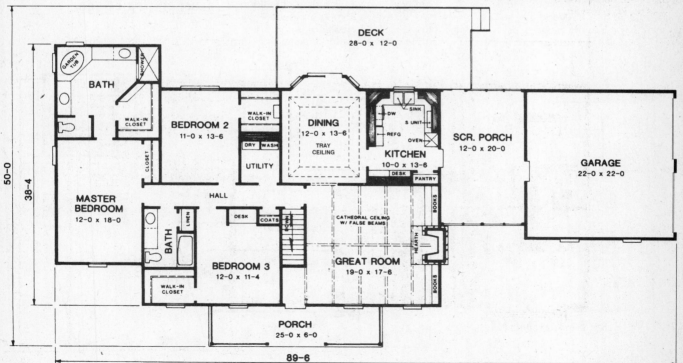

MAIN FLOOR

TO ORDER THIS BLUEPRINT,
CALL TOLL-FREE 1-800-547-5570

Plan C-8905

PRICES AND DETAILS
ON PAGES 12-15

121

Luxurious Recreation

- This fun home blends recreational living with unparalleled luxuries.
- A neat bridge leads from the three-car garage to a welcoming deck, where a bright glass door opens into the foyer.
- The sunken living room straight ahead features a 22½-ft. vaulted ceiling and a cozy fireplace with a raised hearth.
- In the country kitchen, a second fireplace adds a warm glow. The kitchen also boasts an island worktop, a built-in desk and sliding doors to a wraparound deck. Beyond a huge pantry and a laundry room, a lush greenhouse leads to the garage.

- Across the home, the master bedroom features a private deck that is ideal for romantic evenings. The master bath includes two vanities and a raised Jacuzzi tub.
- Nearby, a second bedroom features convenient access to a hall bath.
- A centrally located staircase leads to the second floor, where a loft allows a view of the foyer below. The loft features a ceiling that slopes from 4½ ft. to an impressive 12 ft., 8 inches.
- In the daylight basement, two more bedrooms flank a fun activity room that includes a nice fireplace and sliding glass doors to the backyard. A split bath with two vanities serves the floor.
- Two huge storage rooms and three closets on the lower floor provide ample space for outdoor gear.

Plan LMB-9156

Bedrooms: 4+	**Baths:** 3

Living Area:	
Upper floor	339 sq. ft.
Main floor	2,502 sq. ft.
Greenhouse	252 sq. ft.
Daylight basement (finished)	1,731 sq. ft.
Total Living Area:	**4,824 sq. ft.**
Basement storage areas	647 sq. ft.
Garage and shop	847 sq. ft.

Exterior Wall Framing: 2x4

Foundation Options:

Daylight basement
(All plans can be built with your choice of foundation and framing. A generic conversion diagram is available. See order form.)

BLUEPRINT PRICE CODE: G

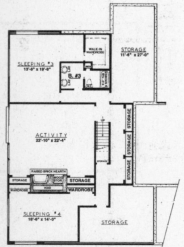

DAYLIGHT BASEMENT

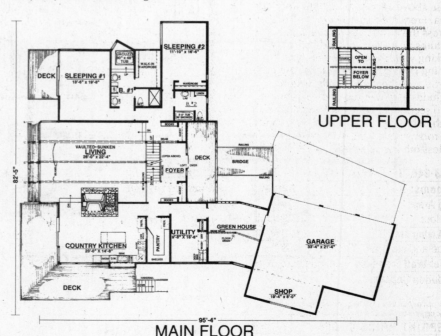

UPPER FLOOR

MAIN FLOOR

TO ORDER THIS BLUEPRINT, CALL TOLL-FREE 1-800-547-5570

Plan LMB-9156

PRICES AND DETAILS ON PAGES 12-15

Compact Luxury

Thoughtful planning has packed this compact home with luxurious details. A stucco exterior, impressive arched windows and a neat tiled roof give the home plenty of curb appeal. Dramatic French doors open directly into the combined living and dining rooms, which are highlighted by a 13-ft. ceiling. The living room features a built-in media center, a see-through fireplace and access to a nice lanai. The fireplace opens through to the breakfast nook and the kitchen, which includes a handy island. Greenhouse glass above allows sunlight to flood the area. French doors open to the lanai. Across the home, the master suite features an 11½-ft. vaulted ceiling, a striking window arrangement and sliding glass doors to the lanai. An arch introduces the master bath, which includes a garden tub and two vanities. Two secondary bedrooms share a hall bath, which includes a dual-sink vanity. All rooms have 9-ft., 4-in. ceilings unless otherwise noted.

Plan B-94013

Bedrooms: 3	**Baths:** 2

Living Area:

Main floor	1,679 sq. ft.
Total Living Area:	**1,679 sq. ft.**
Garage and storage	468 sq. ft.

Exterior Wall Framing: 8-in. concrete block

Foundation Options:

Slab

(All plans can be built with your choice of foundation and framing. A generic conversion diagram is available. See order form.)

BLUEPRINT PRICE CODE:	**B**

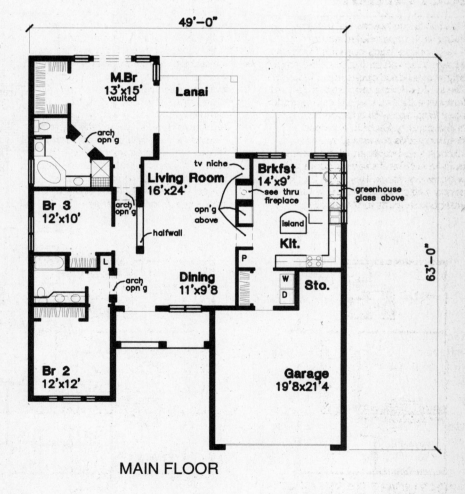

MAIN FLOOR

TO ORDER THIS BLUEPRINT,
CALL TOLL-FREE 1-800-547-5570

Plan B-94013

PRICES AND DETAILS
ON PAGES 12-15

123

REAR VIEW

Rustic Comfort

- A wraparound deck, a cozy woodstove and a sumptuous master suite are just a few of the many stylish features of this comfortable two-story.
- To the left of the entry, a unique kitchen boasts a large island with a breakfast bar and a vegetable sink.
- Adjoining the kitchen, the dining room is brightly lighted by a nice bay window and offers French-door deck access.
- The dining room shares a 20-ft. vaulted ceiling with the living room, which flaunts a charming boxed-out window. A cheery woodstove warms both rooms.
- The luxurious master bedroom sports a boxed-out window and a large walk-in closet. The skylighted master bath boasts a relaxing Jacuzzi tub and a 12-ft., 8-in. vaulted ceiling.
- Upstairs, a quiet bedroom with an 11½-ft. ceiling is serviced by a hall bath. A loft room with an 11½-ft. ceiling may be used as an office.
- The daylight basement offers two large rooms that are perfect for leisurely pastimes. A wine cellar and a large utility room with a half-bath are located near the tuck-under garage.

Plan LMB-9470

Bedrooms: 2+	Baths: 3½
Living Area:	
Upper floor	678 sq. ft.
Main floor	1,330 sq. ft.
Daylight basement	645 sq. ft.
Total Living Area:	**2,653 sq. ft.**
Tuck-under garage	527 sq. ft.
Exterior Wall Framing:	2x6
Foundation Options:	

Daylight basement
(All plans can be built with your choice of foundation and framing. A generic conversion diagram is available. See order form.)

BLUEPRINT PRICE CODE:	D

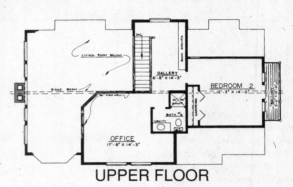

UPPER FLOOR

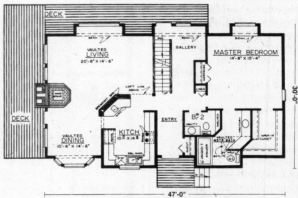

MAIN FLOOR

DAYLIGHT BASEMENT

TO ORDER THIS BLUEPRINT,
CALL TOLL-FREE 1-800-547-5570

Plan LMB-9470

PRICES AND DETAILS
ON PAGES 12-15

Zesty Villa

- Its tile roof and stucco facade, together with high ceiling fans and naturally lighted spaces, give this appealing home a zesty, Spanish villa feel.
- The sidelighted entry is adorned with two plant shelves.
- Straight ahead, four columns define the foyer, which boasts an 11-ft. ceiling.
- A nearby full bath services the front bedroom, which has an 8-ft. ceiling. All other rooms have 10-ft. ceilings.
- To the left of the foyer, the formal dining room is brightened by two skylights.
- To the right, French doors lead to an office or bedroom, which offers built-in bookshelves.
- The spacious family room boasts a fireplace flanked by built-in bookshelves and cabinets with a TV space. French doors with transoms lead to a covered backyard porch.
- A handy serving bar is shared by the open kitchen and the cheerfully bright morning room.
- On the other side of the home, the master suite is highlighted by a garden tub and a separate shower.

Plan DD-1779

Bedrooms: 2+	Baths: 2
Living Area:	
Main floor	1,779 sq. ft.
Total Living Area:	**1,779 sq. ft.**
Standard basement	1,529 sq. ft.
Garage and storage	425 sq. ft.
Exterior Wall Framing:	2x4

Foundation Options:

Standard basement
Crawlspace
Slab
(All plans can be built with your choice of foundation and framing. A generic conversion diagram is available. See order form.)

BLUEPRINT PRICE CODE: B

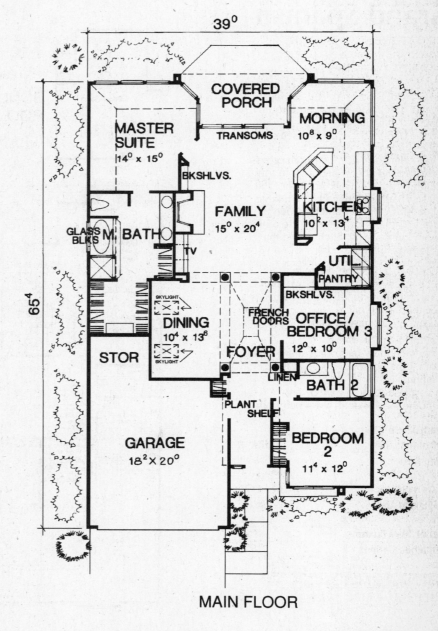

MAIN FLOOR

Grand Spanish

- Majestic arched windows adorn the stucco facade of this appealing one-story home, giving it a grand elegance.
- Double doors give way to a 12-ft.-high foyer, which is open to the formal dining and living rooms. Both rooms boast 12-ft. ceilings.
- To the right, a den may be used as a quiet study or an extra bedroom.
- The secluded master bedroom offers private patio access and a 10-ft. tray ceiling. Past two walk-in closets, the master bath is highlighted by a large glass-block shower and a garden tub.
- Just around the corner from the dining room, the gourmet kitchen and the adjoining breakfast nook share a 10-ft. ceiling. The nook offers French-door patio access.
- An angled serving bar makes entertaining in the family room easy and fun. A central fireplace warms the family room, while a 12½-ft. vaulted ceiling soars overhead.
- Two secondary bedrooms share a hall bath. One bedroom boasts a 10-ft. ceiling.
- A vast bonus room may be converted to a home theater or an extra bedroom.

Plan HDS-99-211

Bedrooms: 3+	Baths: 2
Living Area:	
Main floor	2,322 sq. ft.
Bonus room	370 sq. ft.
Total Living Area:	**2,692 sq. ft.**
Garage	518 sq. ft.
Exterior Wall Framing:	2x4
Foundation Options:	

Slab
(All plans can be built with your choice of foundation and framing.
A generic conversion diagram is available. See order form.)

BLUEPRINT PRICE CODE: D

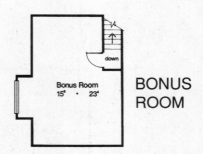

BONUS ROOM

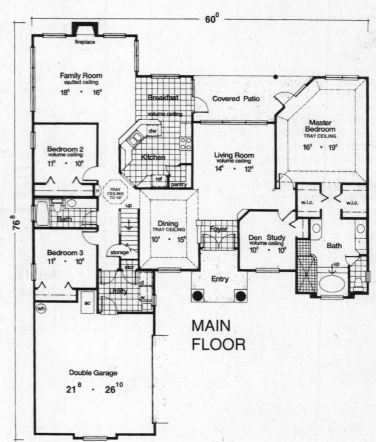

MAIN FLOOR

Plan HDS-99-211

*PRICES AND DETAILS
ON PAGES 12-15*

Marvelous Mediterranean

- A stucco exterior, keystone details and gorgeous gables enhance this marvelous home's Mediterranean style.
- Inside, the foyer extends to the living room and the dining room. A 12-ft. ceiling soars over the whole space.
- The living room leads to the casual living areas, which include the gourmet kitchen, the bayed breakfast nook and the fabulous family room.
- A neat snack bar serves the family room, which boasts a 12½-ft. vaulted ceiling, a warm fireplace and sliding glass doors to a covered patio. A patio wet bar makes summer affairs a snap.
- Beyond the kitchen, two secondary bedrooms share a split bath.
- Across the home, double doors open to the master suite, where a 12-ft. tray ceiling and French doors add style. A garden tub highlights the master bath.
- A quiet study could serve as an additional bedroom, and a bonus room offers more space.
- Unless otherwise noted, every main-floor room boasts a 10-ft. ceiling.

Plan HDS-99-213

Bedrooms: 3+	Baths: 3
Living Area:	
Main floor	2,551 sq. ft.
Bonus room	287 sq. ft.
Total Living Area:	**2,838 sq. ft.**
Garage	435 sq. ft.
Exterior Wall Framing:	2x4

Foundation Options:

Slab
(All plans can be built with your choice of foundation and framing. A generic conversion diagram is available. See order form.)

BLUEPRINT PRICE CODE: D

BONUS ROOM

MAIN FLOOR

Relaxing Retreat

- A peaceful covered porch and a tranquil country air make this home a relaxing retreat for the family.
- Inside, the inviting foyer leads to the large family room, which features ample space and a cozy fireplace with a nice brick hearth.
- Nearby, stately columns and a half-wall introduce the formal dining room, which includes access to a fun deck.
- The roomy kitchen extends to the huge, tiled breakfast nook. The nook boasts a bright corner window and access to a cozy side porch. A handy powder room and garage access are found nearby.
- Across the home, the master suite boasts a private bath with a dual-sink vanity and a separate tub and shower.
- Every room on the main floor is expanded by a 9-ft. ceiling.
- Upstairs, two bedrooms with sloped ceilings share a bath. An optional fourth bedroom is located nearby.

Plan GMA-1829

Bedrooms: 3+	Baths: 2½
Living Area:	
Upper floor	490 sq. ft.
Main floor	1,339 sq. ft.
Total Living Area:	**1,829 sq. ft.**
Optional 4th bedroom	145 sq. ft.
Standard basement	1,339 sq. ft.
Garage	491 sq. ft.
Exterior Wall Framing:	2x4
Foundation Options:	

Standard basement
(All plans can be built with your choice of foundation and framing. A generic conversion diagram is available. See order form.)

BLUEPRINT PRICE CODE:	B

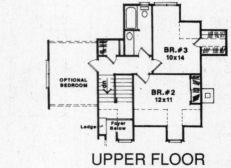

UPPER FLOOR

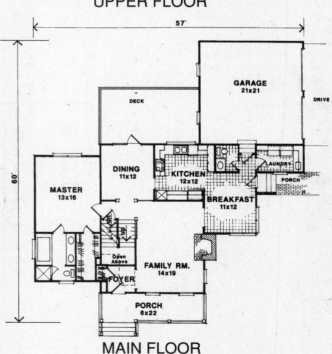

MAIN FLOOR

TO ORDER THIS BLUEPRINT, CALL TOLL-FREE 1-800-547-5570

Plan GMA-1829

PRICES AND DETAILS ON PAGES 12-15

REAR VIEW

All Decked Out!

- All decked out to take full advantage of the outdoors, this stylish home is perfect for a scenic site.
- Entered through a front vestibule, the bright and open floor plan provides an ideal setting for casual lifestyles.
- The sunken living room features a handsome fireplace, a skylighted 19-ft. ceiling and three sets of sliding glass doors that open to an expansive backyard deck.
- The efficient kitchen has a sunny sink and a pass-through with bi-fold doors to the adjoining dining room.
- The main-floor bedroom has a walk-in closet and sliding glass doors to the deck. A half-bath is nearby.
- Upstairs, a railed balcony overlooks the living room. The smaller of the two bedrooms has private access to the bathroom and another deck.

Plan CAR-81007

Bedrooms: 2+	**Baths:** 1½
Living Area:	
Upper floor	560 sq. ft.
Main floor	911 sq. ft.
Total Living Area:	**1,471 sq. ft.**
Standard basement	911 sq. ft.
Exterior Wall Framing:	2x6

Foundation Options:

Standard basement

(All plans can be built with your choice of foundation and framing. A generic conversion diagram is available. See order form.)

BLUEPRINT PRICE CODE: A

UPPER FLOOR

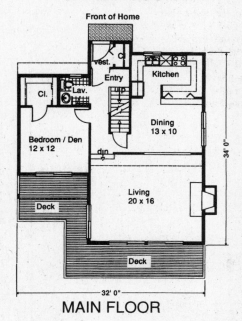

MAIN FLOOR

REAR VIEW

Stunning Estate for Scenic Sites

- A tiered roofline, expansive windows and a magnificent wraparound deck adorn this fantastic home, which is perfect for scenic building sites.
- The main floor is a masterpiece of open design, beginning with the sunny dining room that flows into the unique kitchen. The kitchen features an angled island cooktop/snack bar, a corner sink framed by windows and a nice pantry closet.
- The sunken living room is bordered by railings on two sides, keeping it visually open. A window-filled bay overlooks the deck, while a 12-ft. ceiling heightens the room's spaciousness. Other highlights include built-in bookshelves and a fireplace with a raised hearth and a built-in log bin.
- The luxurious master suite boasts a cozy window seat, a plush bath and a private sitting room with access to the deck.
- Downstairs, the recreation room offers another fireplace and double doors to a covered driveway or patio. One of the two bedrooms here offers a private bath and walk-in closet.
- Ceilings in most rooms are at least 9-ft. high for added spaciousness.

Plan NW-779	
Bedrooms: 3	**Baths:** 3½
Living Area:	
Main floor	1,450 sq. ft.
Daylight basement	1,242 sq. ft.
Total Living Area:	**2,692 sq. ft.**
Exterior Wall Framing:	2x6
Foundation Options:	

Daylight basement

(All plans can be built with your choice of foundation and framing. A generic conversion diagram is available. See order form.)

BLUEPRINT PRICE CODE:	D

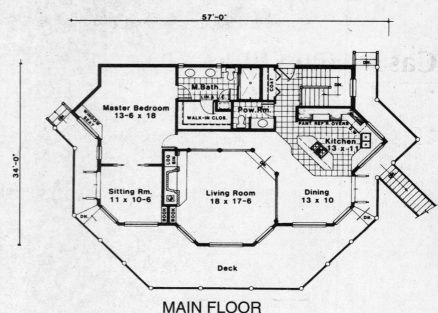

MAIN FLOOR

DAYLIGHT BASEMENT

Plan NW-779

PRICES AND DETAILS ON PAGES 12-15

Casual Flexibility

- This beautifully designed vacation or year-round home is spacious and flexible.
- The interior is brightened by an abundance of windows.
- The open, vaulted living room boasts a central fireplace that makes a great conversation place or a cozy spot for spending cold winter evenings.
- The kitchen opens to the dining room and the scenery beyond through the dramatic window wall with half-round transom.
- The sleeping room and loft upstairs can easily accommodate several guests or could be used as multi-purpose space.

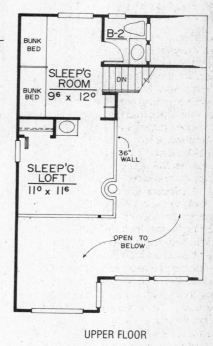

UPPER FLOOR

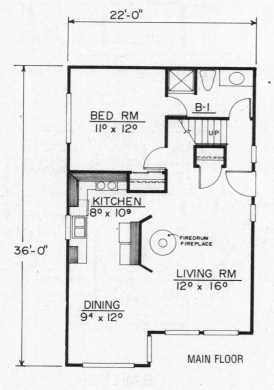

MAIN FLOOR

Plan I-1032-A

Bedrooms: 2-3	Baths: 1½
Living Area:	
Upper floor	288 sq. ft.
Main floor	744 sq. ft.
Total Living Area:	**1,032 sq. ft.**
Exterior Wall Framing:	2x6

Foundation Options:
Crawlspace
(Typical foundation & framing conversion diagram available—see order form.)

BLUEPRINT PRICE CODE: A

TO ORDER THIS BLUEPRINT,
CALL TOLL-FREE 1-800-547-5570

Plan I-1032-A

PRICES AND DETAILS
ON PAGES 12-15

131

REAR VIEW

Angled Solar Efficiency

- Dramatically angled to maximize the benefits of passive-solar technology, this compact one-story home can be adapted to many sites and orientations.
- South-facing rooms, including the combination sun room and den, absorb and store heat energy in thermal floors for nighttime radiation.
- Heavy insulation in exterior walls and ceilings, plus double glazing in windows, keep heat loss to a minimum. During the summer, heat is expelled through an operable clerestory window and through an automatic vent in the sun room.
- The entrance vestibule provides an immediate view of the sun room and the outdoors beyond.
- The living lounge boasts a warm fireplace, a bright bay window and a 14-ft. vaulted ceiling.
- The kitchen features an eating bar, while the attached dining area opens to a large rear terrace.
- The bedrooms are isolated for total privacy. The master suite features a private bath and a large walk-in closet.

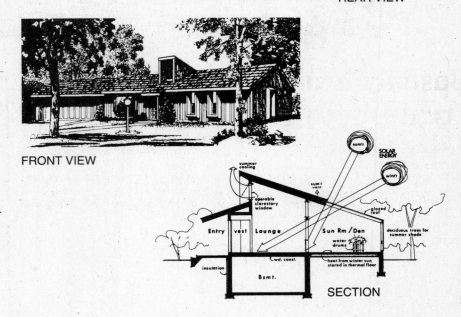

FRONT VIEW

SECTION

Plan K-505-R

Bedrooms: 3	Baths: 2
Living Area:	
Main floor	1,261 sq. ft.
Sun room	164 sq. ft.
Total Living Area:	**1,425 sq. ft.**
Standard basement	1,030 sq. ft.
Garage	466 sq. ft.
Exterior Wall Framing:	2x4 or 2x6

Foundation Options:

Standard basement

Slab

(All plans can be built with your choice of foundation and framing. A generic conversion diagram is available. See order form.)

BLUEPRINT PRICE CODE:	A

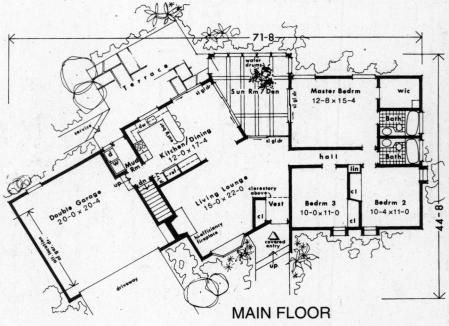

MAIN FLOOR

TO ORDER THIS BLUEPRINT, CALL TOLL-FREE 1-800-547-5570

Plan K-505-R

PRICES AND DETAILS ON PAGES 12-15

Upstairs Suite Creates Adult Retreat

- This multi-level design is ideal for a gently sloping site with a view to the rear.

- Upstairs master suite is a sumptuous "adult retreat" complete with magnificent bath, vaulted ceiling, walk-in closet, private deck and balcony loft.
- Living room includes wood stove area and large windows to the rear. Wood bin can be loaded from outside.
- Main floor also features roomy kitchen and large utility area.

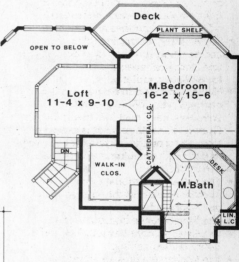

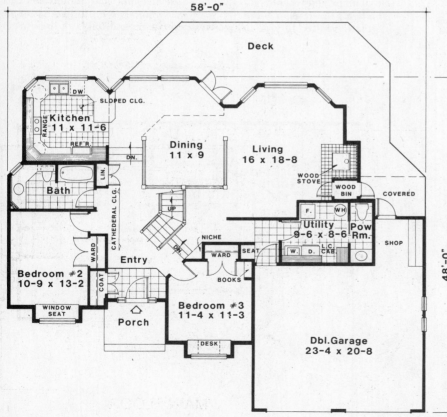

Plan NW-544-S

Plan NW-544-S	
Bedrooms: 3	Baths: 2½
Space:	
Upper floor:	638 sq. ft.
Main floor:	1,500 sq. ft.
Total living area:	2,138 sq. ft.
Garage:	545 sq. ft.
Exterior Wall Framing:	2x6
Foundation options: Crawlspace only. (Foundation & framing conversion diagram available — see order form.)	
Blueprint Price Code:	C

Affordable Alternative

- A rustic contemporary exterior surrounds an efficient plan to create an affordable rec home.
- The design would be well-suited to a ski or water location for winter or summer enjoyment.
- The heart of the plan is the dramatic vaulted fireside living room with fireplace and an optional built-in sofa.
- The informal galley ktichen serves the dining room while enjoying plenty of views on three sides.
- The sleeping quarters upstairs can accommodate up to two bedrooms with a second full bath in-between.

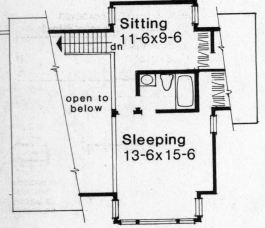

UPPER FLOOR

Plan B-7635

Bedrooms: 1-2	Baths: 2

Space:
Upper floor:	452 sq. ft.
Main floor:	700 sq. ft.

Total living area:	**1,152 sq. ft.**

Exterior Wall Framing:	2x4

Foundation options:
Crawlspace.
(Foundation & framing conversion diagram available — see order form.)

Blueprint Price Code:	A

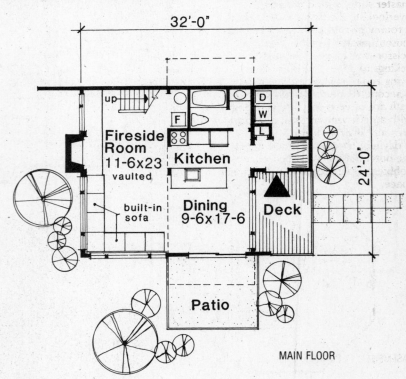

MAIN FLOOR

Plan B-7635

PRICES AND DETAILS ON PAGES 12-15

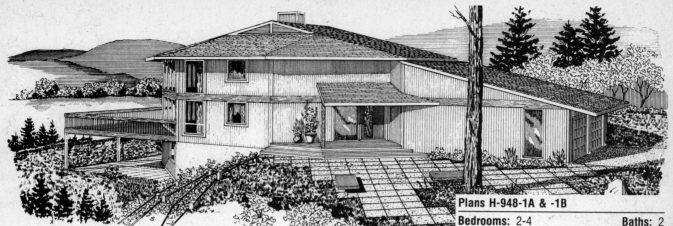

FRONT VIEW

Plans H-948-1A & -1B

Bedrooms: 2-4	Baths: 2

Space:

Upper floor:	700 sq. ft.
Main floor:	1,236 sq. ft.

Total without basement:	1,936 sq. ft.
Daylight basement:	1,236 sq. ft.

Total with basement:	3,172 sq. ft.
Garage:	550 sq. ft.

Exterior Wall Framing:	2x6

Foundation options:
Daylight basement (H-948-1B).
Crawlspace (H-948-1A).
(Foundation & framing conversion
diagram available — see order form.)

Blueprint Price Code:

Without basement:	B
With basement:	E

Octagonal Sunshine Special

Octagon homes offer the ultimate for taking advantage of a view, and are fascinating designs even for more ordinary settings.

This plan offers a huge, house-spanning living/dining area with loads of glass and a masonry collector wall to store solar heat.

The 700-square-foot upper level is devoted entirely to an enormous master suite, with a balcony overlooking the living room below, a roomy private bath and a large closet/dressing area.

Scissor-trusses allow vaulted ceilings over the two-story-high living room and the master suite.

A second roomy bedroom and full bath are offered downstairs, along with an efficient kitchen, a laundry area and inviting foyer.

A daylight basement option offers the potential for more bedrooms, hobbies, work rooms or recreational space.

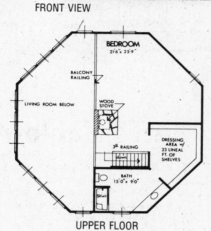

UPPER FLOOR

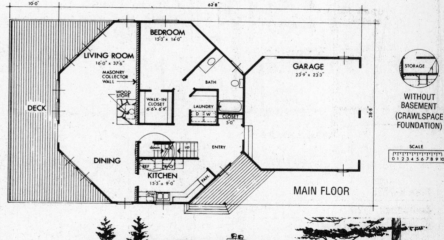

MAIN FLOOR

WITHOUT BASEMENT (CRAWLSPACE FOUNDATION)

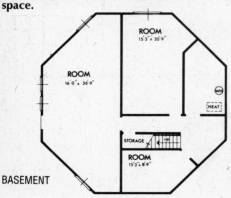

BASEMENT

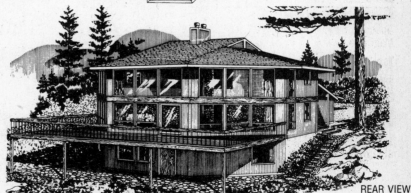

REAR VIEW

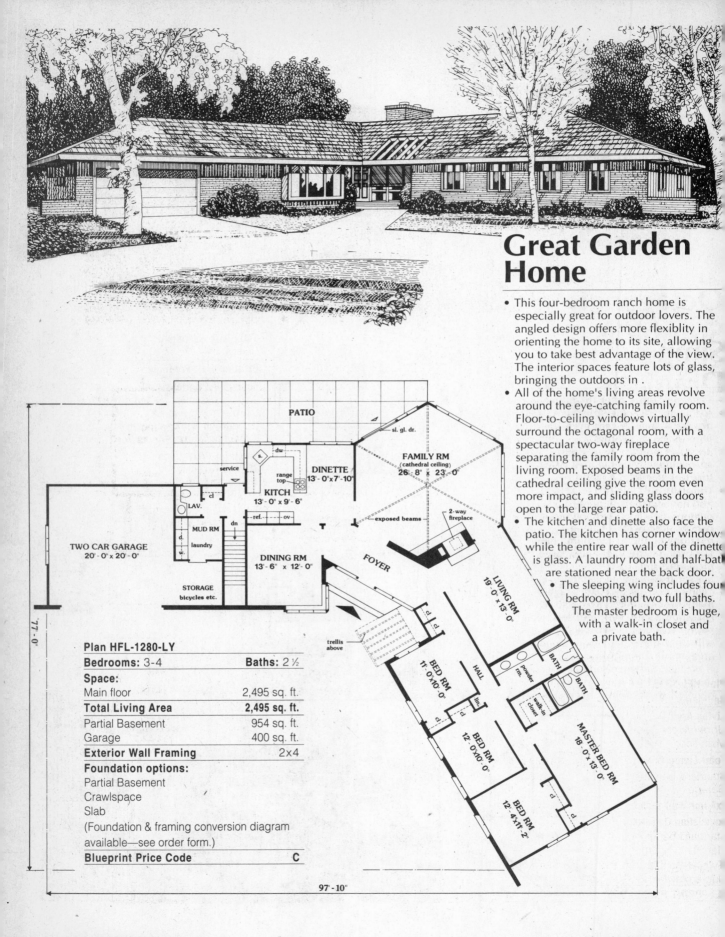

Great Garden Home

- This four-bedroom ranch home is especially great for outdoor lovers. The angled design offers more flexiblity in orienting the home to its site, allowing you to take best advantage of the view. The interior spaces feature lots of glass, bringing the outdoors in .
- All of the home's living areas revolve around the eye-catching family room. Floor-to-ceiling windows virtually surround the octagonal room, with a spectacular two-way fireplace separating the family room from the living room. Exposed beams in the cathedral ceiling give the room even more impact, and sliding glass doors open to the large rear patio.
- The kitchen and dinette also face the patio. The kitchen has corner windows while the entire rear wall of the dinette is glass. A laundry room and half-bath are stationed near the back door.
- The sleeping wing includes four bedrooms and two full baths. The master bedroom is huge, with a walk-in closet and a private bath.

PATIO

sl. gl. dr.

FAMILY RM
(cathedral ceiling)
26'-8" x 23'-0"

service

DINETTE
13'-0"x 7'-10"

KITCH
13'-0" x 9'-6"

range top

dw

s.

cl

LAV.

ref. — ov.

exposed beams

2-way fireplace

MUD RM

dn

laundry

TWO CAR GARAGE
20'-0" x 20'-0"

DINING RM
13'-6" x 12'-0"

FOYER

STORAGE
bicycles etc.

trellis above

LIVING RM
19'-0 x 13'-0"

BED RM
11'-0"x10'-0"

HALL

lin.

powder rm.

BATH

BATH

BED RM
12'-0"x10'-0"

walk-in closet

MASTER BED RM
18'-0"x 13'-0"

BED RM
12'-4"x11'-2"

77'-0"

97'-10"

Plan HFL-1280-LY

Bedrooms: 3-4	**Baths: 2 ½**

Space:

Main floor	2,495 sq. ft.
Total Living Area	**2,495 sq. ft.**
Partial Basement	954 sq. ft.
Garage	400 sq. ft.
Exterior Wall Framing	2x4

Foundation options:

Partial Basement
Crawlspace
Slab
(Foundation & framing conversion diagram
available—see order form.)

Blueprint Price Code	**C**

Plan HFL-1280-LY

PRICES AND DETAILS
ON PAGES 12-15

Simple, but Dramatic

- A dramatic sloped roof exterior and interior living room with sloped ceiling, floor-to-ceiling windows, an adjoining deck and wood stove give this home an interesting, but easy and affordable structure under 1,500 square feet.
- The attached kitchen and dining area also has access to the deck, for an outdoor dining alternative; a pantry and convenient laundry room is secluded to the rear.

The main-level bedroom could ideally be used as the master; it offers dual closets and nearby bath.

Off the two-story foyer is the stairway to the second level which ends in a balcony area that overlooks the living room. Two good-sized bedrooms, one with unique dressing vanity, share the upper level with a second bath.

Plan HFL-1382

Bedrooms: 3	Baths: 2
Living Area:	
Upper floor	465 sq. ft.
Main floor	963 sq. ft.
Total Living Area:	**1,428 sq. ft.**
Standard basement	811 sq. ft.
Garage	220 sq. ft.
Exterior Wall Framing:	2x6

Foundation Options:
Standard basement
Slab
(Typical foundation & framing conversion diagram available—see order form.)

BLUEPRINT PRICE CODE: A

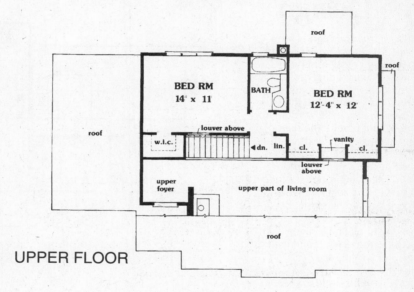

UPPER FLOOR

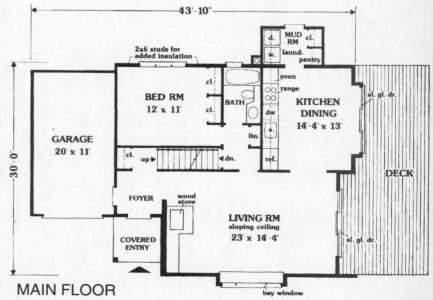

MAIN FLOOR

Striking Hillside Home Design

- This striking home is designed for a sloping site. The two-car garage and sideyard deck are nestled into the hillside, while cedar siding and a shake roof blend in nicely with the terrain.
- Clerestory windows brighten the entry and the living room, which unfold from the covered front porch. The huge living/dining area instantly catches the eye, with its corner fireplace, 17-ft. sloped ceiling and exciting window treatments. The living room also offers an inviting window seat, while the dining room has sliding glass doors to the large deck.
- The adjoining nook and kitchen also have access to the deck, along with lots of storage and work space.
- The isolated bedroom wing includes a master suite with his-and-hers closets and a private bath. The two smaller bedrooms share a hall bath.
- The daylight basement hosts a laundry room, a recreation room with a fireplace and a bedroom with two closets, plus a large general-use area.

Plan H-2045-5

Bedrooms: 4	Baths: 3
Living Area:	
Main floor	1,602 sq. ft.
Daylight basement	1,133 sq. ft.
Total Living Area:	**2,735 sq. ft.**
Tuck-under garage	508 sq. ft.
Exterior Wall Framing:	2x4

Foundation Options:

Daylight basement

(All plans can be built with your choice of foundation and framing. A generic conversion diagram is available. See order form.)

BLUEPRINT PRICE CODE:	D

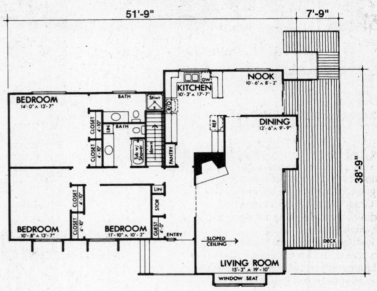

MAIN FLOOR

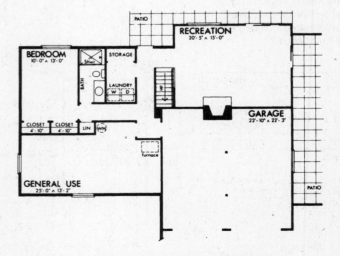

DAYLIGHT BASEMENT

Designed for Today's Family

- Compact and affordable, this home is designed for today's young families.
- The Great Room features corner windows, an impressive fireplace and a 12-ft.-high vaulted ceiling.
- The kitchen/dining room combination offers space for two people to share food preparation and clean-up chores.
- The master suite is impressive for a home of this size, and includes a cozy window seat, a large walk-in closet and a private bath.
- Another full bath serves the remainder of the main floor. The optional third bedroom could be used as a den or as an expanded dining area.

Plan B-8317

Bedrooms: 2+	Baths: 2
Living Area:	
Main floor	1,016 sq. ft.
Total Living Area:	**1,016 sq. ft.**
Exterior Wall Framing:	2x4

Foundation Options:

Slab

(All plans can be built with your choice of foundation and framing. A generic conversion diagram is available. See order form.)

BLUEPRINT PRICE CODE: **A**

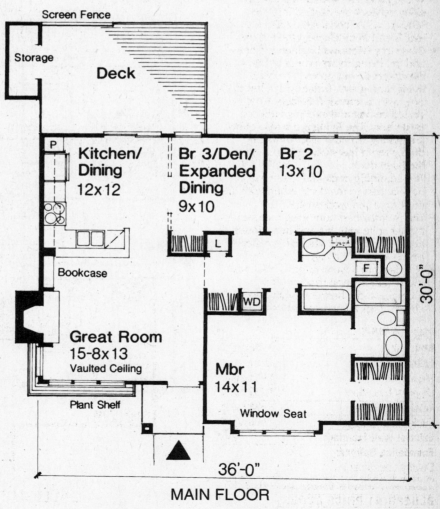

MAIN FLOOR

TO ORDER THIS BLUEPRINT,
CALL TOLL-FREE 1-800-547-5570

Plan B-8317

PRICES AND DETAILS
ON PAGES 12-15

139

Circular Dining Room Featured

- An attractive stone facade, innovative architectural features and a functional, light-filled floor plan are the hallmarks of this attractive design.
- Guests are welcomed in the skylighted gallery, which boasts an 11-ft.-high sloped ceiling. The living room features a stone fireplace and opens to the circular dining room.
- The dining room is highlighted by a curved wall of windows and an 11-ft. domed ceiling, making an expansive space for entertaining.
- The open kitchen is set up for efficient operation and adjoins the sunny dinette and the cozy family room.
- The bedrooms are zoned to the left, with the master suite including a private bath, a large walk-in closet and access to an outdoor terrace. The additional bedrooms share another full bath.

Plan K-663-N

Bedrooms: 3	Baths: 2
Living Area:	
Main floor	1,682 sq. ft.
Total Living Area:	**1,682 sq. ft.**
Standard basement	1,645 sq. ft.
Garage	453 sq. ft.
Exterior Wall Framing:	2x4 or 2x6

Foundation Options:

Standard basement
Slab
(All plans can be built with your choice of foundation and framing. A generic conversion diagram is available. See order form.)

BLUEPRINT PRICE CODE: B

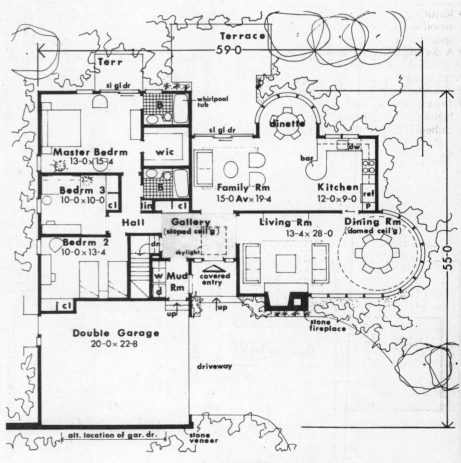

MAIN FLOOR

TO ORDER THIS BLUEPRINT, CALL TOLL-FREE 1-800-547-5570

Plan K-663-N

PRICES AND DETAILS ON PAGES 12-15

Spacious Home with Studio

- Rustic exterior overtones of stone and wood siding surround this home's spacious interior.
- A decorative planter serves as an attractive conversation piece that separates the entry from the formal dining room beyond.
- The tremendous sunken living room is highlighted by a breathtaking 20-ft. cathedral ceiling and a fireplace.

- The impressive U-shaped kitchen offers a windowed sink and ample counter space. The adjacent breakfast room boasts a large front window.
- The private master suite includes a walk-in closet and private access to a compartmentalized bath.
- Two additional bedrooms at the rear of the home share a unique bath with twin toilets and sinks.
- An upper-floor studio, study or play area overlooks the living room.
- The two-car garage offers two storage areas, one of which can be accessed from the breakfast room.

Plan C-7113	
Bedrooms: 3+	**Baths:** 2
Living Area:	
Upper floor	260 sq. ft.
Main floor	2,213 sq. ft.
Total Living Area:	**2,473 sq. ft.**
Daylight basement	2,213 sq. ft.
Garage	410 sq. ft.
Storage and utility	120 sq. ft.
Exterior Wall Framing:	2x4

Foundation Options:

Daylight basement
Crawlspace
Slab
(All plans can be built with your choice of foundation and framing. A generic conversion diagram is available. See order form.)

BLUEPRINT PRICE CODE:	C

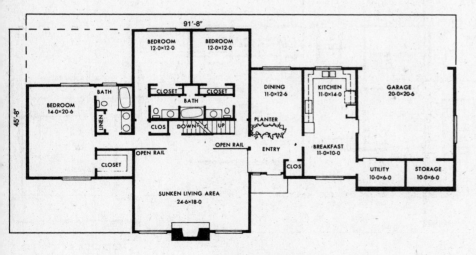

MAIN FLOOR

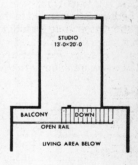

UPPER FLOOR

TO ORDER THIS BLUEPRINT,
CALL TOLL-FREE 1-800-547-5570

Plan C-7113

PRICES AND DETAILS
ON PAGES 12-15

141

Spacious Home for Scenic Lots

- Vertical wood siding, stone accents, large windows and a spectacular deck make this home ideal for a mountain, lake, golf course or other scenic site.
- The front porch opens to a spacious foyer, which unfolds to the formal dining room.
- The sunken family room is set off from the hall with an open rail and boasts a 20-ft. cathedral ceiling, a stone fireplace and access to a large deck.

- The U-shaped kitchen opens to a bright breakfast room with deck access.
- A laundry/utility room is conveniently located between the breakfast room and the two-car garage.
- The master suite is removed from the secondary bedrooms and offers a roomy walk-in closet. The compartmentalized master bath includes a separate dressing area with a dual-sink vanity.
- Two additional bedrooms share a unique bath with separate vanities and dressing areas.
- A fabulous upstairs studio is brightened by tall, angled windows and could provide extra space for guests.

Plan C-7710

Bedrooms: 3+	**Baths:** 2

Living Area:	
Upper floor	248 sq. ft.
Main floor	2,192 sq. ft.
Total Living Area:	**2,440 sq. ft.**
Daylight basement	2,192 sq. ft.
Garage	431 sq. ft.
Storage and utility	132 sq. ft.
Exterior Wall Framing:	2x4

Foundation Options:

Daylight basement
Crawlspace
Slab
(All plans can be built with your choice of foundation and framing. A generic conversion diagram is available. See order form.)

BLUEPRINT PRICE CODE:	C

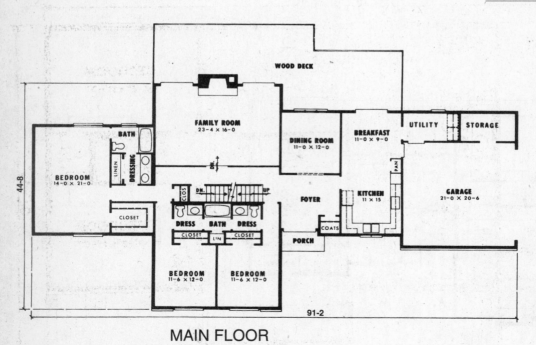

MAIN FLOOR

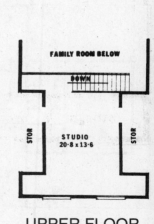

UPPER FLOOR

Plan C-7710
PRICES AND DETAILS ON PAGES 12-15

Rustic Appeal

- Stone and wood combine with high angled windows to give this rustic home an appealing facade.
- The entry opens directly from a wide front deck to the majestic living room, which is accented by a 15-ft. cathedral ceiling with exposed beams. A massive central stone fireplace is the focal point of the room, while tall windows overlook the deck.
- Behind the fireplace, the cathedral ceiling continues into the adjoining

dining room, which offers ample space for formal occasions.
- The galley-style kitchen features a sunny sink and easy service to the dining room. Just a step away, a pantry, a laundry closet and access to the carport are also available.
- The master suite boasts a walk-in closet, a private master bath and sliding glass doors to the deck.
- Across the home, two additional bedrooms share another full bath.
- Two handy storage areas are attached to the carport.

Plan C-7360	
Bedrooms: 3	**Baths:** 2
Living Area:	
Main floor	1,454 sq. ft.
Total Living Area:	**1,454 sq. ft.**
Daylight basement	1,454 sq. ft.
Carport	400 sq. ft.
Storage	120 sq. ft.
Exterior Wall Framing:	2x4

Foundation Options:
Daylight basement
Crawlspace
Slab
(All plans can be built with your choice of foundation and framing. A generic conversion diagram is available. See order form.)

BLUEPRINT PRICE CODE:	A

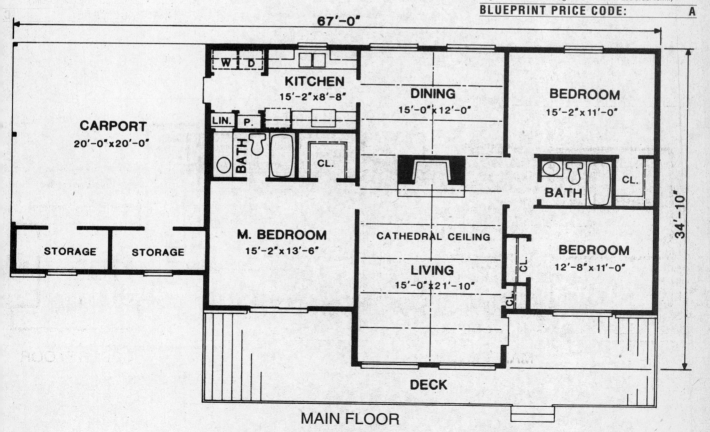

MAIN FLOOR

TO ORDER THIS BLUEPRINT,
CALL TOLL-FREE 1-800-547-5570

Plan C-7360

PRICES AND DETAILS
ON PAGES 12-15

143

Living with Sun Power

- Angled wood siding accentuates the geometrical architecture of this flexible leisure home.
- Designed to exploit sun power and conserve energy, this home's focal point is an expansive living lounge with a fireplace, a sloped ceiling and a glass wall that opens to a wraparound sun deck. The deck offers a unique outdoor eating bar.
- The roomy L-shaped kitchen provides a second eating bar and services the adjacent dining area.
- The three bedrooms are isolated from noise and traffic and share a hall bath.
- As an option, two solar collectors may be installed on the roof, either over the living lounge or on the opposite roof, depending on the southern exposure. Solar equipment may be installed now or in the future.

Plan K-166-T	
Bedrooms: 3	**Baths:** 1
Living Area:	
Main floor	1,077 sq. ft.
Total Living Area:	**1,077 sq. ft.**
Exterior Wall Framing:	2x4 or 2x6
Foundation Options:	

Crawlspace
(All plans can be built with your choice of foundation and framing. A generic conversion diagram is available. See order form.)

BLUEPRINT PRICE CODE:	**A**

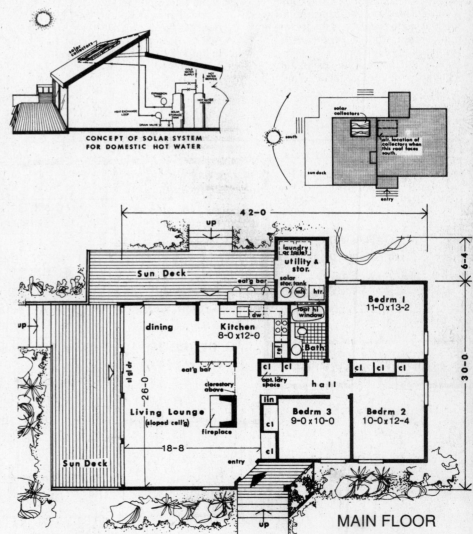

CONCEPT OF SOLAR SYSTEM FOR DOMESTIC HOT WATER

MAIN FLOOR

Practical and Cozy

This three-bedroom, two-bath eye-catcher blends plenty of practicality with a hideaway coziness. Its multi-level design places two bedrooms and one bath upstairs, ideal as the separate children's area that many parents prize. They will also enjoy the lavish master suite that awaits on the main floor, complete with its pass-through walk-in wardrobe and over-sized vanity counter.

Within outside dimensions of 34' wide by 48' deep, this home appears to far exceed its 1,346 sq. ft. Vaulted ceilings sweep up to meet an exposed beam that spans the entire diagonal length of the immense Great Room and dining areas. Another exposed beam merges with the first to extend its vaulted ceilings over a sunny morning room that opens to an intimate private patio. Note the stylish kitchen design, with its convenient access to the two adjacent eating areas.

Main floor:	963 sq. ft.
Upper floor:	383 sq. ft.
Total living area: (Not counting garage)	1,346 sq. ft.

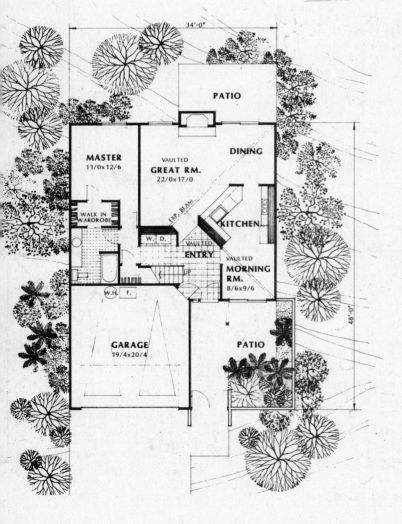

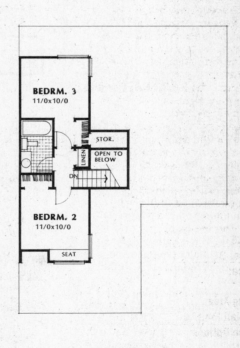

PLAN P-6564-3A
WITHOUT BASEMENT

Unique Octagon Design

- Irregularly shaped rooms are oriented around an entrance hall paralleling the octagonal exterior.
- Short directional hallways eliminate cross-room traffic and provide independent room access to the front door.
- Spacious living and dining rooms form a continuous area more than 38' wide.
- Oversized bathroom serves a large master suite which features a deck view and dual closets.
- This plan is also available with a stucco exterior (Plans H-942-2, with daylight basement, and H-942-2A, without basement).

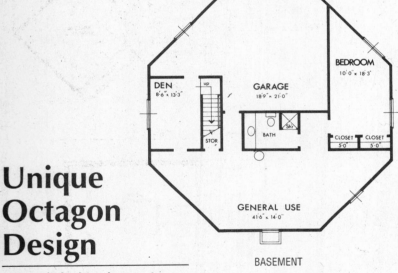

BASEMENT

1/16" = 1'

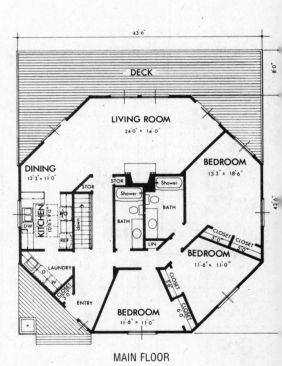

MAIN FLOOR

Plans H-942-1 & -1A (Wood)
Plans H-942-2 & -2A (Stucco)

Bedrooms: 3-4	Baths: 2-3

Space:
Main floor:	1,564 sq. ft.
Basement:	approx. 1,170 sq. ft.

Total with basement:	2,734 sq. ft.
Garage:	394 sq. ft.

Exterior Wall Framing:	2x6

Foundation options:
Daylight basement (Plans H-942-1 & -2).
Crawlspace (Plans H-942-1A & -2A).
(Foundation & framing conversion diagram available — see order form.)

Blueprint Price Code:
Without basement:
With basement:

Spacious and Striking

- Alluring angles and an open, airy floor plan distinguish this impressive home, designed to take advantage of a sloping lot.
- A gorgeous covered deck and patio give guests a royal welcome.
- Designed for both entertaining and family gatherings, the home's main floor features a bright family room with an 11-ft.-high vaulted ceiling and fabulous windows. A two-way fireplace with a lovely semi-round planter is shared with the adjoining dining room.
- The combination kitchen and breakfast area features a 10-ft. vaulted ceiling, a center island and a high pot shelf.
- The roomy master suite boasts a 10-ft. vaulted ceiling and double doors to a private balcony. The sumptuous master bath includes a beautiful Jacuzzi, a separate shower and a walk-in closet.
- Three more bedrooms and three full baths are located on the lower floor.
- A second family room includes a wet bar and double doors to a large covered patio.

Plan Q-3080-1A

Bedrooms: 4	Baths: 4½
Living Area:	
Main floor	1,575 sq. ft.
Lower floor	1,505 sq. ft.
Total Living Area:	**3,080 sq. ft.**
Garage	702 sq. ft.
Exterior Wall Framing:	2x4

Foundation Options:

Slab

(All plans can be built with your choice of foundation and framing. A generic conversion diagram is available. See order form.)

BLUEPRINT PRICE CODE: E

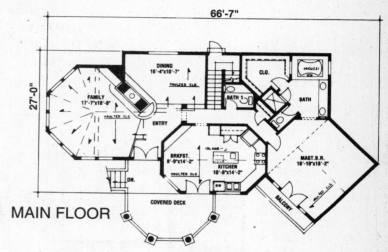

MAIN FLOOR

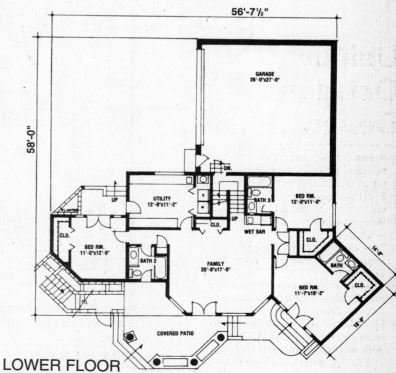

LOWER FLOOR

TO ORDER THIS BLUEPRINT,
CALL TOLL-FREE 1-800-547-5570

Plan Q-3080-1A

PRICES AND DETAILS
ON PAGES 12-15

147

Bold New Economic Plan

- The inviting entry of this economical three-bedroom ranch flows directly into the spacious living room.
- Warmed by a fireplace, the living room is easily served from the kitchen's angled snack counter. The adjoining dining area enjoys access to a covered backyard patio.
- The charming master bedroom offers a private bath, a dressing area and a roomy walk-in closet.
- Two additional bedrooms boast walk-in closets and are served by a nearby hallway bath.
- The convenient laundry/utility room accesses the two-car garage, which includes extra storage space.
- At only 46 ft. wide, this design would be suitable for a narrow lot.

Plan SDG-81115

Bedrooms: 3	Baths: 2
Living Area:	
Main floor	1,296 sq. ft.
Total Living Area:	**1,296 sq. ft.**
Garage	400 sq. ft.
Exterior Wall Framing:	2x4

Foundation Options:

Slab

(All plans can be built with your choice of foundation and framing. A generic conversion diagram is available. See order form.)

BLUEPRINT PRICE CODE: A

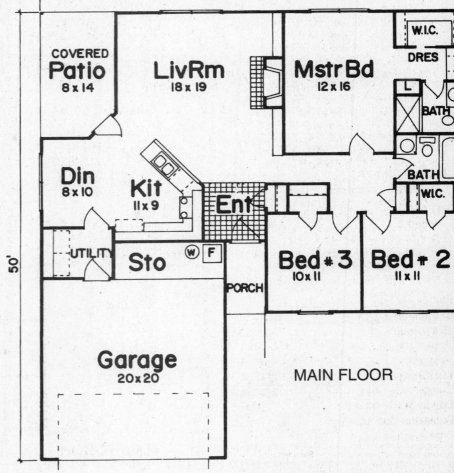

MAIN FLOOR

Plan SDG-81115

PRICES AND DETAILS ON PAGES 12-15

Comfort on a Narrow Lot

- With its narrow width of only 24 ft., this home is well suited for zero-lot developments or duplex construction.
- The covered entry opens to an efficient foyer that leads traffic into the living room or the family room. Also note the convenient powder room off the entry.
- The unique living room contains an impressive fireplace and a 16-ft. vaulted ceiling. The adjoining family room provides additional entertainment space, with sliding glass doors that lead to a corner patio.
- The kitchen is efficient and open, with a laundry area conveniently close.
- Upstairs, the master bedroom includes a generous-sized walk-in closet and a private bath. A railing offers views of the living room below.
- Two secondary bedrooms share a second full bath.

Plan H-1427-1A

Bedrooms: 3	Baths: 2½
Living Area:	
Upper floor	755 sq. ft.
Main floor	655 sq. ft.
Total Living Area:	**1,410 sq. ft.**
Garage	404 sq. ft.
Exterior Wall Framing:	2x4

Foundation Options:

Crawlspace
(All plans can be built with your choice of foundation and framing. A generic conversion diagram is available. See order form.)

BLUEPRINT PRICE CODE: A

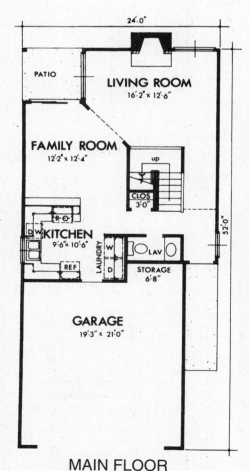

MAIN FLOOR

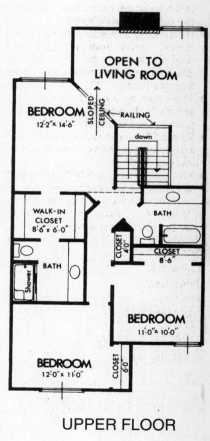

UPPER FLOOR

TO ORDER THIS BLUEPRINT,
CALL TOLL-FREE 1-800-547-5570

Plan H-1427-1A

PRICES AND DETAILS
ON PAGES 12-15

149

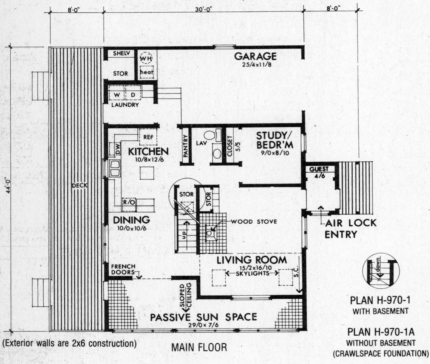

Main floor labels:

8'-0" | 30'-0" | 8'-0"

44'-0"

DECK

SHELV | STOR | WH heat
W | D
LAUNDRY

GARAGE
25/4x11/8

DW | REF
KITCHEN
10/8x12/6

PANTRY | LAV | CLOSET 5/5

STUDY/
BEDR'M
9/0x8/10

R/O

GUEST
4/6

STOR | STOR
WOOD STOVE

DINING
10/0x10/6

UP

LIVING ROOM
15/2x16/10
SKYLIGHTS

AIR LOCK
ENTRY

FRENCH
DOORS

SLOPED
CEILING

PASSIVE SUN SPACE
29/0x7/6

(Exterior walls are 2x6 construction) MAIN FLOOR

PLAN H-970-1
WITH BASEMENT

PLAN H-970-1A
WITHOUT BASEMENT
(CRAWLSPACE FOUNDATION)

down

Second floor labels:

SKYLIGHTS | LINEN | LINEN | CLOSET 5/6 | CLOSET 5/6
Tub w/ Shower
BATH
BEDROOM
10/0 x 13/6
DESK | CLOSET 4/9
down
SKYLIGHTS
DESK | CLOSET
BEDROOM
15/2 x 16/6
STORAGE
SKYLIGHTS

SECOND FLOOR

First floor:	817 sq. ft.
Sunspace:	192 sq. ft.
Second floor:	563 sq. ft.
Total living area: (Not counting basement or garage)	1,572 sq. ft.
Airlock entry:	40 sq. ft.
Garage:	288 sq. ft.

The Simple Life at Its Best in a Passive Solar Design

This home's rustic exterior is suggestive of Carpenter Gothic Style homes or early barn designs. The wood shake roof and "board-and-batten" style siding help to carry out this theme. An air-lock entry provides a protected place to remove outer garments as well as serving as an energy-conserving heat loss barrier. As you pass from the entry into the cozy living room, there is an immediate perception of warmth and light. This room features a centrally located woodstove and two skylights.

Between the living room and the sun space are two double-hung windows to provide heat circulation as well as admit natural light. Further inspection of the ground floor reveals a delightful flow of space. From the dining room it is possible to view the kitchen, the wider portion of the sun space and part of the living room. An open staircase connects this room with the second floor.

The kitchen boasts modern appliances, large pantry and storage closets and a convenient peninsula open to the dining room. The remainder of the first floor includes a handy laundry room, an easily accessible half-bath and a bonus room with an unlimited number of possibilities. One such use may be as a home computer/study area. Upstairs, two bedrooms with an abundance of closet space share the fully appointed, skylighted bathroom.

A word about the passive sun room: It seems that solar design has come full circle, returning us to the concept that less is more. This sun room uses masonry floor pavers as heat storage and natural convection as the primary means of heat circulation. This serves to reduce both the potential for system failures and the heavy operating workload often found in more elaborate solar designs, not to mention the high cost of such systems.

Blueprint Price Code B

Plans H-970-1 & H-970-1A

PRICES AND DETAILS ON PAGES 12-15

Attractive, Sunny Design

- This versatile plan features a striking exterior and numerous energy-saving extras, like passive-solar heating, glazed roof panels with adjustable shades, and operable skylights.
- An air-lock vestibule, which minimizes heat loss, leads into the spacious living room. This room has a stone fireplace, an operable clerestory window, a 14½-ft. sloped ceiling and sliding doors to the glass-roofed solar room.
- The adjacent dining room also has a sloped ceiling and offers sliding glass doors to a backyard terrace.
- The U-shaped kitchen features a laundry closet, a handy pantry and an eating bar for informal dining.
- The skylighted upper-floor hallway leads to the master suite, which offers a private balcony and a personal bath with a whirlpool tub.
- Two additional bedrooms, one with a bay window, share a second full bath.

Plan K-521-C	
Bedrooms: 3	**Baths: 2½**
Living Area:	
Upper floor	686 sq. ft.
Main floor	690 sq. ft.
Solar room	106 sq. ft.
Total Living Area:	**1,482 sq. ft.**
Standard basement	690 sq. ft.
Garage	437 sq. ft.
Exterior Wall Framing:	2x4 or 2x6
Foundation Options:	
Standard basement	
Slab	

(All plans can be built with your choice of foundation and framing. A generic conversion diagram is available. See order form.)

BLUEPRINT PRICE CODE: **A**

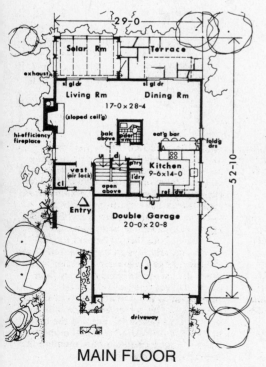

MAIN FLOOR

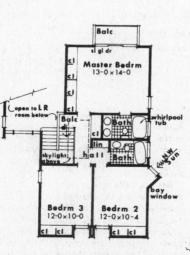

UPPER FLOOR

VIEW INTO LIVING ROOM AND SOLAR ROOM

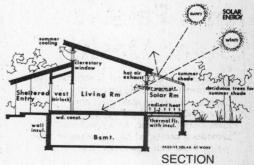

SECTION

Suspended Sun Room

- This narrow-lot design is a perfect combination of economical structure and luxurious features.
- The living and dining rooms flow together to create a great space for parties or family gatherings. A 16-ft. sloped ceiling and clerestory windows add drama and brightness. A fabulous deck expands the entertaining area.
- An exciting sun room provides the advantages of passive-solar heating.
- The sunny, efficient kitchen is open to the dining room.
- A full bath serves the two isolated main-floor bedrooms.
- The optional daylight basement includes an additional bedroom and bath as well as a tuck-under garage and storage space.

Plans H-951-1A & -1B

Bedrooms: 2+	Baths: 1-2
Living Area:	
Main floor	1,075 sq. ft.
Sun room	100 sq. ft.
Daylight basement	662 sq. ft.
Total Living Area:	**1,175/1,837 sq. ft.**
Tuck-under garage	311 sq. ft.
Exterior Wall Framing:	2x6
Foundation Options:	**Plan #**
Daylight basement	H-951-1B
Crawlspace	H-951-1A

(All plans can be built with your choice of foundation and framing. A generic conversion diagram is available. See order form.)

BLUEPRINT PRICE CODE:	**A/B**

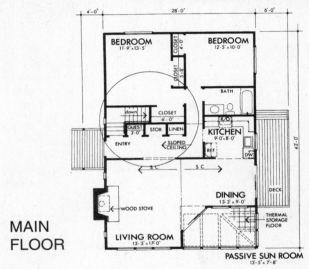

MAIN FLOOR

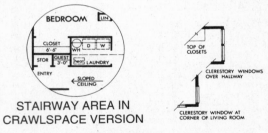

STAIRWAY AREA IN CRAWLSPACE VERSION

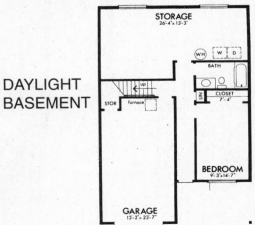

DAYLIGHT BASEMENT

TO ORDER THIS BLUEPRINT, CALL TOLL-FREE 1-800-547-5570

Plans H-951-1A & -1B

PRICES AND DETAILS ON PAGES 12-15

Cozy Home for Retirees or New Families

Total living area: 1,283 sq. ft.
(Not counting basement or garage)

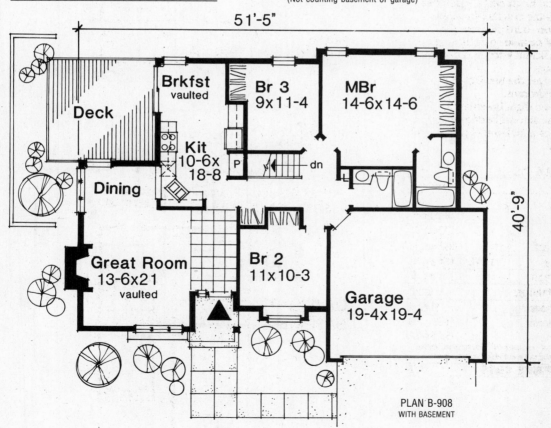

51'-5"

40'-9"

Deck

Brkfst
vaulted

Br 3
9x11-4

MBr
14-6x14-6

Kit
10-6x
18-8

Dining

dn

P

Great Room
13-6x21
vaulted

Br 2
11x10-3

Garage
19-4x19-4

PLAN B-908
WITH BASEMENT

Blueprint Price Code A
Plan B-908

PRICES AND DETAILS
ON PAGES 12-15

Warm, Rustic Appeal

- This quaint home has a warm, rustic appeal with a stone fireplace, paned windows and a covered front porch.
- Just off the two-story-high foyer, the living room hosts a raised-hearth fireplace and flows into the kitchen.
- The open L-shaped kitchen offers a pantry closet and a bright sink as it merges with the bayed dining room.
- The secluded master bedroom boasts a walk-in closet and a private bath with a dual-sink vanity. A laundry closet and access to a backyard deck are nearby.
- Upstairs, a hall balcony overlooks the foyer. A full bath serves two secondary bedrooms, each with a walk-in closet and access to extra storage space.
- Just off the dining room, a stairway descends to the daylight basement that contains the tuck-under garage.

Plan C-8339

Bedrooms: 3	Baths: 2
Living Area:	
Upper floor	660 sq. ft.
Main floor	1,100 sq. ft.
Total Living Area:	**1,760 sq. ft.**
Daylight basement/garage	1,100 sq. ft.
Exterior Wall Framing:	2x4

Foundation Options:

Daylight basement

(All plans can be built with your choice of foundation and framing. A generic conversion diagram is available. See order form.)

BLUEPRINT PRICE CODE:	**B**

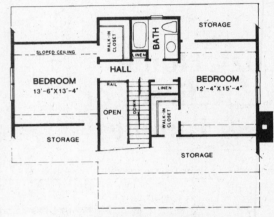

UPPER FLOOR

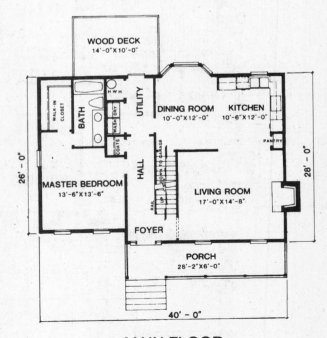

MAIN FLOOR

Plan C-8339

FRONT VIEW

Ever-Popular Brick Rambler

Total living area: 1,231 sq. ft.
(Not counting basement or garage)

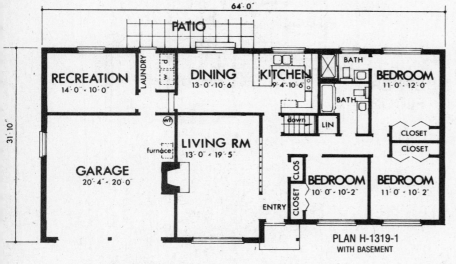

PLAN H-1319-1
WITH BASEMENT

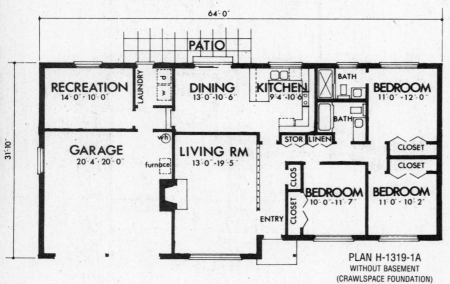

PLAN H-1319-1A
WITHOUT BASEMENT
(CRAWLSPACE FOUNDATION)

The simple rectangular shape and small square footage of this design make it a good choice for first-home buyers or for retirees. But this home is more than the basic rambler. The low-slung roof is staggered to form two levels and is capped with a modified hip roof — sometimes known as a "Tahitian roof" — for a look of refinement. The exterior walls are covered with 4" thick brick veneer, with corbeled brick used to trim the windows.

The interior hosts all the features today's homeowners are looking for while keeping the total living area under 1,250 sq. ft. The main entry provides a warm reception area for guests. To the left is the living room and fireplace, sectioned off from the hallway by a 9' wide half-wall with turned posts extending to the ceiling. The main hall has a guest closet and intersects with the hallways leading to the kitchen and the bedrooms.

The U-shaped kitchen features a breakfast bar that provides seating space for four people. The refrigerator, drop-in range and sink are positioned in a step-saving triangle, with plenty of counter space in between. The adjacent dining room has sliding glass doors opening onto the backyard patio.

Another rear entrance leads into the laundry room, which is also accessible from the garage. The laundry and recreation rooms are a step down from the main part of the house and can be closed off from the dining room.

All three bedrooms are equipped with 2' x 7' closets, with more storage space outside the main bath. The master bedroom features a bath of its own.

The optional basement includes a family room with a fireplace, plus a bathroom, fourth bedroom and a general-use area.

Country Kitchen Centerpiece

- This charming home features a rustic combination of stone and wood, which is offset by two half-round windows in the attention-getting gables.
- The centerpiece of the floor plan is the spacious country kitchen, featuring ample work surfaces, a nice-sized eating area with built-in bookshelves and access to a large backyard deck.
- The formal dining area is highlighted by a dramatic three-sided fireplace that is shared with the adjoining living room. The living room is enhanced by a dramatic 17-ft. vaulted ceiling.
- A powder room and a deluxe laundry room are easily reached from all of the main-floor rooms as well as the garage.
- Upstairs, the master bedroom boasts a 12-ft. vaulted ceiling that reveals a plant shelf above the entrance to the private bath and the walk-in closet.
- The two smaller bedrooms are separated by a full bath. The front-facing bedroom features an arched window set into a high-ceilinged area.

Plan B-87107

Bedrooms: 3	Baths: 2½
Living Area:	
Upper floor	722 sq. ft.
Main floor	834 sq. ft.
Total Living Area:	**1,556 sq. ft.**
Standard basement	834 sq. ft.
Garage	470 sq. ft.
Exterior Wall Framing:	2x4

Foundation Options:

Standard basement

(All plans can be built with your choice of foundation and framing. A generic conversion diagram is available. See order form.)

BLUEPRINT PRICE CODE:	**B**

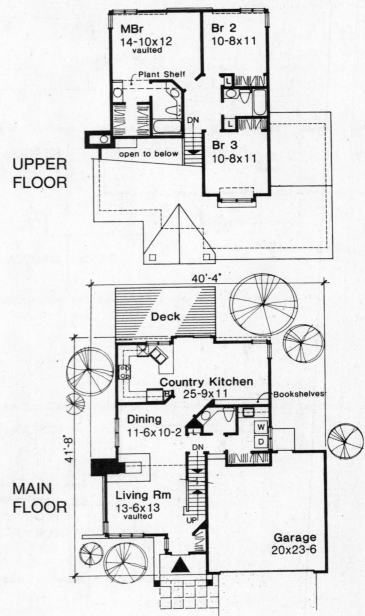

UPPER FLOOR

MAIN FLOOR

TO ORDER THIS BLUEPRINT, CALL TOLL-FREE 1-800-547-5570

Plan B-87107

PRICES AND DETAILS ON PAGES 12-15

BASEMENT

UPPER FLOOR

Upper floor labels:
SKYLIGHTS
Tub w/ Shower
LINEN | LINEN | CLOSET 5/6 | CLOSET 5/6
BATH
BEDROOM 10/0 x 13/6
DESK
CLOSET 4/9
down
BEDROOM 15/2 x 16/6
SKYLIGHTS
DESK | CLOSET
SKYLIGHTS
STORAGE

Main floor labels:
8'-0" | 30'-0" | 8'-0"
44'-0"
SHELV
STOR
WH heat
GARAGE 25/4 11/8
W | D
LAUNDRY
DECK
REF
DW
KITCHEN 10/8 x 12/6
PANTRY
LAV
CLOSET 5/5
STUDY/ BEDR'M 9/0 x 8/10
GUEST 4/6
R/O
STOR | STOR
WOOD STOVE
AIR LOCK ENTRY
DINING 10/0 x 10/6
UP
FRENCH DOOR
SUN ROOM 13/3 x 7/6
SLOPED CEILING
LIVING ROOM 15/2 x 21/10 SKYLIGHTS
S.C.

MAIN FLOOR

A Home for All Seasons

- Battened and barnlike, this rustic facade conceals a treasure of contemporary living.
- The airlock entry allows access without loss of heat, while the passive sun room collects heat. Other efficiencies include skylights and a woodstove.
- The step-saving kitchen offers a central work island and a pantry, plus easy access to the convenient main-floor laundry room.
- The study or extra bedroom could also be used as a den or home office.
- Two spacious bedrooms are located on the upper level, both with skylights, a built-in desk, and abundant closet space.

Plans H-970-2 & -2A

Bedrooms: 2-3	**Baths:** 1½
Living Area:	
Upper floor	563 sq. ft.
Main floor	1,009 sq. ft.
Total Living Area:	**1,572 sq. ft.**
Standard basement	768 sq. ft.
Garage	288 sq. ft.
Exterior Wall Framing:	2x6
Foundation Options:	**Plan #**
Standard basement	H-970-2
Crawlspace	H-970-2A

(Typical foundation & framing conversion diagram available—see order form.)

BLUEPRINT PRICE CODE: **B**

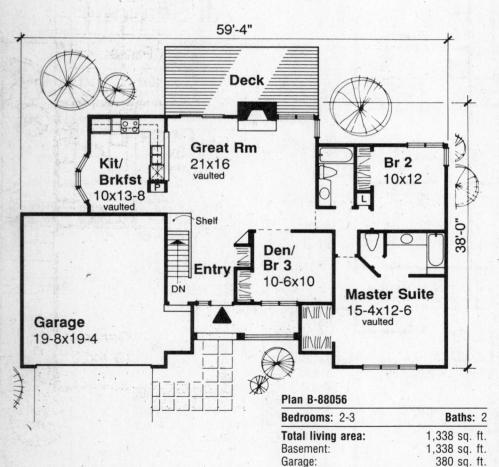

Deck

Great Rm
21x16
vaulted

**Kit/
Brkfst**
10x13-8
vaulted

Br 2
10x12

Shelf

DN

Entry

**Den/
Br 3**
10-6x10

Garage
19-8x19-4

Master Suite
15-4x12-6
vaulted

59'-4"

38'-0"

Spacious Great Room Featured

- A spacious Great Room takes this modest-sized home out of the ordinary.
- Great Room includes an impressive fireplace and easy access — both physically and visually — to a large deck.
- The kitchen/breakfast area includes sunny bay windows and a vaulted ceiling.
- The master suite also features a vaulted ceiling, and has a private, compartmentalized bath and large walk-in closet.
- The optional third bedroom would make an attractive and convenient home office.
- Basement stairs are convenient to both the front entry and garage door.

Plan B-88056

Bedrooms: 2-3	Baths: 2
Total living area:	1,338 sq. ft.
Basement:	1,338 sq. ft.
Garage:	380 sq. ft.
Exterior Wall Framing:	2x4

Foundation options:
Standard basement only.
(Foundation & framing conversion diagram available — see order form.)

Blueprint Price Code:

Economical Starter Home

- This economical one-story is ideal for a first home or small family.
- Two or three bedrooms can be finished, as needed.
- A generous sized vaulted living room with large fireplace and corner windows and dining room overlook the rear patio.
- The kitchen offers convenient laundry facilities.

Plan B-88003

Bedrooms: 2-3	Baths: 2

Space:

Main floor:	1,159 sq. ft.
Total living area:	**1,159 sq. ft.**
Garage:	425 sq. ft.

Exterior Wall Framing:	2x4

Foundation options:
Slab.
(Foundation & framing conversion diagram available — see order form.)

Blueprint Price Code:	A

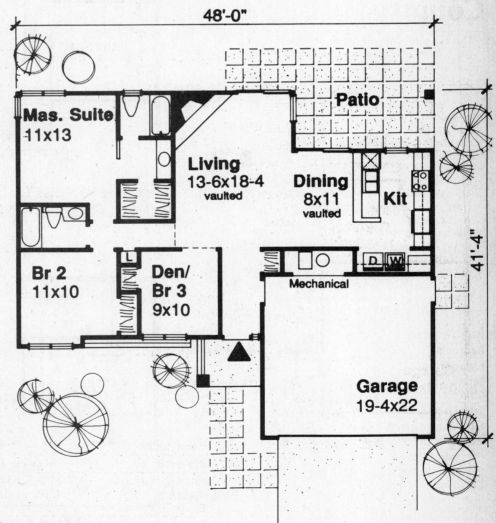

48'-0"
41'-4"

Mas. Suite 11x13

Living 13-6x18-4 vaulted

Patio

Dining 8x11 vaulted

Kit

Br 2 11x10

Den/ Br 3 9x10

Mechanical

Garage 19-4x22

Relax in the Country

- This country home provides plenty of room to relax, with its covered porches and wide-open living spaces.
- Just off the front porch, the living room boasts a two-story-high cathedral ceiling and a soothing fireplace with a raised brick hearth.
- The adjoining dining room opens to the backyard porch and merges with the bright walk-through kitchen.
- In between the kitchen and the main-floor master bedroom are a pantry, a full bath with a whirlpool tub and a laundry closet housing a stackable washer and dryer.
- The master bedroom boasts two closets, views of the front porch and private access to the bath.
- An open stairway with an oak rail leads to the upper-floor bedroom, which features a window seat, a pair of closets and access to extra storage space.

Plan J-90016

Bedrooms: 2	**Baths:** 1

Living Area:	
Upper floor	203 sq. ft.
Main floor	720 sq. ft.
Total Living Area:	**923 sq. ft.**
Standard basement	720 sq. ft.
Exterior Wall Framing:	2x6

Foundation Options:
Standard basement
Crawlspace
Slab
(All plans can be built with your choice of foundation and framing.
A generic conversion diagram is available. See order form.)

BLUEPRINT PRICE CODE: A

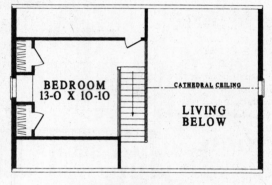

UPPER FLOOR

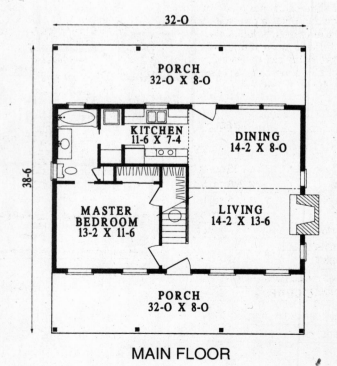

MAIN FLOOR

Plan J-90016

PRICES AND DETAILS
ON PAGES 12-15

Luxurious Country Home

- This country cottage hosts many luxuries, such as an expansive Great Room, good-sized sleeping areas and a large screened back porch.
- The rustic front porch opens into the Great Room, which offers a handsome fireplace and access to the large screened back porch.
- The bright kitchen features a huge work island, and unfolds to both the formal dining room and the breakfast bay. A handy laundry closet and access to the garage are also offered.
- The removed master suite has views of the front porch and offers a private bath with two walk-in closets, a dual-sink vanity, a spa tub and a separate shower.
- Upstairs are two oversized bedrooms, each with a dressing room that accesses a common bath.

Plan C-8535

Bedrooms: 3	Baths: 2½
Living Area:	
Upper floor	765 sq. ft.
Main floor	1,535 sq. ft.
Total Living Area:	**2,300 sq. ft.**
Daylight basement	1,535 sq. ft.
Garage	424 sq. ft.
Exterior Wall Framing:	2x4

Foundation Options:

Daylight basement

(All plans can be built with your choice of foundation and framing. A generic conversion diagram is available. See order form.)

BLUEPRINT PRICE CODE: **C**

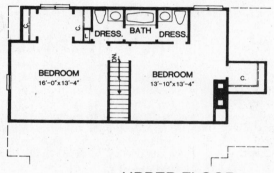

UPPER FLOOR

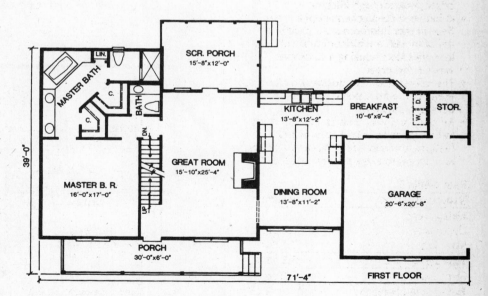

MAIN FLOOR

TO ORDER THIS BLUEPRINT,
CALL TOLL-FREE 1-800-547-5570

Plan C-8535

PRICES AND DETAILS
ON PAGES 12-15

161

Traditional Retreat

- This traditional vacation retreat maximizes space by offering an open, flowing floor plan.
- The spacious living room's luxurious features include a cathedral ceiling, fireplace and wet bar; its openness is extended by an exciting adjoining covered deck.
- Sweeping diagonally from the living room is the formal dining room with both front-facing and roof windows.

- The merging kitchen is separated from the living areas by a counter bar.
- The first floor bedroom features a unique triangular window seat, a dressing area and a full bath.
- The second floor is devoted entirely to a private master suite, complete with a lovely window seat, walk-in closet and attached bath.

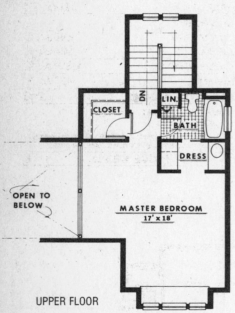

CLOSET

DN

LIN.

BATH

DRESS

OPEN TO BELOW

MASTER BEDROOM
17' x 18'

UPPER FLOOR

Plan NW-334

Bedrooms: 2	Baths: 2

Space:

Upper floor:	438 sq. ft.
Main floor:	1,015 sq. ft.
Total living area:	1,453 sq. ft.
Carport:	336 sq. ft.

Exterior Wall Framing: 2x6

Foundation options:
Crawlspace.
(Foundation & framing conversion diagram available — see order form.)

Blueprint Price Code: A

48'

BATH

BEDROOM 2
13'-6" x 12'

STOR.

ENTRY

PORCH

DRESS

COAT

BAR

38'

LOG BIN

LIVING ROOM
18'-6" x 12'
CATHEDRAL CEILING

UTILITY

W.
D.

KITCHEN
12' x 9'

CAR PORT
14' x 24'

COVERED DECK

DINING
12' x 10'

MAIN FLOOR

Modern Country Charm

- Charming window treatments, a covered porch and detailed railings give this modern home a country feeling.
- The inviting entry flows into the elegant living room, which features a 10-ft. ceiling and a striking corner fireplace.
- The sunny kitchen is built into a beautiful bay and easily serves the formal dining room.

- The spacious sunken family room enjoys bright windows and offers sliding glass doors to a backyard patio.
- A half-bath, a laundry/utility room and a storage area are conveniently located off the garage entrance.
- Upstairs, the master bedroom includes a private garden bath, a walk-in closet and a separate dressing area with a dual-sink vanity.
- Two additional upper-floor bedrooms share a full bath and a linen closet. Both rooms are enhanced by sizable closets and cozy window seats.

Plan NW-836	
Bedrooms: 3	**Baths:** 2½
Living Area:	
Upper floor	684 sq. ft.
Main floor	934 sq. ft.
Total Living Area:	**1,618 sq. ft.**
Garage	419 sq. ft.
Exterior Wall Framing:	2x6

Foundation Options:

Crawlspace
(All plans can be built with your choice of foundation and framing. A generic conversion diagram is available. See order form.)

BLUEPRINT PRICE CODE: B

MAIN FLOOR

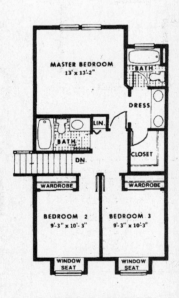

UPPER FLOOR

Outstanding One-Story

- Vaulted living spaces add to the spacious feel of this outstanding home, which would be ideal for a narrow lot.
- The focal point is the spacious Great Room and dining room area, enhanced by a 13½-ft. vaulted ceiling and a large fireplace flanked by windows to overlook the lovely patio and backyard.
- The dining room offers access to a secluded side courtyard.
- A beautiful bay window in the adjoining kitchen brightens the room and overlooks a front garden. A 10½-ft. vaulted ceiling and a functional snack bar are also featured.
- The master suite offers a sitting room with sliding glass doors to the patio. A private bath and a walk-in closet are also included.
- The two remaining bedrooms share the hall bath.

Plans P-6588-2A & -2D

Bedrooms: 3	Baths: 2

Living Area:

Main floor (crawlspace version)	1,362 sq. ft.
Main floor (basement version)	1,403 sq. ft.
Total Living Area:	**1,362/1,403 sq. ft.**
Daylight basement	1,303 sq. ft.
Garage	427 sq. ft.
Exterior Wall Framing:	**2x6**
Foundation Options:	**Plan #**
Daylight basement	P-6588-2D
Crawlspace	P-6588-2A

(All plans can be built with your choice of foundation and framing. A generic conversion diagram is available. See order form.)

BLUEPRINT PRICE CODE:	**A**

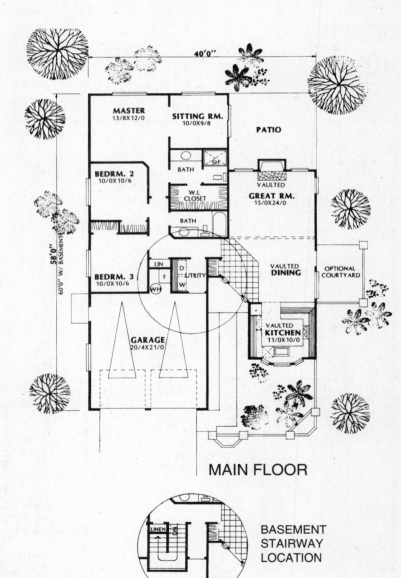

MAIN FLOOR

BASEMENT STAIRWAY LOCATION

Plans P-6588-2A & -2D
PRICES AND DETAILS ON PAGES 12-15

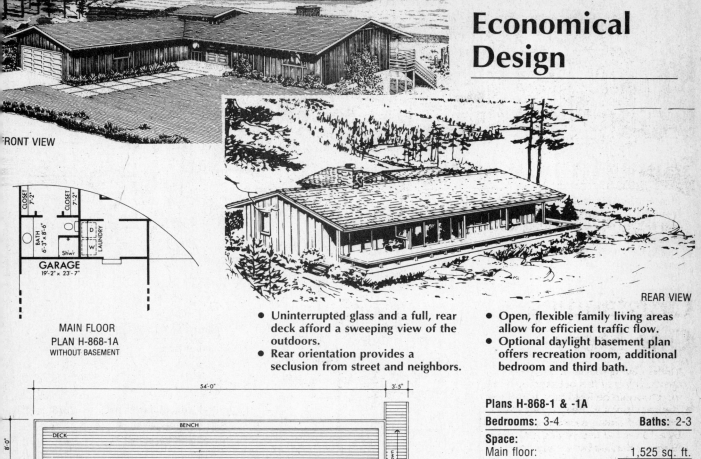

Economical Design

FRONT VIEW

REAR VIEW

MAIN FLOOR
PLAN H-868-1A
WITHOUT BASEMENT

- Uninterrupted glass and a full, rear deck afford a sweeping view of the outdoors.
- Rear orientation provides a seclusion from street and neighbors.
- Open, flexible family living areas allow for efficient traffic flow.
- Optional daylight basement plan offers recreation room, additional bedroom and third bath.

Plans H-868-1 & -1A	
Bedrooms: 3-4	**Baths:** 2-3

Space:	
Main floor:	1,525 sq. ft.
Total living area:	1,525 sq. ft.
Basement:	1,420 sq. ft.
Garage:	426 sq. ft.

Exterior Wall Framing:	2x4

Foundation options:
Daylight basement (Plan H-868-1).
Crawlspace (Plan H-868-1A).
(Foundation & framing conversion diagram available — see order form.)

Blueprint Price Code:
Without basement	B
With basement	D

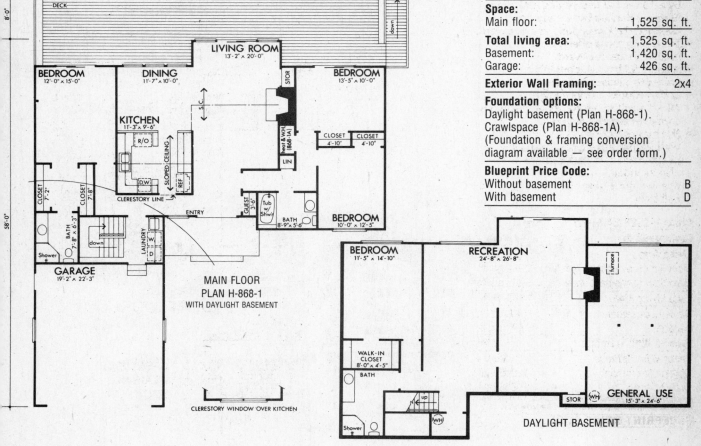

MAIN FLOOR
PLAN H-868-1
WITH DAYLIGHT BASEMENT

CLERESTORY WINDOW OVER KITCHEN

DAYLIGHT BASEMENT

TO ORDER THIS BLUEPRINT,
CALL TOLL-FREE 1-800-547-5570

Plans H-868-1 & -1A

PRICES AND DETAILS
ON PAGES 12-15

165

FRONT VIEW

Sunny Family Living

- Pleasant-looking and unassuming from the front, this plan breaks into striking, sun-catching angles at the rear.
- The living room sun roof gathers passive solar heat, which is stored in the tile floor and the two-story high masonry backdrop to the wood stove.
- A 516-square-foot master suite with private bath and balcony makes up the second floor.
- The main floor offers two more bedrooms and a full bath.

UPPER FLOOR

WITHOUT BASEMENT
(CRAWLSPACE FOUNDATION)

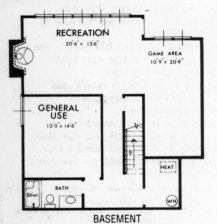

BASEMENT

MAIN FLOOR

Plans H-947-1A & -1B

Bedrooms: 3	Baths: 2-3
Space:	
Upper floor:	516 sq. ft.
Main floor:	1,162 sq. ft.
Total without basement:	1,678 sq. ft.
Daylight basement:	966 sq. ft.
Total with basement:	2,644 sq. ft.
Garage:	279 sq. ft.
Exterior Wall Framing:	2x6

Foundation options:
Daylight basement (H-947-1B).
Crawlspace (H-947-1A).
(Foundation & framing conversion diagram available — see order form.)

Blueprint Price Code:
Without basement:	B
With basement:	D

REAR VIEW

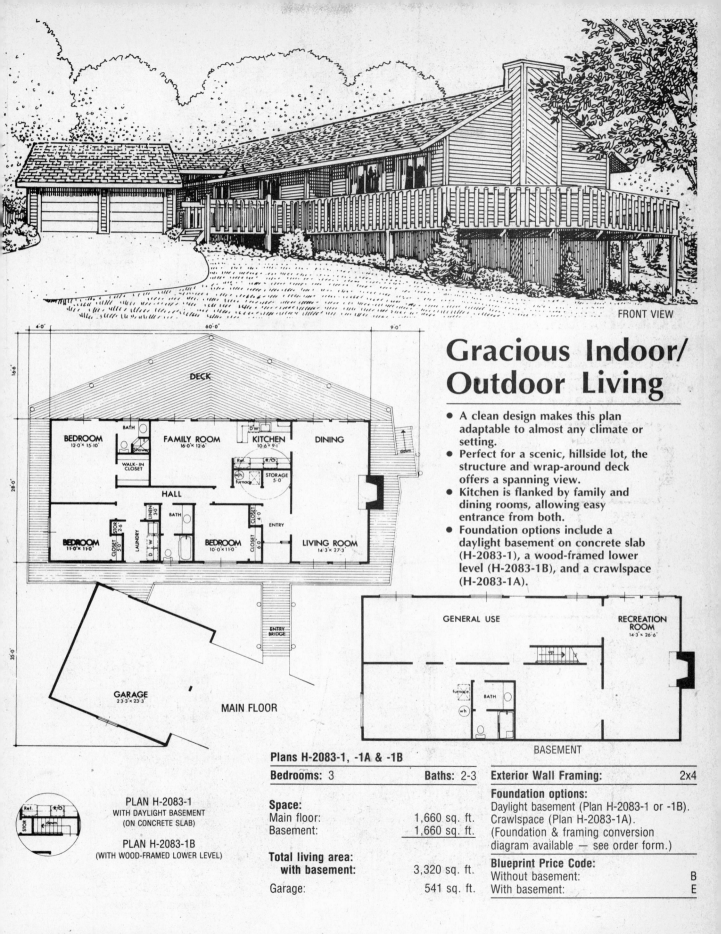

FRONT VIEW

Gracious Indoor/ Outdoor Living

- A clean design makes this plan adaptable to almost any climate or setting.
- Perfect for a scenic, hillside lot, the structure and wrap-around deck offers a spanning view.
- Kitchen is flanked by family and dining rooms, allowing easy entrance from both.
- Foundation options include a daylight basement on concrete slab (H-2083-1), a wood-framed lower level (H-2083-1B), and a crawlspace (H-2083-1A).

DECK

BEDROOM 12-0 × 15-10

BATH

FAMILY ROOM 16-0 × 12-6

KITCHEN 10-6 × 9-1

DINING

WALK-IN CLOSET

Shower

D W

Ref.

R/O

STORAGE 5-0

w.h. furnace

HALL

down

BEDROOM 11-0 × 11-0

CLOSET 5-0 STOR 2-6

LINEN 3-0

BATH

LAUNDRY D W

BEDROOM 10-0 × 11-0

CLOSET 4-0

CLOSET 6-0

ENTRY

LIVING ROOM 14-3 × 27-3

ENTRY BRIDGE

GARAGE 23-3 × 23-3

MAIN FLOOR

GENERAL USE

RECREATION ROOM 14-3 × 26-6

up

furnace

BATH

w.h.

BASEMENT

PLAN H-2083-1
WITH DAYLIGHT BASEMENT
(ON CONCRETE SLAB)

PLAN H-2083-1B
(WITH WOOD-FRAMED LOWER LEVEL)

Plans H-2083-1, -1A & -1B

Bedrooms: 3	Baths: 2-3

Space:
Main floor:	1,660 sq. ft.
Basement:	1,660 sq. ft.

Total living area:
with basement:	3,320 sq. ft.
Garage:	541 sq. ft.

Exterior Wall Framing: 2x4

Foundation options:
Daylight basement (Plan H-2083-1 or -1B).
Crawlspace (Plan H-2083-1A).
(Foundation & framing conversion diagram available — see order form.)

Blueprint Price Code:
Without basement:	B
With basement:	E

REAR VIEW

FRONT VIEW

Luxurious Living Areas

- This striking exterior design also provides plenty of excitement inside as well, with its angles, curves and bay windows.
- Especially note the eye-popping entry, with its curving stairway soaring through the two-story high foyer.
- The large family room is surrounded by a spacious deck, and a sunny nook adjoins the efficient kitchen.
- The upper floor is devoted mostly to a luxurious master suite with a spa bath and large closet. An adjoining space can serve as a nursery, library or den.

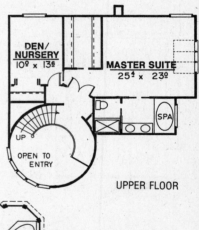

DEN/ NURSERY
10⁰ x 13⁹

MASTER SUITE
25⁴ x 23⁰

SPA

UP

OPEN TO ENTRY

UPPER FLOOR

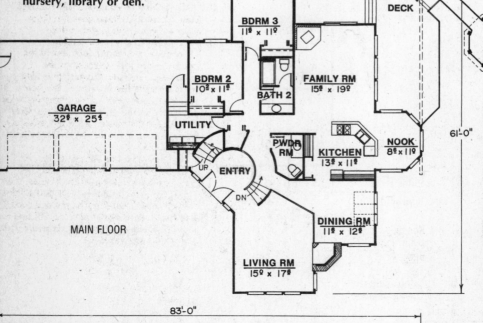

DECK

BDRM 3
11⁹ x 11⁹

BDRM 2
10² x 11⁹

BATH 2

FAMILY RM
15⁹ x 19⁰

SPA

GARAGE
32⁹ x 25⁴

UTILITY

PWDR RM

KITCHEN
13⁹ x 11⁹

NOOK
8⁹ x 11⁹

UP ENTRY

DN

MAIN FLOOR

DINING RM
11⁹ x 12⁹

LIVING RM
15⁰ x 17⁹

61'-0"

83'-0"

Plan I-2686	
Bedrooms: 3	Baths: 2½

Space:	
Upper floor:	785 sq. ft.
Main floor:	1,901 sq. ft.

Total living area:	2,686 sq. ft.
Basement: approx.	1,900 sq. ft.
Garage:	823 sq. ft.

Exterior Wall Framing:	2x6

Foundation options:
Standard basement.
Crawlspace.
Slab.
(Foundation & framing conversion diagram available — see order form.)

Blueprint Price Code: D

Plan I-2686

PRICES AND DETAILS ON PAGES 12-15

Popular Contemporary

This low-slung contemporary design contains a lot more space than is apparent from the outside. Oriented towards the outdoor sideyard, it features a pair of sliding glass doors offering outside access from both the living and dining room.

Effective zoning is the rule here: Bedrooms are secluded on one side to the rear; living areas and active kitchen space are grouped on the opposite side of the home.

All of these rooms are easily reached from a central hallway that provides excellent traffic flow, precluding unnecessary cross-room traffic.

Note the convenient location of the laundry room and staircase to the basement. Access to the garage is also available from the interior of the home. A generous assortment of plumbing facilities is grouped at the rear of the home. One bath serves the master bedroom privately. Another complete unit serves the balance of the house.

The attractive low silhouette is embellished with architectural touches such as the interesting window seats, the extension of the masonry wall that shields the side patio, and the low pitched roof.

Overall width of the home is 58' and greatest depth measures 36'. Exterior walls are 2x6 construction.

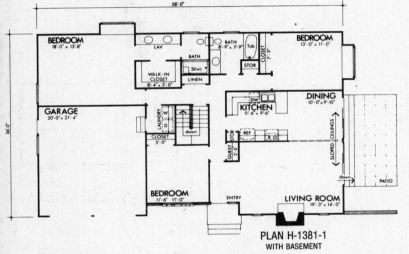

PLAN H-1381-1
WITH BASEMENT

Total living area: 1,596 sq. ft.
(Not counting basement or garage)

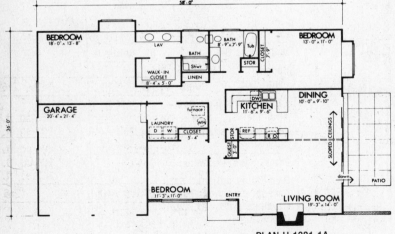

PLAN H-1381-1A
WITHOUT BASEMENT
(CRAWLSPACE FOUNDATION)

Total living area: 1,587 sq. ft.
(Not counting garage)

Spacious Octagon

- Highly functional main floor plan makes traffic easy and minimizes wasted hall space.
- Double-sized entry opens to spacious octagonal living room with central fireplace and access to all rooms.
- U-shaped kitchen and attached dining area allow for both informal and formal occasions.
- Contiguous bedrooms each have independent deck entrances.
- Exciting deck borders entire home.

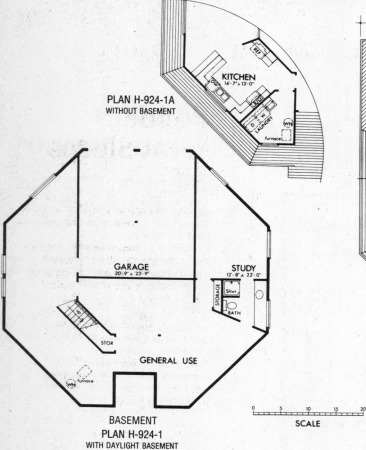

PLAN H-924-1A
WITHOUT BASEMENT

KITCHEN
14'-7" x 13'-0"

GARAGE
20'-9" x 23'-9"

STUDY
12'-8" x 22'-0"

STORAGE

STOR

BATH

GENERAL USE

furnace

BASEMENT
PLAN H-924-1
WITH DAYLIGHT BASEMENT

SCALE

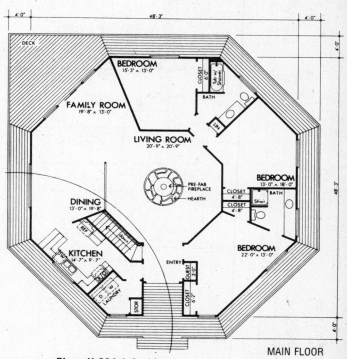

DECK

BEDROOM
15'-3" x 13'-0"

CLOSET
6'-0"

BATH
Tub w/ Shower

FAMILY ROOM
19'-8" x 13'-0"

LIVING ROOM
20'-9" x 20'-9"

PRE-FAB FIREPLACE

HEARTH

BEDROOM
13'-0" x 18'-0"

CLOSET
4'-8"

CLOSET
4'-8"

Sh'w'r

BATH

DINING
13'-0" x 19'-8"

REF

KITCHEN
14'-7" x 9'-7"

ENTRY

CLOSET
3'-0"

BEDROOM
22'-0" x 13'-0"

STOR

CLOSET
6'-2"

D W LAUNDRY

MAIN FLOOR

Plans H-924-1 & -1A

Bedrooms: 3-4	Baths: 2-3
Space: Main floor:	1,888 sq. ft.
Total without basement:	1,888 sq. ft.
Basement:	1,395 sq. ft.
Total with basement:	3,283 sq. ft.
Garage:	493 sq. ft.
Exterior Wall Framing:	2x4

Foundation options:
Daylight basement (Plan H-924-1).
Crawlspace (Plan H-924-1A).
(Foundation & framing conversion diagram available — see order form.)

Blueprint Price Code:

Without basement:	B
With basement:	E

Lakeside Retreat Sleeps Eight

- Four bedrooms border the exterior walls of this lakeside retreat, affording a fair amount of privacy.
- A deck and a vaulted screened-in porch surround the spectacular cathedral-ceilinged Great Room and dining area. The large living space is also loaded with glass so you can enjoy your favorite scenic site.
- The adjoining kitchen features an oversized eating bar and work counter combination.
- Two full baths sit back-to-back, conveniently serving both bedroom wings. A handy main-floor laundry room is also included.

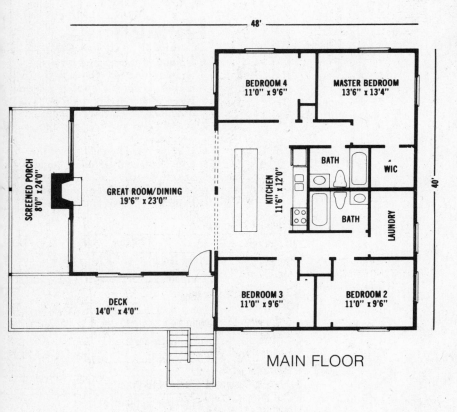

MAIN FLOOR

Plan PH-1600

Bedrooms: 4	Baths: 2
Space:	
Main floor	1,600 sq. ft.
Total Living Area	**1,600 sq. ft.**
Exterior Wall Framing	2x6

Foundation options:

Crawlspace
Pole
Slab
(Foundation & framing conversion diagram available—see order form.)

Blueprint Price Code	B

Striking Vertical Design

- Unique roof deck and massive wrap-around main level deck harbor an equally exciting interior.
- Large sunken living room is brightened by a three-window skylight and also features a log-sized fireplace.
- U-shaped kitchen is just off the entry, adjacent to handy laundry area.
- Second-story balcony overlooks the large living room and entryway below.

Plans H-935-1 & -1A

Bedrooms: 3	Baths: 2
Space:	
Upper floor:	844 sq. ft.
Main floor:	1,323 sq. ft.
Total living area:	**2,167 sq. ft.**
Basement:	approx. 1,323 sq. ft.
Carport:	516 sq. ft.
Exterior Wall Framing:	2x6

Foundation options:
Standard basement (Plan H-935-1).
Crawlspace (Plan H-935-1A).
(Foundation & framing conversion diagram available — see order form.)

Blueprint Price Code: C

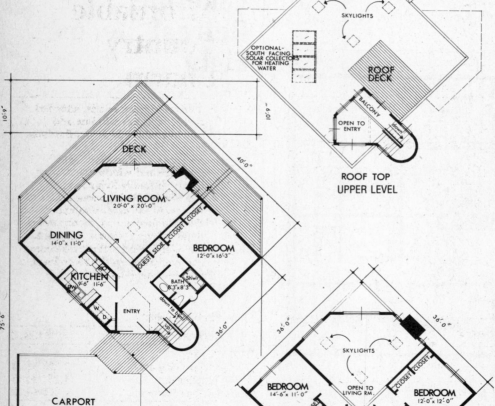

ROOF TOP UPPER LEVEL

MAIN FLOOR

UPPER FLOOR

Plans H-935-1 & -1A

PRICES AND DETAILS ON PAGES 12-15

Affordable Country Charm

- A covered front porch, attached garage, and bay window add appeal to this efficient, affordable home.
- A spacious living room with fireplace and window seat offer plenty of family living space.
- The kitchen/dining room opens to a rear patio for indoor/outdoor living.
- The attached garage incorporates stairs for the optional basement.
- The plan includes three bedrooms and two baths on the same level, a plus for young families.

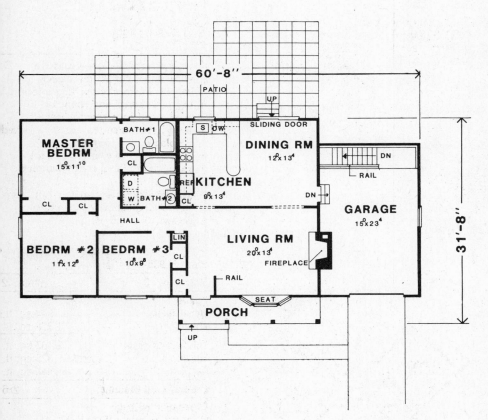

Plan AX-98602

Bedrooms: 3	Baths: 2

Space:

Total living area:	1,253 sq. ft.
Basement:	1,253 sq. ft.
Garage:	368 sq. ft.

Exterior Wall Framing:	2x4

Foundation options:
Standard basement.
Slab.
(Foundation & framing conversion diagram available — see order form.)

Blueprint Price Code:	A

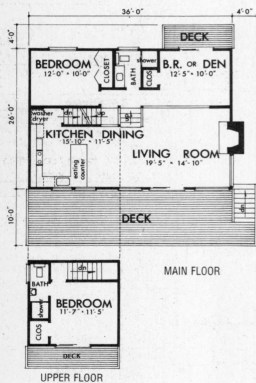

DECK

BEDROOM
12'-0" × 10'-0"

CLOSET

BATH

shower

B.R. OR DEN
12'-5" × 10'-0"

CLOS

washer dryer

dn

up

KITCHEN DINING
15'-10" × 11'-5"

LIVING ROOM
19'-5" × 14'-10"

eating counter

DECK

36'-0"

4'-0"

4'-0"

26'-0"

10'-0"

MAIN FLOOR

BATH

shower

dn

BEDROOM
11'-7" × 11'-5"

CLOS

DECK

UPPER FLOOR

Multi-Level Design

- This open and attractive design features multi-level construction and efficient use of living space.
- Elevated den and high ceilings with exposed rafters enhance the spacious feeling of the living room.
- Washer/dryer and kitchen are separated from the dining area by an eating counter.
- Third level comprises the master bedroom and bath.
- Garage and storage space are combined in the basement level.

Plan H-863-2

Bedrooms: 2-3	Baths: 2

Space:

Upper floor:	252 sq. ft.
Main floor:	936 sq. ft.
Total living area:	**1,188 sq. ft.**
Basement: (includes garage)	approx. 936 sq. ft.

Exterior Wall Framing: 2x4

Foundation options:
Daylight basement only.
(Foundation & framing conversion diagram available — see order form.)

Blueprint Price Code: A

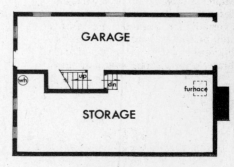

GARAGE

wh

up

dn

furnace

STORAGE

BASEMENT

Plan H-863-2

PRICES AND DETAILS ON PAGES 12-15

Clean, Stylish Lines

The sweeping roofline and arched windows give this home plenty of "presence", even though it is fairly modest in size.

Besides being stylish, the plan is also sturdy and energy-efficient, with 2x6 walls, R-19 perimeter insulation and R-38 in the ceilings.

The sheltered entry leads to an effective foyer which in turn leads visitors to the dining area or living room. These two spaces flow together to create a huge space for entertaining.

The roomy kitchen includes abundant cabinet and counter space. A utility room is in the garage entry area.

A large downstairs bedroom adjoins a full bath and includes a large walk-in closet. This would make a great guest or in-law suite.

Upstairs, another large bedroom features a private bath and walk-in closet.

A versatile loft overlooks the living room below, and provides room for children to play or for adults to keep a library, sewing room, studio or study.

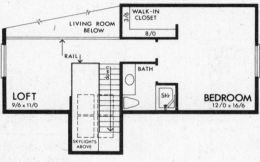

UPPER FLOOR

Plans H-1448-1 & -1A	
Bedrooms: 2-3	Baths: 2
Space:	
Upper floor	487 sq. ft.
Main floor	1,278 sq. ft.
Total Living Area	**1,765 sq. ft.**
Basement	1,278 sq. ft.
Garage	409 sq. ft.
Exterior Wall Framing	**2x6**
Foundation options:	Plan #
Standard Basement	H-1448-1
Crawlspace	H-1448-1A
(Foundation & framing conversion diagram available—see order form.)	
Blueprint Price Code	**B**

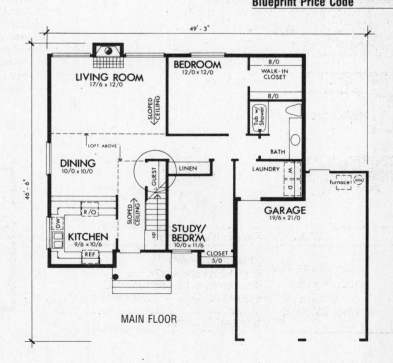

MAIN FLOOR

BASEMENT

At One with the Sun

- This two-bedroom ranch home combines an open floor plan with large expanses of glass to get the most out of the sun.
- The vaulted kitchen faces a cheerful sun porch on one side and opens to the dining and living rooms on the other.
- The dining and living rooms are combined to create one huge area, which is enhanced by vaulted ceilings and views of the large rear deck. A corner fireplace radiates warmth to the entire living area.
- The master bedroom has twin walk-in closets and a private bath. Another full bath, a laundry closet and a den or second bedroom complete the efficient plan.
- The full basement offers more potential living space.

Plan B-91012

Bedrooms: 2	**Baths: 2**

Space:

Main floor	1,421 sq. ft.
Total Living Area	**1,421 sq. ft.**
Basement	1,421 sq. ft.
Garage	440 sq. ft.
Exterior Wall Framing	**2x4**

Foundation options:
Standard Basement
(Foundation & framing conversion diagram available—see order form.)

Blueprint Price Code	**A**

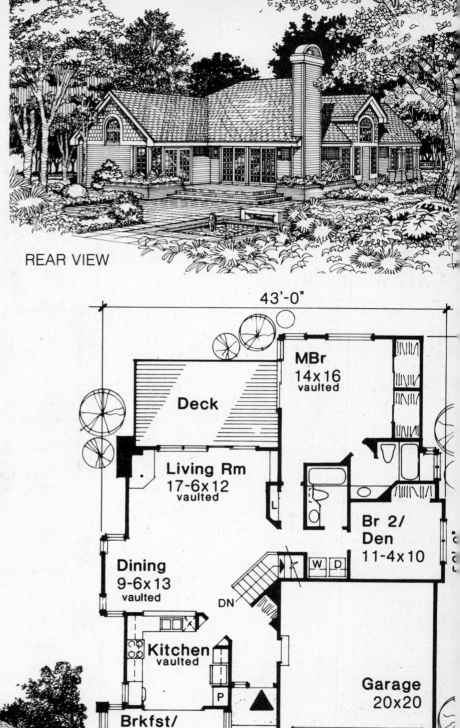

REAR VIEW

43'-0"

Deck

MBr
14x16
vaulted

Living Rm
17-6x12
vaulted

Br 2/
Den
11-4x10

Dining
9-6x13
vaulted

DN

W D

Kitchen
vaulted

P

Garage
20x20

Brkfst/
Sun Porch
7-3x14-6

FRONT VIEW

MAIN FLOOR

Plan B-91012

PRICES AND DETAILS
ON PAGES 12-15

Cozy Bungalow

- This pleasing L-shaped design packs a lot of living space into its floor plan.
- The large family room at the center of the home extends to two outdoor living spaces: a screened porch and a big patio or deck. For colder days, the warm fireplace will come in handy.
- Formal occasions will be well received in the spacious living/dining room at the front of the home. Each area offers a nice view of the front porch.
- The airy kitchen includes a pantry, a windowed sink and lots of counter space. Attached is a cozy breakfast bay and, beyond that, a laundry room.
- Secluded to the rear of the sleeping wing, the master suite boasts a private symmetrical bath with a garden tub, a separate shower and his-and-hers vanities and walk-in closets.
- Two secondary bedrooms and another full bath complete the sleeping wing.

Plan C-8620

Bedrooms: 3	Baths: 2
Living Area:	
Main floor	1,950 sq. ft.
Total Living Area:	**1,950 sq. ft.**
Daylight basement	1,950 sq. ft.
Garage	420 sq. ft.
Exterior Wall Framing:	2x4

Foundation Options:

Daylight basement

Crawlspace

Slab

(All plans can be built with your choice of foundation and framing. A generic conversion diagram is available. See order form.)

BLUEPRINT PRICE CODE:	B

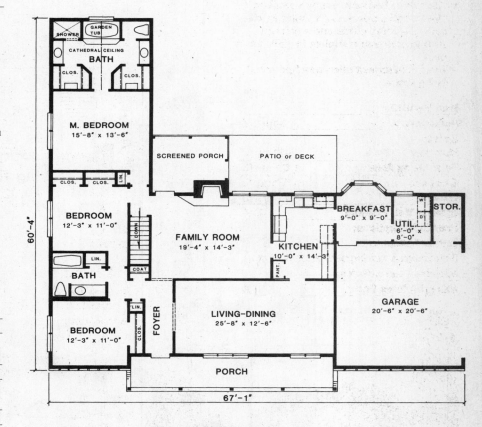

MAIN FLOOR

Southwestern Standout

- Contemporary styling with a traditional touch makes this house a standout in any neighborhood.
- The generously sized kitchen contains abundant counter space, a handy pantry and corner windows overlooking an enticing backyard patio. The kitchen is open to the family room and nook for informal living.
- The family room and kitchen can be totally closed off to provide extra privacy for the formal dining and living rooms. Both the family room and the living room feature fireplaces.
- The master bedroom has a private bath and is highlighted by a sunny alcove with a French door that opens to the patio
- The laundry room is handy to the garage and to the bedrooms.

Plan R-1039

Bedrooms: 3	Baths: 2
Space:	
Main floor	1,642 sq. ft.
Total Living Area	**1,642 sq. ft.**
Garage	517 sq. ft.
Exterior Wall Framing	2x6

Foundation options:

Slab

Crawlspace

(Foundation & framing conversion diagram available—see order form.)

Blueprint Price Code	B

53'-0"

64'-8"

Nook
8/6x8/6

Master
14/0x15/0

Kit.

Dining
10/0x10/0

Family
13/0x17/0

ref. pan

Bedrm. 2
10/0x11/0

Living
13/0x17/0

Entry

w h f.

d w

Bedrm. 3
10/0x10/0

Garage
22/0x23/6

Creatively Efficient

- This attractive one-story design shows that a home can have creativity and flair in an economical floor plan.
- The covered front porch beckons visitors into the sidelighted, tiled foyer, which includes a large guest closet.
- Decorative columns and a 36-in.-high railing set off the bay-windowed living and dining room. A fireplace adds to the comfortable ambience.
- The cozy family room and breakfast nook combination features a built-in entertainment center and sliding glass doors to an enticing patio.
- The wraparound kitchen is brightened by fluorescent lighting and boasts a handy sit-down snack bar with a sink.
- A skylighted hallway leads to three quiet bedrooms and two baths. The secluded master suite features a private, compartmentalized bath.

Plan S-41493

Bedrooms: 3	Baths: 2

Living Area:

Main floor	1,320 sq. ft.
Total Living Area:	**1,320 sq. ft.**
Standard basement	1,285 sq. ft.
Garage	387 sq. ft.
Exterior Wall Framing:	**2x6**

Foundation Options:

Standard basement

Crawlspace

Slab

(All plans can be built with your choice of foundation and framing. A generic conversion diagram is available. See order form.)

BLUEPRINT PRICE CODE:	**A**

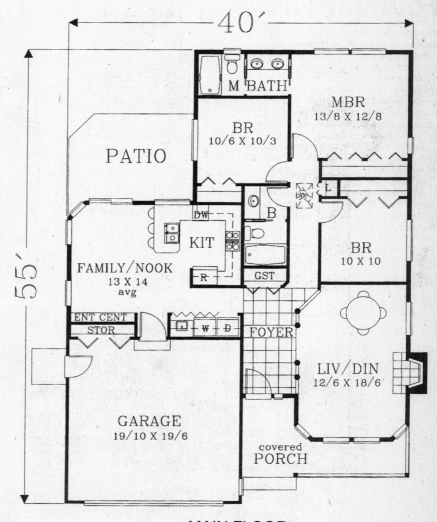

MAIN FLOOR

FRONT VIEW

Luxury on a Compact Foundation

Sky-lighted sloped ceilings, an intriguing stairway and overhead bridge and a carefully planned first floor arrangement combine to delight the senses as one explores this spacious 2737 sq. ft. home. A major element of the design is the luxurious master suite that is reached via the stairway and bridge. An abundance of closet space and an oversized bath are welcome features here.

Two bedrooms, generous bath facilities and a large family room provide lots of growing room for the younger members of the household.

All these features are available within a mere 36′ width which allows the house to be built on a 50′ wide lot — a real bonus these days.

Main floor:	1,044 sq. ft.
Upper level:	649 sq. ft.
Lower level:	1,044 sq. ft.
Total living area: (Not counting garage)	2,737 sq. ft.

(Exterior walls are 2x6 construction)

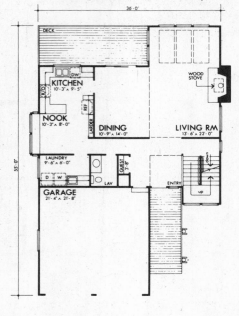

MAIN FLOOR
1044 SQUARE FEET

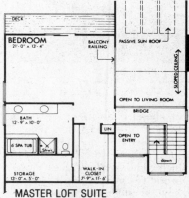

MASTER LOFT SUITE
649 SQUARE FEET

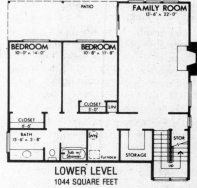

LOWER LEVEL
1044 SQUARE FEET

REAR VIEW

Blueprint Price Code D

Plan H-2110-1B

Easy, Open Floor Plan

- This attractive home flaunts a mixture of vertical and horizontal wood siding, and the wide-open floor plan permits easy traffic flow.
- A large, central living room merges with a dining area at the back of the home. The skylighted living room features a 10-ft. ceiling, a handsome fireplace and a patio door to a covered side porch.
- The roomy U-shaped kitchen includes a pantry and a convenient eating bar. Nearby, a utility room offers garage access and extra freezer space.
- The isolated master suite boasts a sunny sitting area and a large walk-in closet. The private master bath has two sets of double doors and offers an exciting oval tub, a separate toilet room and his-and-hers sinks in a long, angled vanity.
- Two more bedrooms and another full bath are at the other end of the home.

Plan E-1430

Bedrooms: 3	**Baths:** 2

Living Area:

Main floor	1,430 sq. ft.
Total Living Area:	**1,430 sq. ft.**
Garage and storage	465 sq. ft.
Exterior Wall Framing:	2x4

Foundation Options:

Crawlspace

Slab

(All plans can be built with your choice of foundation and framing. A generic conversion diagram is available. See order form.)

BLUEPRINT PRICE CODE: **A**

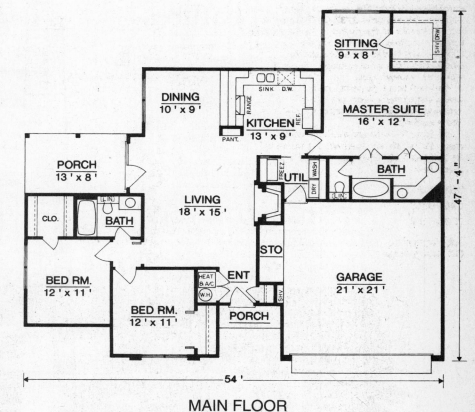

MAIN FLOOR

A-Frame Chalet with Popular Features

Ski chalets bring to mind Alpine comforts and evenings by the hearth. Schussing down nearby slopes is much more enjoyable when you don't have to worry about long drives home. Also, being on hand means you won't miss the fresh snowfall. In addition, summer time finds the mountain setting ideal for refreshing weekends away from the crowds and heat.

This class A-Frame is designed for optimum comfort and minimum cost, yet allows for variety and individual taste in setting and decor. Your home away from home can vary from plush to rustic, depending on personal preferences.

A special feature of this plan is the natural stone fireplace located where it can be enjoyed from indoors and outdoors. It serves the dual function of being a standard fireplace indoors and a handy barbecue outdoors. Two sleeping rooms on the main floor are a further advantage. Upstairs, there is a third bedroom plus a half bath. A balcony room provides space for overflow guests or a playroom for the kids. All the rooms in the house have "knee walls" so the space is usable right to the wall. These walls provide handy storage places as well as space for insulation.

First floor:	845 sq. ft.
Second floor:	375 sq. ft.
Total living area:	1,220 sq. ft.

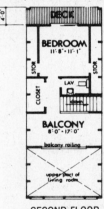

PLAN H-6
WITHOUT BASEMENT
(CRAWLSPACE FOUNDATION)

SECOND FLOOR
375 SQUARE FEET

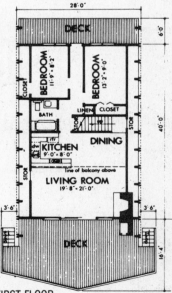

FIRST FLOOR
845 SQUARE FEET

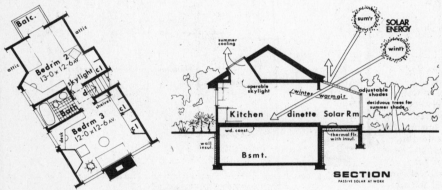

SECOND FLOOR PLAN

SECTION
PASSIVE SOLAR AT WORK

SOLAR ENERGY

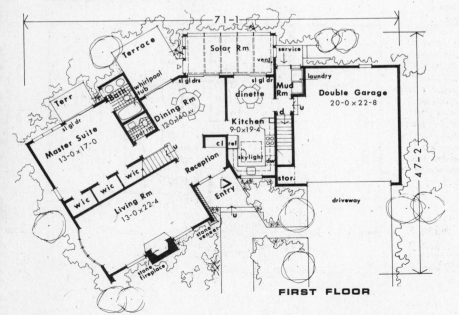

FIRST FLOOR

Passive Solar Home Meets Modern Demands

The exterior of this two-story plan is thoroughly contemporary. The layout is angled to give it added distinction in any neighborhood. Optional orientations in relation to the street allow this plan to adapt to a variety of plot shapes. Inside, the reception hall immediately presents a pleasing view of the rear terrace and solar room. To the left is the living room, which is graced by a stone fireplace.

In winter months, light and solar heat enter through the glass and heat is stored in the ceramic tiled floor of the solar room; after the sun sets, this warmth is released to the house. In summer months, the sun rises higher and its rays are blocked by adjustable shades built into glazed ceiling panels; automatic vent guards against heat buildup.

Generously sized, the master bedroom features extensive glass to the south side, a personal bath and sliding glass doors that lead out to a private terrace.

Total living area, excluding the solar room, is 1,132 sq. ft. on the first floor and 416 sq. ft. on the second. Optional basement is 1,176 sq. ft.; garage, mud room, etc., come to 560 sq. ft. (Alternate slab-on-grade foundation plan is included.)

Total living area: 1,548 sq. ft.

Blueprint Price Code B

Plan K-513-A

TO ORDER THIS BLUEPRINT,
CALL TOLL-FREE 1-800-547-5570

PRICES AND DETAILS
ON PAGES 12-15   **183**

Warm Rural Feel

- Round-top windows, a wrap-around covered porch and brick chimney give a warm rural feel to this innovative plan.
- The entry opens to the spacious living room with fireplace and soaring ceiling, leading the eye up the stairs to the second floor family room with dormer and balcony.
- The kitchen overlooks the dining room, with French doors to the side porch.
- Two secondary bedrooms are located on the main level, while the lavish master suite with dormered sitting area and private bath is on the second level.

Plan NW-297

Bedrooms: 3	Baths: 2

Space:

Upper floor:	663 sq. ft.
Main floor:	1,470 sq. ft.
Total living area:	**2,133 sq. ft.**
Exterior Wall Framing:	**2x6**

Foundation options:
Crawlspace.
(Foundation & framing conversion diagram available — see order form.)

Blueprint Price Code: C

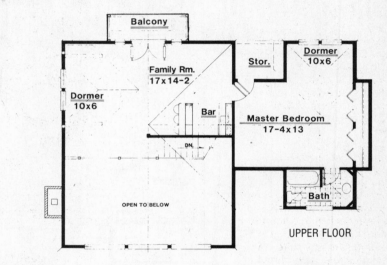

UPPER FLOOR

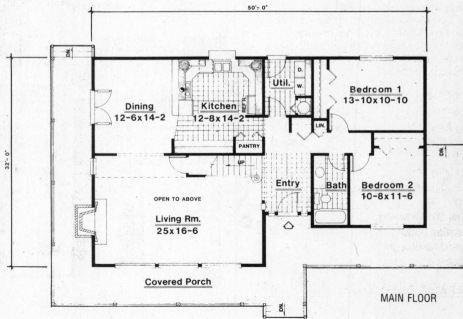

MAIN FLOOR

xceptional
Multi-Level

A dramatic circular stairway sets a tone of elegance and intrigue in this stunning contemporary home.

The double-door entry flows into the bright living room, which features a railed overlook to the formal dining room below. An angled fireplace warms both rooms.

Three steps down, the kitchen offers a curved eating bar that is echoed by a breakfast nook set into a curved wall of sunny windows.

The large family room boasts a corner woodstove to warm indoor activities, while a two-level deck with a hot tub provides outdoor fun.

Upstairs, the unique master suite features a secluded den, a whirlpool tub, a shower and a private deck.

The circular stairway continues up to a railed roof deck. This large open-air entertainment space is highlighted by a barbecue that cleverly utilizes the fireplace chimney.

an I-2700

drooms: 3	**Baths:** 2½
ing Area:		
per floor		715 sq. ft.
in floor		1,985 sq. ft.
al Living Area:		**2,700 sq. ft.**
ndard basement		1,985 sq. ft.
rage		582 sq. ft.
erior Wall Framing:		2x6

undation Options:
ndard basement
awlspace
b

UEPRINT PRICE CODE: D

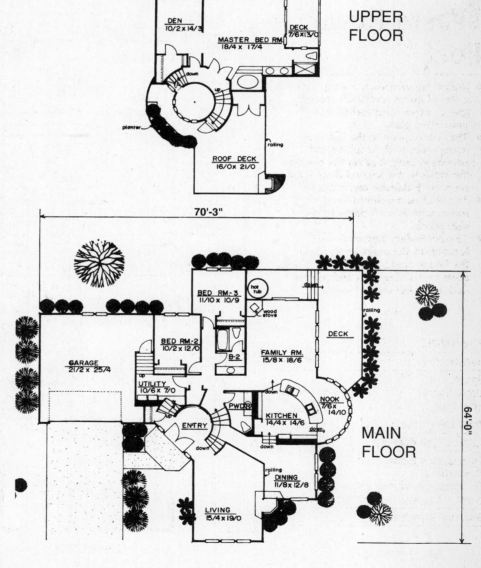

UPPER FLOOR

DEN 10/2 x 14/3
MASTER BED RM. 18/4 x 17/4
DECK 7/6 x 13/0
down
up
planter
railing
ROOF DECK 16/0 x 21/0

70'-3"

64'-0"

BED RM.-3 11/10 x 10/9
hot tub
down
railing
wood stove
BED RM.-2 10/2 x 12/0
B-2
FAMILY RM. 15/8 x 18/6
DECK
GARAGE 21/2 x 25/4
UTILITY 10/6 x 7/0
up
PWDR.
NOOK 7/6 x 14/10
down
KITCHEN 14/4 x 14/6
down
ENTRY
down
up
down
railing
DINING 11/8 x 12/8
LIVING 15/4 x 19/0

MAIN FLOOR

FRONT VIEW

Dramatic Western Contemporary

REAR VIEW

- Dramatic and functional building features contribute to the comfort and desire of this family home.
- Master suite offers a spacious private bath and luxurious hydro spa.
- Open, efficient kitchen accommodates modern appliances, a large pantry, and a snack bar.
- Skylights shed light on the entryway, open staircase, and balcony.
- Upper level balcony area has private covered deck, and may be used as a guest room or den.

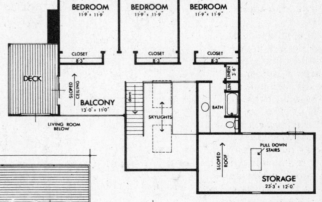

BEDROOM 11'-9" x 11'-9"
BEDROOM 11'-9" x 11'-9"
BEDROOM 11'-9" x 11'-9"
CLOSET 8'-3"
CLOSET 8'-3"
CLOSET 8'-3"
LINEN 3'-6"
DECK
SLOPED CEILING
BALCONY 13'-0" x 11'-0"
BATH
SKYLIGHTS
LIVING ROOM BELOW
PULL DOWN STAIRS
SLOPED ROOF
STORAGE 23'-3" x 12'-0"

UPPER FLOOR

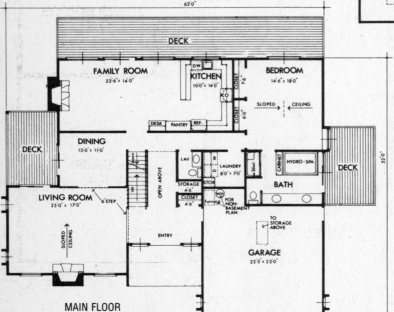

62'-0"
DECK
FAMILY ROOM 23'-6" x 14'-0"
KITCHEN 10'-0" x 14'-0"
DW
CLOSET 7'-6"
BEDROOM 14'-6" x 18'-0"
SLOPED | CEILING
DESK
PANTRY
REF.
CLOSET 6'-0"
DECK
DINING 13'-0" x 11'-0"
LAV
LAUNDRY 8'-0" x 7'-0"
CABINET
HYDRO - SPA
DECK
52'-0"
OPEN ABOVE
STORAGE 4'-6"
STOR.
BATH
LIVING ROOM 23'-0" x 17'-0"
6" STEP
CLOSET 4'-6"
WH
FURNACE
FOR NON-BASEMENT PLAN
SLOPED CEILING
ENTRY
TO STORAGE ABOVE
GARAGE 23'-3" x 22'-0"

MAIN FLOOR

Plans H-3708-1 & -1A

Bedrooms: 4	Baths: 2

Space:

Upper floor:	893 sq. ft
Main floor:	2,006 sq. ft

Total living area:	**2,899 sq.**
Basement:	approx. 2,006 sq.
Garage:	512 sq.

Exterior Wall Framing:	2x

Foundation options:
Daylight basement (Plan H-3708-1).
Crawlspace (Plan H-3708-1A).
(Foundation & framing conversion diagram available — see order form.)

Blueprint Price Code:

Bring the Outdoors In!

- This home is filled with features that meld the interior spaces with the outdoors, yet is affordably sized.
- Cathedral ceilings, angled walls, skylights and rear-facing views are key elements that add light, space and intensity to the home.
- The boxed-out kitchen, which overlooks a covered rear deck or patio, is easily reached from the dining room.
- The family room offers a cathedral ceiling, a window wall facing the backyard and access to the deck.
- The living room is highlighted by a beautiful Palladian window. Framed by a cathedral ceiling and a deep ledge, the window floods the living room and the adjoining dining room with light.
- The master suite is enhanced by double doors, angled walls and a large window facing the side yard. A walk-in closet and a private bath are also included.
- Two secondary bedrooms are positioned at the rear of the home for picturesque views as well as for privacy. A full bathroom, a linen closet and a laundry closet are nearby.

Plan NW-864

Bedrooms: 3	Baths: 2
Living Area:	
Main floor	1,449 sq. ft.
Total Living Area:	**1,449 sq. ft.**
Garage	390 sq. ft.
Exterior Wall Framing:	2x6

Foundation Options:

Crawlspace

(All plans can be built with your choice of foundation and framing. A generic conversion diagram is available. See order form.)

BLUEPRINT PRICE CODE: **A**

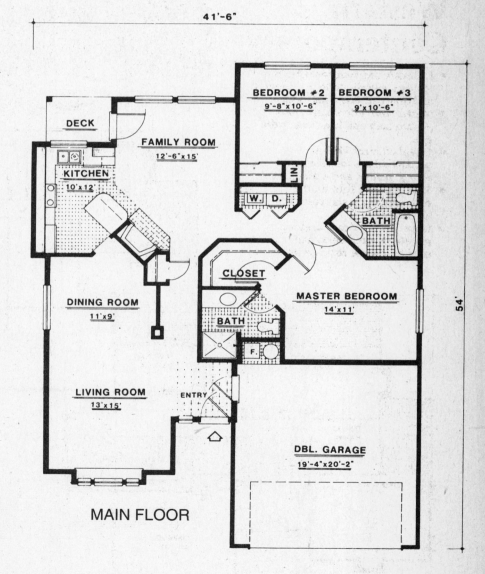

MAIN FLOOR

REAR VIEW

Vacation Living

- An expansive deck across the back of the home sets a casual outdoor living theme for this compact plan.
- Two bedrooms flank the entry and share a roomy bath.
- The kitchen, the dining room and the 16½-ft. vaulted living room are several steps down from the entry level for a dramatic effect. The kitchen provides a handy snack counter and has easy access to the laundry room. The living room's handsome fireplace warms the

entire area. Sliding glass doors extend functions to the outdoors.
- Upstairs, a hideaway bedroom includes an 11½-ft. open-beam vaulted ceiling, a personal bath, a walk-in closet and a romantic private deck.
- The optional daylight basement (not shown) features a large recreation room with a fireplace and sliding glass doors to a patio underneath the rear deck.
- A fourth bedroom and a third bath are also included, in addition to large area that could be used for a hobby room or a children's play area.

Plans H-877-1 & -1A	
Bedrooms: 3+	**Baths: 2-3**
Living Area:	
Upper floor	320 sq. ft.
Main floor	1,200 sq. ft.
Daylight basement	1,200 sq. ft.
Total Living Area:	**1,520/2,720 sq. ft.**
Garage	155 sq. ft.
Exterior Wall Framing:	2x6
Foundation Options:	**Plan #**
Daylight basement	H-877-1
Crawlspace	H-877-1A

(All plans can be built with your choice of foundation and framing. A generic conversion diagram is available. See order form.)

BLUEPRINT PRICE CODE:	**B/D**

FRONT OF HOME

BASEMENT
STAIRWAY
LOCATION

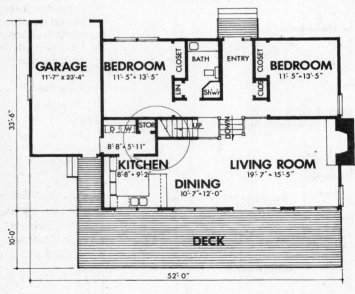

MAIN FLOOR

UPPER FLOOR

TO ORDER THIS BLUEPRINT, CALL TOLL-FREE 1-800-547-5570   Plans H-877-1 & -1A   *PRICES AND DETAILS ON PAGES 12-15*

Soaring Prows

- This unique vacation-style home features prows on all four sides.
- Dramatic window treatments and stunning views are found throughout.
- The exciting Great Room boasts a cathedral ceiling open to the upper level, a fireplace and a front wall of sliding glass doors topped by triangular transoms.
- The spacious kitchen and dining area features an angled bay and a cathedral ceiling also open to the upper level.
- A laundry closet and a full bath are located near the spacious main-floor master bedroom.
- A second bath and two extra bedrooms share the upper level.

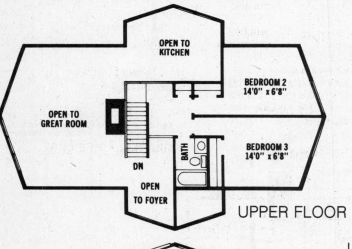

UPPER FLOOR

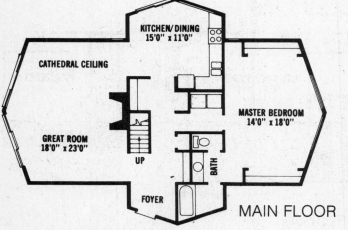

MAIN FLOOR

Plan PH-1841	
Bedrooms: 3	**Baths:** 2
Space:	
Upper floor	518 sq. ft.
Main floor	1,323 sq. ft.
Total Living Area	**1,841 sq. ft.**
Basement	1,323 sq. ft.
Exterior Wall Framing	2x6
Foundation options:	
Standard Basement	
Daylight Basement	
Crawlspace	
Slab	
Pole	
(Foundation & framing conversion diagram available—see order form.)	
Blueprint Price Code	B

TO ORDER THIS BLUEPRINT,
CALL TOLL-FREE 1-800-547-5570

Plan PH-1841

PRICES AND DETAILS
ON PAGES 12-15

189

ELEVATION A

ELEVATION B

ELEVATION C

Three Attractive Facades

- The impressive entrance to this versatile one-story reveals the openness and pleasantries found throughout.
- A lovely kitchen and breakfast nook offer a pass-thru to the busy, vaulted Great Room beyond.
- The family room section features a cozy fireplace and a generous view of the attached patio outside.
- An attractive solarium lies between the master bedroom and bath, the bedroom with vaulted ceilings and a full-length closet, the bath with dual vanities and a separate shower and tub.
- The two secondary bedrooms share a bath.
- NOTE: All three elevation choices are included in the plans.

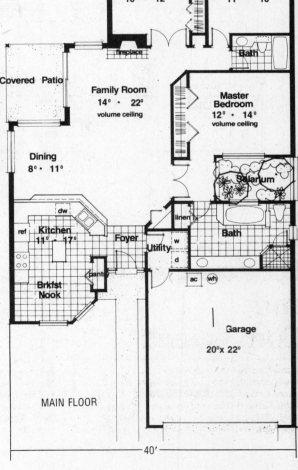

Plan HDS-90-820

Bedrooms: 3	Baths: 2

Space:

Total living area:	1,576 sq. ft.
Garage:	440 sq. ft.

Exterior Wall Framing: concrete block

Foundation options:
Slab.
(Foundation & framing conversion diagram available — see order form.)

Blueprint Price Code: B

Plan HDS-90-820

**PRICES AND DETAILS
ON PAGES 12-15**

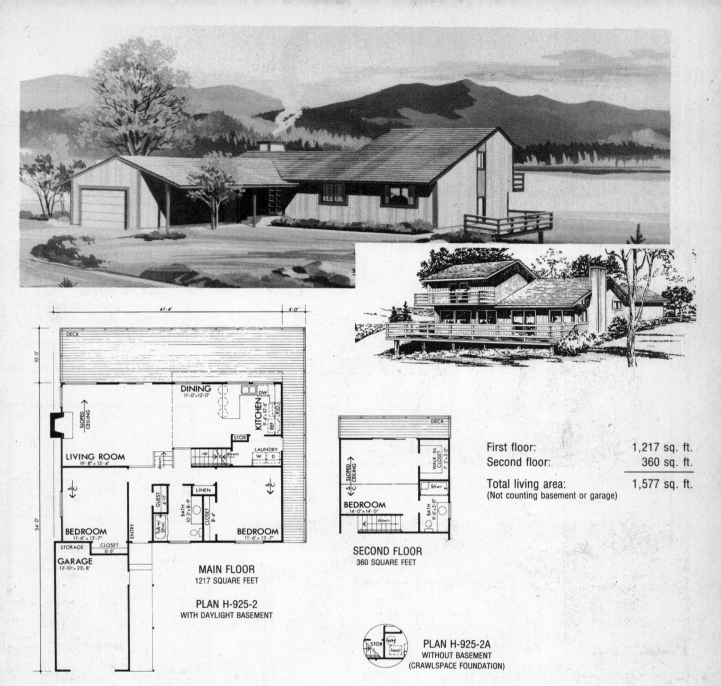

First floor: 1,217 sq. ft.
Second floor: 360 sq. ft.

Total living area: 1,577 sq. ft.
(Not counting basement or garage)

MAIN FLOOR
1217 SQUARE FEET

PLAN H-925-2
WITH DAYLIGHT BASEMENT

SECOND FLOOR
360 SQUARE FEET

PLAN H-925-2A
WITHOUT BASEMENT
(CRAWLSPACE FOUNDATION)

Economical and Convenient

In an effort to merge the financial possibilities and the space requirements of the greatest number of families, the designers of this home restricted themselves to just over 1,200 sq. ft. of ground cover (exclusive of garage), and still managed to develop a superior three-bedroom design.

From a covered walkway, one approaches a centralized entry hall which effectively distributes traffic throughout the home without causing interruptions. Two main floor bedrooms and bath as well as the stairway to the second floor master suite are immediately accessible to the entry. Directly forward and four steps down finds one in the main living area, consisting of a large living room with vaulted ceiling and a dining-kitchen combination with conventional ceiling height. All these rooms have direct access to an outdoor living deck of over 400 sq. ft. Thus, though modest and unassuming from the street side, this home evolves into eye-popping expansion and luxury toward the rear.

To ease homemaking chores, whether this is to be a permanent or vacation home, the working equipment, including laundry space, is all on the main floor. Yet the homemaker remains part of the family scene because there is only a breakfast counter separating the work space from the living area.

Tucked away upstairs, in complete privacy, one finds a master bedroom suite equipped with separate bath, walk-in wardrobe and a romantic private deck.

The plan is available with or without a basement and is best suited to a lot that slopes gently down from the road.

Blueprint Price Code B

Plans H-925-2 & -2A

TO ORDER THIS BLUEPRINT,
CALL TOLL-FREE 1-800-547-5570

PRICES AND DETAILS
ON PAGES 12-15   191

Simple, Spacious, Easy to Build

For a simple, spacious, easy-to-construct home away from home, you should definitely consider this plan.

Entrance to the home is by way of the lower level or the side door to the living room, or both, where grade levels permit. This has the advantage of elevating the second floor to take advantage of a view that otherwise may be blocked out by surrounding buildings.

The living area, consisting of the living room, dining room and kitchen, occupies 565 sq. ft. of the main floor. The open room arrangement allows the cook to remain part of the family even when occupied with necessary chores.

The design's basically simple rectangular shape allows for easy construction, and the home could be built by any moderately experienced do-it-yourselfer. All you have to do is order the plan that fits your setting.

Plan H-833-5 has the garage entry to the street side. H-833-6 puts the garage under the view-side deck.

Upper floor:	1,200 sq. ft.
Lower level:	876 sq. ft.
Total living area: (Not counting garage)	2,076 sq. ft.

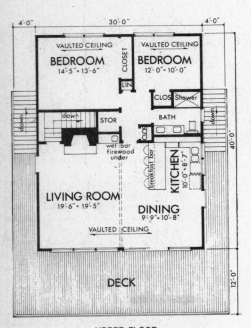

UPPER FLOOR
1200 SQUARE FEET

LOWER FLOOR
876 SQUARE FEET
PLAN H-833-5

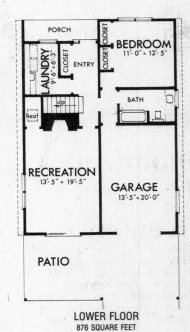

LOWER FLOOR
876 SQUARE FEET
PLAN H-833-6

Blueprint Price Code C

Plans H-833-5 & -6

PRICES AND DETAILS
ON PAGES 12-15